A Publication of the National Center
for Postsecondary Governance and Finance

How Colleges Work

Robert Birnbaum

How Colleges Work

*The Cybernetics
of Academic Organization
and Leadership*

Jossey-Bass Publishers

San Francisco   •   London   •   1988

HOW COLLEGES WORK
The Cybernetics of Academic Organization and Leadership
by Robert Birnbaum

Copyright © 1988 by: Jossey-Bass Inc., Publishers
350 Sansome Street
San Francisco, California 94104
&
Jossey-Bass Limited
28 Banner Street
London EC1Y 8QE

Library of Congress Cataloging-in-Publication Data

Birnbaum, Robert.
How colleges work.

(The Jossey-Bass higher education series)
Bibliography: p.
Includes index.
1. Universities and colleges—United States—
Administration. 2. Cybernetics—United States.
I. Title. II. Series.
LB2341.B48   1988   378.73   88-4277
ISBN 1-55542-126-1

Manufactured in the United States of America

The paper in this book meets the guidelines for
permanence and durability of the Committee on
Production Guidelines for Book Longevity of the
Council on Library Resources.

JACKET DESIGN BY WILLI BAUM

 A Publication of the National Center
for Postsecondary Governance and Finance

FIRST EDITION

Code 8847

The Jossey-Bass
Higher Education Series

Contents

ix

Preface

Every year I end my introductory course in college and university organization and administration with an exercise in which students simulate four years of college functioning. Over an eight-hour period, participants play the roles of trustees, administrators, faculty, and students. They select a president, administer a budget, raise money, teach courses, write articles for publication, take final examinations, and work out the problems that arise out of their various roles, personalities, interactions with the environment, and the rules of the college. My students call this exercise "the college in a box," because when the materials for the simulation are not in use, they are stored in a small box on a bookshelf in my office.

What is a college? An educator might respond that a college is an institution offering comparatively advanced instruction leading to a degree. An administrator might answer that a college is an organization consisting of people in certain roles whose authority, responsibilities, and relationships are defined by legal documents, job descriptions, and organizational charts. A policy maker might look at a college as a goal-directed organization that serves a number of important societal functions, such as training the young for occupations, encouraging scientific development, or providing for social mobility. Each of these responses describes part of the truth. But after watching my students each year, I think I could also defend the proposition that a college is in its essence an interrelated system of ideas that can be activated by the materials contained in a box small enough to fit on my bookshelf.

These definitions are of more than theoretical interest. The beliefs held by administrators and others who influence institutional life affect how they behave, how they interpret their experiences, and even what they "see." The primary objective of *How Colleges Work* is to help administrators think in more complex ways about their work, and thereby improve their performance. Unlike many other volumes on organization and governance, however, it will not propose a single "best solution" to institutional problems. Neither will it offer any proven steps to effective planning or advocate any particular administrative procedures or organizational structure. Instead, it will suggest some ways in which we can usefully change perceptions about how organizations of higher education work.

For those who view organizational life as being relatively straightforward—although often perverse—the outcome of reading this book will be to add richness, dimension, and texture, for with complexity come understanding and appreciation of subtleties. For those who know of the many elements that can influence the course of institutional life but who consider institutional processes all too random and not amenable to administrative direction, the aim of this volume will be to develop alternative ways of viewing relationships and interactions. In both cases, my purpose is to encourage administrators to expand their repertoire of interpretations, to suggest alternative ways of responding to problems and situations, and to assess the likelihood that these responses will be effective.

Some of what happens in life may appear random, but mathematicians are now finding that patterns exist even in chaos. *How Colleges Work* is predicated on the belief that there are patterns in organizational life as well. Ineffective administrators fail to see these patterns and often act foolishly. Effective administrators recognize existing patterns and act sensibly. The most creative administrators are those who not only perceive complex patterns and relationships but also discover or invent new patterns where others find only confusion.

Ideas matter, and this is a book based on ideas that have been developed by many scholars in a number of fields over a period of more than fifty years. Some of these ideas will be relatively familiar to many administrators but others of them are likely to be new and in some instances may even seem a trifle bizarre. Whether new or old, these ideas about organization are presented in a way that particularly illuminates their implications for higher education. In doing this I have sometimes ignored the more esoteric aspects of an idea and avoided the use of extensive scholarly citations. In many places I have used illustrations to illuminate and simplify—and therefore inevitably to somewhat distort—important concepts. Without apology, I have resolved conflicts between scholarly accuracy and completeness, on the one hand, and clarity and a focus on higher education, on the other, in favor of the latter.

In order to illustrate important concepts, I have created five fictional institutions. Huxley College, led by President Quincey Wagstaff, is used in Parts One and Three of the book to provide examples of organizational processes and systems applicable to colleges and universities in general. The other four institutions, presented in Part Two, are Heritage College, People's Community College, Regional State University, and Flagship University. All four are successful institutions, and each has developed a different system of organization, administration, and governance. There are more than 3,200 colleges and universities in this country. They have many similarities as well as enormous differences. My fictional campuses cannot fully capture the great diversity in institutions, but they can serve as simplified examples for understanding the dynamics of organization and management in institutions of different kinds.

This book is not intended to be a complete summary of organization theory for scholars; it is a selective consideration of ideas that may help college and university administrators develop a more coherent and integrated view of the institutions they inhabit and, therefore, to be more effective as they work in them. Kurt Lewin's aphorism that there is nothing as useful as a good theory is particularly appropriate in the field of higher education, and organization theory is too important to be left only to the theorists. I believe that the only thing more useful to an administrator than a good theory is several good theories—particularly if they happen to be in conflict with one another.

Audience

Readers familiar with the literature of higher education will recognize that this book is quite different from other works dealing with leadership, management, and governance. Part of that difference is in this book's strong foundation in organization theory. But of equal importance is the attempt to provide a coherent integration of models of college and university organization and governance that have previously been viewed as separate and for the most part unrelated. The intended audience for this book includes trustees, administrators at all institutional levels, faculty involved in governance, and those who teach and learn in graduate programs of higher education.

Overview of the Contents

This book is divided into three parts. In Part One I analyze the elements that define colleges and universities; the chapters in this part provide the conceptual bases for the rest of the book. Chapter One summarizes key ideas about college and university organization and governance and indicates some of the major reasons why understanding and managing these institutions has proven to be so problematical. In Chapter Two I introduce ideas about systems that will be put to work in my later discussion of organizational dynamics. Important concepts, such as open and nonlinear systems, loose coupling, and casual loops, are explained and illustrated. In Chapter Three I suggest that the major purpose of organizations is not decision making, but "sense making." That is the process by which people in an organization arrive at acceptable agreements about what is real and important. This conflict between being rational and being sensible leads institutions to develop elaborate shared perceptions of reality, establishes powerful constraints on the behavior of administrators, and even determines what institutions and administrators must do to be considered effective.

In Part Two I describe several models that have been proposed by others to explain how colleges and universities are organized and managed. The collegial model, often referred to as the community of scholars, is the subject of Chapter Four. In Chapter Five I consider the college as a bureaucracy and examine the characteristic processes that typify these complex, hierarchically structured, and highly rational systems. In Chapter Six I analyze the university as a political system—one in which interest groups contend over the development of policies and resource allocations in an effort to influence organizational outcomes. In Chapter Seven I present a fictional institution with particular properties that have caused it to be called an organized anarchy.

In Part Three I integrate the models previously discussed and suggest how administrators can influence institutions by using ongoing organizational processes. Understanding organizational life would indeed be simplified if all the processes of any institution consistently reflected elements of a single model. However, while some organizations frequently appear to reflect some of the characteristics of one model, there are no colleges or universities in the real world that reflect one model's characteristics all of the time. In Chapter Eight I present a new model of colleges and universities as cybernetic organizations that rely on negative feedback to be adaptive and self-correcting. The cybernetic view does not replace the other models; it integrates them to create a more complete understanding of the dilemmas and complexities of how colleges work. Finally, in Chapter Nine I offer some advice to administrators to help them understand the organizational aspects of their problems and to suggest how they can discover or invent ways to be more effective.

Acknowledgments

A number of colleagues at Teachers College, Columbia University; the National Center for Postsecondary Governance and Finance; and other institutions have been exceptionally generous in reading all or part of several drafts of the manuscript for this book and offering their criticisms and suggestions. I am particularly grateful to Richard E. Anderson, Estela M. Bensimon, Lee G. Bolman, Ellen Earle Chaffee, Richard P. Chait, Judith Eaton, Joseph N. Hankin, Joseph Katz, Joseph F. Kauffman, Anna Neumann, Richard C. Richardson, David Riesman, Kathryn T. Theus, Wagner Thielens, Jr., William G. Tierney, and several anonymous reviewers for their criticism and wise counsel. These colleagues are not responsible for sins of omission or commission in this book, but by challenging and correcting some of my thoughts they certainly have improved it.

This book was prepared pursuant to a grant from the Office of Educational Research and Improvement/Department of Education (OERI/ED). However, the opinions expressed herein do not necessarily reflect the position or policy of the OERI/ED, and no official endorsement by the OERI/ED should be inferred.

New York, New York   Robert Birnbaum
August 1988

The Author

Robert Birnbaum is associate director of the National Center for Postsecondary Governance and Finance—where his current responsibilities include directing a major five-year study of institutional leadership—and professor of higher education at Teachers College, Columbia University. He received his B.A. degree (1958) in psychology from the University of Rochester and his M.A. (1964) and Ed.D. (1967) degrees in higher education from Teachers College, Columbia University.

Birnbaum has held administrative positions in a number of academic settings, including the positions of vice chancellor at City University of New York, vice chancellor at the New Jersey Department of Higher Education, and chancellor at the University of Wisconsin–Oshkosh. He has also been a professor of higher education at the University of Miami.

His research findings have been published in many scholarly and professional journals. He is the author or coauthor of *Creative Academic Bargaining: Managing Conflict in the Unionized College and University* (1980), *Maintaining Diversity in Higher Education* (1983), and *Cooperation in Academic Negotiations: A Guide to Mutual Gains Bargaining* (1985, with

James P. Begin and Bert R. Brown). As well, Birnbaum is the editor of the *ASHE Reader in Organization and Governance in Higher Education* (1983, 1984). His recent articles on topics such as the latent organizational roles of faculty senates, presidential searches and the discovery of organizational goals, the effects of cognitive biases on administrative judgments, and the organizational changes related to leader succession reflect his current interest in studying colleges and universities as cognitive and symbolic systems.

How Colleges Work

Part One

Understanding Colleges and Universities as Organizations

Learning how colleges and universities work requires seeing them as organizations, as systems, and as inventions. When we study them as organizations, we see groups of people filling roles and working together toward the achievement of common objectives within a formal social structure. When we view them as systems, particular roles and structures seem less important, and our concern is focused on the dynamics through which the whole and its parts interact. While all systems share certain characteristics, there are differences between them as well. Biological or physical systems such as amoebas or galaxies have independent physical realities, but social systems such as institutions of higher education in large measure are symbolic inventions that exist because we believe in them. The three perspectives—organizational, systemic, and symbolic—are different but complementary. They are the topics of this first part.

Colleges and universities differ in many ways from other organizations (Baldridge, Curtis, Ecker, and Riley, 1978; Carnegie Commission on Higher Education, 1973; Corson, 1960, 1979; Perkins, 1973b; Whetton, 1984), and this book begins with a consideration of some of their unique characteristics. In

1

some portions of Chapter One, I make use of the traditional practice of comparing colleges with business enterprises, because many of our ideas about organization and management come from studies of business firms. Identifying some of the differences between the two types of organization helps illuminate why a comprehensive understanding of college and university functioning remains elusive and why their management and governance are so problematic.

The consideration of colleges and universities as systems in Chapter Two emphasizes how their parts interact with each other and with the larger systems of which they themselves are parts. The important elements of an institution, and the different patterns by which they can be combined, make institutions look different even though the processes by which they function as systems are comparable. Certain properties of systems make some problems of administration inherent and intractable, and administrators must learn to cope with what they cannot control.

Chapter Three looks at the usefulness of some common ideas about organizational rationality, goals, and effectiveness and shows why these ideas often are not helpful to administrators. The important thing about colleges and universities is not the choices that administrators are presumed to make but the agreement people reach about the nature of reality. People create organizations as they come over time to agree that certain aspects of the environment are more important and that some kinds of interaction are more sensible than others. These agreements coalesce in institutional cultures that exert profound influence on what people see, the interpretations they make, and how they behave.

Chapter 1

Problems of Governance, Management, and Leadership in Academic Institutions

American colleges and universities are the most paradoxical of organizations. On the one hand, it has been said that "they constitute one of the largest industries in the nation but are among the least businesslike and well managed of all organizations" (Keller, 1983, p. 5). On the other hand, many believe that our institutions of higher education exhibit levels of diversity, access, and quality that are without parallel. At a time when American business and technology suffer an unfavorable trade deficit and are under siege from foreign competition, our system of higher education maintains a most favorable "balance of trade" by enrolling large numbers of students from other countries. Our system remains the envy of the world.

The apparent paradox that American colleges and universities are poorly run but highly effective is easily resolved if either or both of these judgments are wrong. But what if they are both right? Such a state of affairs would lead to several interesting speculations. For example, it might be that the success of the system has come about *in spite of* bad management, and that if management could somehow be improved, the system could be made even more effective than it is today. Or it might be that, contrary to our traditional expectations, at least in colleges and universities, management and performance are not closely related. If this is true, then improvements in management might not yield comparable benefits in organizational accomplishment. Or, strangest of all, it might be that to at least some extent our colleges and universities are successful *because* they are poorly managed, at least as *management* is often defined in other complex organizations. If this is true, then attempts to "improve" traditional management processes might actually diminish rather than enhance organizational effectiveness in institutions of higher education. This book is in large part an exploration of these possibilities.

The concept that best reflects the ways in which institutions of higher education differ from other organizations is *governance,* and I shall use it extensively in this chapter. There is no single and generally accepted definition of governance; it has been variously discussed in terms of structures, legal relationships, authority patterns, rights and responsibilities, and decision-making processes. I shall use the word *governance* in a very broad way to refer to the structures and processes through which institutional participants interact with and influence each other and communicate with the larger environment. A governance system is an institution's answer—at least temporarily—to the enduring question that became a plaintive cry during the campus crisis of the late 1960s and early 1970s: "Who's in charge here?"

Problems of Governance

The authority to establish a college or university belongs to the state, which exercises it by forming through statute, charter, or constitutional provision an institution with a corporate existence and a lay governing board. An uncomplicated view of governance need go no further than this fact, because legally the governing board *is* the institution (Glenny and Dalglish, 1973). But the reality of governance today is much different from what this strict legal interpretation would suggest. In fact, "decision making is spread among trustees, presidents, and faculty, and although the legal status of the trustees has not changed, there is ambivalence about how much power they should have" (Carnegie Foundation for the Advancement of Teaching, 1982, p. 72).

Trustees and Faculty. In earlier times, institutions were small, trustees were clergymen, and administration and faculty might consist of a president and a handful of tutors. Boards could—and often did—exercise the full authority that they legally possessed. Governance was not an issue; it was the will of the board. But as institutions became more complex, boards delegated de facto authority to presidents. And as the faculty became more professionalized during the early part of the twentieth century, much authority on many campuses, particularly in curriculum and academic personnel matters, was further delegated to faculties. Some reached the point where "the faculty . . . tend to think of themselves as being the university. This leaves the board of trustees with little authority over the [major] function of the university, instruction" (Besse, 1973, p. 109).

As a result, different campus constituencies now assert their claim to primacy in areas over which boards retain legal obligations and responsibilities. Radical remedies to clarify governance rights have occasionally been suggested. One such suggestion argued that the board should take back from the faculty authority for the curriculum, since the board has full legal responsibility for all aspects of the institution (Ruml and Morrison, 1959). More recently it has been suggested that trustees consider simplifying governance by stripping all campus groups of governance prerogatives except insofar as they might be granted as a privilege by the president acting as the board's exclusive agent (Fisher, 1984). Proposals such as these cannot be taken seriously, but more moderate and responsible calls for greater trustee involvement in governance are increasing (Carnegie Foundation for the Advancement of Teaching, 1982).

Tensions between trustees and faculty are not new. Probably the most outspoken observer and critic of this conflict was Thorsten Veblen ([1918] 1957), whose 1918 book *The*

Higher Learning in America railed against the effects of boards of trustees increasingly made up of businessmen whose interest was focused on efficiency and who did not understand the unique nature of the academic enterprise. In their view, he said, "the university is conceived as a business house dealing in merchantable knowledge, placed under the governing hand of a captain of erudition, whose office it is to turn the means at hand to account in the largest feasible output" (Veblen, [1918] 1957, p. 62). In contrast, said Veblen, scholars pursue their work individually, each in his or her own way. It is not amenable to the orderly and systematic procedures of the administrator and cannot be reduced to the bottom line of a balance sheet. The administrative role is not to govern scholars but rather to serve as their assistants and cater to their idiosyncratic needs. To the extent that this is not done, the university will lose effectiveness, because "a free hand is the first and abiding requisite of scholarly and scientific work" (p. 63). Veblen's acerbic comments set forth the governance issue clearly if simplistically: shall the university be controlled by trustees and administrators or by faculty?

The answer to this question is important, because faculty and lay trustees have different backgrounds and values. Approximately 40 percent of all board members are businesspeople ("College Governing Boards," 1986), who are more likely than faculty to see their institutions as comparable to business firms in their structure and authority patterns and to support ideas of "top-down" management. Trustees are also likely to have a lesser understanding and support of principles of academic freedom than do faculty and are more likely than faculty to believe that certain academic decisions do not require faculty involvement. In general, "trustees differ markedly from those occupying the academic positions 'beneath' them. In terms of political party affiliation and ideology, and attitudes about higher education, the trustees are generally more conservative than the faculty" (Hartnett, 1969, p. 51).

Administrators and Faculty. The days of amateur administration when faculty temporarily assumed administrative positions and then returned to the classroom are long since over at most institutions. As institutions become larger and more complex, knowledge of legal precedents, federal regulations, management information systems, student financial aid procedures, grant and contract administration, and many other areas of specialized expertise is needed to accomplish many administrative tasks. Faculty and administrators fill different roles, encounter and are influenced by different aspects of the environment, and have different backgrounds. The increasing numbers and importance of managers at all levels have led to the "administered university" (Lunsford, 1970, p. 91), in which administrators are separated from the rest of the university. As a consequence, university executives and faculty form separated and isolated conclaves in which they are likely to communicate only with people similar to themselves. The use of more sophisticated management techniques can make things even worse. "In a context in which faculty members are less privileged and in which they often feel oppressed beneath the weight of administrative authority, the innovations wrought by the new devices of management may widen the gulf between faculty and administration and thus intensify the antagonism, latent and overt, which has traditionally existed between the administrative and the academic cultures" (Rourke and Brooks, 1964, p. 180).

Administration and management can become so complex that even those faculty who are interested in governance may not have the time or the expertise to fully understand the processes of decision making or resource acquisition and allocation that are at the heart of many governance issues. Because of these changes, administrators become identified in the faculty mind with red tape, constraints, and outside pressures that seek to alter the institution. They come to be seen by the faculty as ever more remote from the central academic concerns that define the institution. Faculty in turn come to be seen by the administration as self-interested, unconcerned with controlling costs, or unwilling to respond to legitimate requests for accountability.

Normative Statements on Governance. It might be thought that uncertainty and conflict concerning governance

roles and procedures could be moderated by authoritative statements that enunciate the elements of sound practice. Several
important normative statements of this kind exist, perhaps the
most influential of which is the "Joint Statement on Government of Colleges and Universities" (American Association of
University Professors, 1984) published in 1967. The document
articulated the concept of governance as a shared responsibility
and joint effort involving all important constituencies of the
academic community, with the weight given to the views of
each group dependent on the specific issues under discussion.
In particular, while recognizing the legal authority of the board
and the president, the document identified the faculty as having
primary responsibility for the fundamental areas of curriculum,
instruction, faculty status, and the academic aspects of student
life. The term *primary responsibility* was specifically defined to
mean that "the governing board and president . . . should con-
cur with the faculty judgment except in rare instances and for
compelling reasons which should be stated in detail" (p. 109).
This appears to give the de facto authority of the faculty more
weight than the de jure authority of the board in those areas
that in fact define the institution—what shall be taught, who
shall teach, and who shall study. In the eyes of some, this mud-
dled the problem further rather than clarifying solutions.

A major problem with the "Joint Statement"—as well as
with the content of other normative statements—is that while it
presents positions of high principle that can be endorsed by
many campus constituencies, it is less successful in identifying
the specific structures and processes that would implement
these principles. The behavioral implications of the statement
are unclear and can be interpreted in quite different ways. The
statement has also been criticized for failing to describe how
governance *really* functions in many institutions, for assuming
that governance is characterized by shared aims and values
without giving proper weight to the conflict and competition
that exist between constituencies, and for ignoring the ways in
which the external environment affects governance (Mortimer
and McConnell, 1978). The "Joint Statement" is thus seen by
some as an academic Camelot—devoutly to be wished for but
not achievable by mere mortals.

The "Joint Statement" has another weakness, which has been less widely noticed: it does not fully appreciate the differences between various kinds of institutions. The diversity of American higher education is reflected in significant differences in such critical matters as purpose, size, sponsorship, tradition, and values. Policies appropriate and fruitful for one type of institution may be harmful for another. Recommendations of policies that treat "*the* faculty" or "*the* administration" as alike in all institutions (and that speak as if these groups were monolithic within institutions) ignore the reality that the background and expectations of faculty and administrators at community colleges and at research universities, for example, might well produce very different approaches to governance.

Problems of Organization

Dualism of Controls. If a college is compared to a business firm, it is possible to consider the confused relationships between boards, administration, and faculty that we have just discussed as reflecting disorganization, willfulness, or the pursuit of self-interest in preference to college interests. Corson (1960) was among the first observers to ascribe a different cause when he identified the administration of colleges and universities as presenting "a unique dualism in organizational structure" (p. 43). Corson saw the university as including two structures existing in parallel: the conventional administrative hierarchy and the structure through which faculty made decisions regarding those aspects of the institution over which they had jurisdiction. This dual system of control was further complicated by the fact that neither system had consistent patterns of structure or delegation. The faculty governance structure on every campus was different, and each administration seemed to "have been established to meet specific situations in particular institutions or to reflect the strengths and weaknesses of individuals in various echelons" (p. 45).

The two control systems not only were structurally separate but were based on different systems of authority as well (Etzioni, 1964). In most business organizations, major goal activities are directed and coordinated by a hierarchy of administrators who decide questions such as what products should be made, in what number, and with what characteristics. Those higher in rank rely on administrative authority, derived from their position in the organizational structure, to direct the activities of others. These organizations also have need for experts who are not involved in coordinating the institution's goal activities. These experts rely on professional authority to provide specialized knowledge and judgment in one or more professional areas. Their judgments are individual acts that are not governed by the directives of others.

Administrative authority is predicated on the control and coordination of activities by superiors; professional authority is predicated on autonomy and individual knowledge. These two sources of authority are not only different but in mutual disagreement. In business organizations, the administrative line officers direct the primary goal activities of the institution, and the staff professionals provide secondary support activities and knowledge. Conflict caused by the incompatibility of administrative and professional authority is resolved by recognizing the supremacy of administrative authority. But in professional organizations, such as colleges and universities, the resolution is far more problematic. These organizations have staffs composed predominantly of professionals who produce, apply, preserve, or communicate knowledge (Etzioni, 1964) and who are also responsible for setting organizational goals and maintaining standards of performance (Scott, 1981). Etzioni suggests that "although administrative authority is suitable for the major goals activities in private business, in professional organizations administrators are in charge of secondary activities; they administer *means* to the major activity carried out by professionals. In other words, to the extent that there is a staff-line relationship at all, professionals should hold the major authority and administrators the secondary staff authority" (p. 81). This reversal of the patterns seen in other settings makes the organization of colleges and universities difficult to understand.

Mission and Management. Clarity and agreement on organizational mission are usually considered a fundamental principle for establishing systems of accountability. It is commonly stated that "in a business corporation there is always one quantifiable measure of performance . . . the rate of earnings on the capital invested. Because dollar profits are both the objective of the activity and the measure of performance, the operation of the company is keyed to accountability for the profit achieved" (Besse, 1973, p. 110). This relationship between performance and profit can then be translated into systems for identifying responsibility, measuring costs, and preparing periodic reports and analyses.

Although it is too simple to say that the mission of a business enterprise is to make money, that assertion contains an underlying truth that to a great extent provides a clarity of purpose and an integration of management that are absent in higher education. As colleges and universities become more diverse, fragmented, specialized, and connected with other social systems, institutional missions do not become clearer; rather, they multiply and become sources of stress and conflict rather than integration. The problem is not that institutions cannot identify their goals but rather that they simultaneously embrace a large number of conflicting goals (Gross and Grambsch, 1974).

There is no metric in higher education comparable to money in business, and no goal comparable to "profits." This is so in part because of disagreement on goals and in part because neither goal achievement nor the activities related to their performance can be satisfactorily quantified into an educational "balance sheet." Does a core curriculum produce more liberally educated students than a program built on the great books? Should a college measure its performance by the percentage of students who graduate, the percentage who get jobs, the percentage who are satisfied, or the percentage who participate in civic activities? The accountability techniques of the business corporation are of little benefit to the educational purposes of higher education.

Lack of clarity and agreement on institutional goals and mission has equally important effects on organization and management. The list of legitimate institutional missions is a lengthy one, but the problem can be seen in a consideration of only the three commonly articulated missions of teaching, research, and service. Each of these three missions is likely to rely on different structures for its effective implementation. For example, while the academic department may serve as the focus for teaching, funded research is based primarily on the activities of individual faculty members and requires different, and incompatible, management systems, budgeting processes, and organizational units. At the same time, the central coordination that supports service activities not only often operates outside existing faculty units but also conflicts with traditional notions of faculty autonomy and academic freedom (Perkins, 1973a). Teaching, research, and service are interrelated and mutually reinforcing production processes in the higher education system as a whole. However, on many campuses these activities are performed by different people operating within overlapping yet competing structures. Most faculty have their primary affiliation with either an academic department that supports their teaching, an institute within which they engage in research, or an extension division or other unit that provides community service. Few faculty are affiliated with all three. No single organizational design can optimize all legitimate organizational interests; a structure that provides the most effective support for research, for example, will be quite different from a structure that seeks to closely integrate undergraduate teaching activities.

Although some have suggested that higher education institutions could be managed more effectively if their missions were clarified, this has proved to be impossible to do in larger and more complex organizations. A more sensible suggestion might be to redefine management so that it can function usefully within a context of conflicting objectives. Given the differences in the clarity of goals, we should not be too surprised to find that effective management in colleges and universities would differ from that seen in business firms.

Power, Compliance, and Control. Power is the ability to produce intended change in others, to influence them so that they will be more likely to act in accordance with one's own preferences. Power is essential to coordinate and control the activities of people and groups in universities, as it is in other organizations. There are many ways of thinking about power. One influential typology has identified five kinds of power in social groups: coercive power, reward power, legitimate power, referent power, and expert power (French and Raven, 1959). Coercive power is the ability to punish if a person does not accept one's attempt at influence. Reward power is the ability of one person to offer or promise rewards to another or to remove or decrease negative influences. Legitimate power exists when both parties agree to a common code or standard that gives one party the right to influence the other in a specific range of activities or behaviors and obliges the other to comply. A major source of legitimate power in our society is the acceptance of a hierarchical authority structure in formal groups. Referent power results from the willingness to be influenced by another because of one's identification with the other. Expert power is exercised when one person accepts influence from another because of a belief that the other person has some special knowledge or competence in a specific area.

The exercise of power may cause alienation, and responses by faculty and others to various forms of power in institutions of higher education may pose problems for their organization and administration. Coercive power always alienates those subject to it. The use of reward power or legitimate power may or may not produce alienation, depending on the circumstances and the expectations of those subject to it. Neither referent power nor expert power results in alienation.

Different forms of power are typically used in different kinds of organizations, and they have different effects on the responses of organizational participants. One approach has identified coercive, utilitarian, and normative organizations as representing three major patterns (Etzioni, 1961). Coercive organizations, such as prisons, rely predominantly on the punishments and threats of coercive power, and they produce alienated involvement of participants. Utilitarian organizations, such as business firms, emphasize reward power and legitimate power to control participants. People calculate the costs and benefits of involvement in order to decide whether or not to participate.

Normative organizations, such as colleges and universities, rely on referent and expert power that is less likely to cause alienation and that produces committed participants who are influenced through the manipulation of symbols. This does not mean that faculty are indifferent to money, or that they will not become disaffected if they do not consider their salaries to be reasonable. But it is true that faculty members on many campuses are likely to be influenced more by internalized principles of academic freedom and ethical behavior, and by communications from colleagues who are seen as sharing their values, than by salary increases or threats of administrative sanctions.

The means by which faculty behavior can be influenced are therefore very different from what would be effective in traditional business firms emphasizing utilitarian power. Trying to control faculty by offering material benefits, such as money, or by giving orders might affect their behavior but at the same time would increase their alienation and decrease the effectiveness of normative power. The autonomous focus of professional authority and the unwillingness of professionals to accept administrative authority require that higher education take a different approach to the problems of management and governance.

Institutional and Organizational Constraints

Many factors have increasingly limited the discretion and flexibility of academic leaders (Commission on Strengthening Presidential Leadership, 1984). Some of these factors develop as institutions interact with other institutions in their environments, while some arise within the institution itself. Environmental constraints include more federal and state controls, greater involvement by the courts in academic decision making, more layers of governance, particularly in institutions that are part of statewide systems, fewer opportunities for growth and consequently for changes accompanying growth, questions of the importance of the missions of higher education, less acceptance of authority in general, and fewer potential applicants and therefore greater responsiveness to the student market. Within institutions themselves, constraints to leadership arise from greater involvement by faculties in academic and personnel decisions, faculty collective bargaining, greater goal ambiguity, greater fractionation of the campus into interest groups, leading to a loss of consensus and community, greater involvement by trustees in campus operations, and increased bureaucracy and specialization among campus administrators. The dual system of authority, the expectation of participation as an element of shared authority, the linkages of faculty with groups external to the campus—these and related factors already noted severely limit the influence of administrators.

Institutions and Environments. Institutions must be responsive to their environments to survive, and the responses made by colleges and universities have had profound effects on their governance structures and processes. The number and pervasiveness of these environmental forces have increased almost exponentially at many institutions over the past decades. Two examples showing the effects of external sources of support and power serve to illustrate the problem in different ways.

The confusion in governance that results when both faculty and administration lose the ability to understand and control the processes of their institutions was noted over a quarter of a century ago (Mooney, 1963). The loss of faculty control is related to increased institutional size and complexity and the division of faculty into different departments, committees, and other units. This fractionation prevents the development of a holistic faculty perspective. The loss of administrative control is related to the presence of external funding and control agencies that bypass and weaken institutional administration. As a consequence, neither faculty nor administration feels able to take command, since neither group fully understands the enterprise or has control of enough of its resources. As individuals and groups lose their ability to affect their institution through the implementation of positive and constructive programs, they increasingly tend to assert their influence and status by acting as veto blocs, thus increasing institutional conservatism. The result, says Clark Kerr (1982, p. 30), is more commitment "to the status quo—the status quo is the only solution that cannot be vetoed." The same forces that limit the power of faculty groups affect deans and presidents as well, so that the power of administrators in many cases is determined by their right to block programs they consider unwise or improper (Bok, 1983, p. 85).

The major external force limiting institutional autonomy is the exercise of increased authority by the states. The growth of the public sector of higher education during the past quarter century, as well as support in some states of nonpublic institutions, has led to increased state funding of—and therefore concern for—the programs and management of both public and independent colleges and universities. Coordinating or consolidated governing boards in almost all states exercise increasing influence over matters reserved in the past to the campus. Other state executive or legislative agencies become involved in program review, administrative operations, budgeting, and planning. The rationale often offered is the need for public accountability, but the consequence is often chaos and confusion (Carnegie Foundation for the Advancement of Teaching, 1982). Individual institutions become part of larger regional or statewide systems in which single boards have authority for several campuses and not enough time or energy to become familiar with any of them. As the locus of influence moves from the campus to the state, public-sector presidents may find themselves becoming more like middle managers than campus leaders. Faculty may respond to increased centralization of control by centralizing their own participation through processes of collective bargaining that often ritualize disruptive conflict. The loss of ability to exert local influence leads to mutual scapegoating by faculty and administration, end runs to state offices that further reduce administrative authority, and a diminished sense of both campus responsibility and accountability. The sense of powerlessness comes not just from the recognition of one's own limited ability to exert influence upward but also from the realization that those higher in the organization cannot exert much upward influence either.

Decentralization. The centralization of authority at levels above the campus has influenced the distribution of influence at many institutions in two quite different ways. Institutions have become more administratively centralized because of requirements to rationalize budget formats, implement procedures that will pass judicial tests of equitable treatment, and speak with a single voice to powerful external agencies. At the same time, increased faculty specialization and decreased administrative authority have fostered decentralization of educational decision making at many institutions, which leads to further faculty specialization and continued reduction of administrative authority. As faculty become more specialized, they assert their expertise as a requirement for designing curriculum and assessing the qualifications of colleagues. Particularly in larger and more complex institutions, schools or departments become the locus of decision making, sometimes reinforced by an "every tub on its own bottom" management philosophy that makes these subunits responsible for their own enrollment and financial affairs as well. In such cases, the larger institution may become an academic holding company, presiding over a federation of quasi-autonomous subunits. Unable to influence the larger institution, faculty retreat into the small subunit for which they feel affinity and from which they can defend their influence and status.

Inflexibility of Resources. The ability of groups to significantly influence their campus through participation in governance is severely constrained by both the paucity of resources available and the short-term difficulties in internally reallocating those resources that do exist. Some important intangible campus resources, such as institutional prestige or attractiveness to students or to potential donors, are tied into networks of external relationships that are virtually impossible to change in the short run and difficult to alter even over long periods of time. Internally, the personnel complement on most campuses is largely fixed through tenure and contractual provisions, program change is constrained by faculty interests and structures as well as facilities limitations, and yearly planning begins with the largest share of the budget precommitted. In the public sector, institutions are subject to state personnel, purchasing, and construction regulations, as well as budget management restrictions that make certain expenditures impossible even when resources are available. But resources are not always available, and when last year's expenditures exceed this year's projected income, major changes are rare. Even on campuses that stress rational planning and budgeting, opportunities for short-term effects are minimal. For example, one relatively wealthy institution found that its extensive planning program accounted for less than 6 percent of the variance in the budget over ten years. An observer commented that "it may be hard to believe that any effort above a minimal level is justifiable" but added that "since so much of the budget is virtually fixed, especially in the short run, the small portion that is free to vary assumes tremendous importance" (Chaffee, 1983, p. 402).

Confusion of Organizational Levels. Organizations can be thought of as composed of three levels of responsibility and control—technical, managerial, and institutional (Thompson, 1967). In colleges or universities, the technical level includes the research, teaching, and service responsibilities carried out primarily by the faculty. The responsibility of the organization's institutional level, which in higher education is represented by boards of trustees and presidents, is to ensure that the organization is able to respond appropriately to the uncertainty of external social forces. The managerial level is represented by the administration, which is charged with mediating between these two levels and buffering the faculty and researchers who make up the technical core against disruption caused by problems in the acquisition of funding, fluctuations in student enrollments, or governmental interference.

Organizations are presumed to be most effective when the institutional level specializes in coping with uncertainty and the technical level specializes in functioning effectively in conditions of certainty. This specialization is not uncommon in business organizations in which senior officers are responsible for monitoring the environment (Katz and Kahn, 1978, p. 4). But in higher education, distinctions among the three levels can be difficult if not impossible to maintain, particularly in certain types of colleges and universities. For example, there are institutions in which faculty (technical level) are also members of the board of trustees (institutional level). At many institutions, faculty are expected by tradition as well as law (*NLRB* v.*Yeshiva University*, 444 U.S. 672 [1980]) to exercise responsibilities for personnel and for program that in other types of organizations would be considered managerial. Faculty in some types of institutions, through their professional associations, funded research, and consulting activities, often have direct access to major actors and resources in the environment and so bypass the managerial level. And major participants may sequentially (or simultaneously) be both administrators and faculty and therefore participants in both the managerial and technical levels, while the products of the technical level as alumni may become trustees at the institutional level. There are probably few organizations in our society in which someone who is a member of the union bargaining team one day can become the organizational president the next, but it has happened in higher education!

Distinctions among the institutional, managerial, and technical levels are clearer in some institutions than in others (church-related institutions or community colleges, for example). This should make the technical core more rational and management able to be more bureaucratized without creating problems. Other organizations, such as research universities, have technical cores that resist rationality and separation from the environment; faculty engaged in state-of-the-art research often cannot determine their research plans in advance, and they must keep in constant communication with colleagues and funding agencies. In such situations, arbitrary bureaucratic boundaries would be disruptive.

Cosmopolitans and Locals: Prestige and Rank. The growing professionalism and specialization of faculty have tended to create faculty orientations to their institutions and to their disciplines that can be considered across a continuum. The two polar types have been referred to as "cosmopolitans" and "locals" (Gouldner, 1957). Cosmopolitans are faculty whose peers are colleagues across the country—or the world—who share their specialized scholarly interests. They tend to do research and publish, to find their rewards and satisfactions in their disciplinary activities, and to use their institutions as bases for their external activities. Cosmopolitans are less likely to be concerned with parochial campus issues and would tend to think of themselves primarily as independent professionals and scholars and secondarily (if at all) as faculty members at a particular university. Locals, on the other hand, are faculty whose major commitments are to their campuses. They tend to be integrated into the life of the campus community, to focus their attention on teaching, and to be concerned with and participate in institutional activities. They might think of themselves primarily as faculty members at a particular university and secondarily (if at all) as independent professionals and scholars.

The proportions on a faculty of cosmopolitans and locals can have a major effect on campus governance and patterns of influence. In traditional business organizations, prestige and rank are synonymous. The president at the top of the pyramid has both the greatest degree of prestige and the highest status (or rank) in the organization. A vice-president has less prestige and rank than the president but more than a subordinate officer. The organization confers both rank and prestige, and they are mutually reinforcing.

In higher education, however, prestige and rank may not be identical. While the institution may confer rank, prestige may be conferred by professional groups outside the university. A senior department chairperson may have less prestige (and peer influence) than an assistant professor who has just won a national award; a dean with a strong record of scholarship may be more influential with faculty than a vice-president for academic affairs. Particularly in institutions with large proportions of cosmopolitans, the conflicts between rank and prestige may weaken administrative authority and increase the difficulties in coordinating activities.

Other Organizational Differences. A number of organizational principles that differentiate colleges and universities from other organizations have already been suggested; there are other differences as well. If a "typical" business organization and "typical" university were compared, the university would exhibit less specialization of work activities (assistant professors and full professors do essentially the same things), a greater specialization by expertise ("unnecessary" history professors cannot be assigned to teach accounting when enrollments shift), a flatter hierarchy (fewer organizational levels between the faculty "workers" and the chief executive), lower interdependence of parts (what happens in one academic department is likely to have little effect on another), less control over "raw materials" (particularly in public institutions where student admission is nonselective), low accountability (because the administrative hierarchy and control system is less involved in directing goals activities), and less visible role performance (faculty usually carry out their professional teaching responsibilities unseen by either administrators or other professionals).

The differences between academic institutions and business firms are significant enough that systems of coordination and control effective in one of these types of organization might not have the same consequences in the other. In particular, it might be expected that colleges and businesses might require different approaches to leadership.

The Problem of Leadership

Our common notions of leadership arise from the perception that the success of business organizations depends on the directives of hard-driving, knowledgeable, and decisive executives. There are those who also see colleges and universities as the long shadows of great leaders or who assert that "our future rests on the bold, decisive leadership of college and university presidents nationwide" (Fisher, 1984, p. 11). On the other hand, it has been said that "the view of the university as the shadow of a strong president is unrealistic now, however, if indeed it was ever accurate" (Walker, 1979, p. 118) and even that "the presidency is an illusion" (Cohen and March, 1974, p. 2).

How important are administrative leaders to college and university performance? Do presidents make a difference? Because of what we think we see in business organizations, and what experts say about leaders in higher education, questions such as these may appear foolish. Lists identify the 100 most effective presidents ("The 100 Most Effective . . . ," 1986), and blue-ribbon panels argue that "strengthening presidential leadership is one of the most urgent concerns on the agenda of higher education" (Commission on Strengthening Presidential Leadership, 1984, p. 102). Leadership is treated as something identifiable, tangible, measurable, and efficacious. From the way we talk, it appears that we know what leadership is and how it should be practiced. Fine tuning may be required, of course, but the problems of higher education would presumably diminish if only leaders would be willing to exercise leadership—or if we would have the courage to replace them with others who would.

Calling for leadership is easy. But despite thousands of essays, research studies, and other scholarly and practical works, the fact remains that little is actually known about the phenomenon we refer to as "leadership." There is still no agreement on how leadership can be defined, measured, assessed, or linked to outcomes, and "no clear and unequivocal understanding exists as to what distinguishes leaders from nonleaders, and perhaps more important, what distinguishes effective leaders from ineffective leaders" (Bennis and Nanus, 1985, p. 4).

Leadership Theories. Most studies of leadership have taken place in business organizations, the military, and governmental agencies, with little attention given to higher education. The study of leadership is even more difficult in colleges and universities than in other settings because of the dual control systems, conflicts between professional and administrative authority, unclear goals, and the other unique properties of professional, normative organizations. In particular, the relationship between those identified as leaders and those whom they presume to lead is problematic. Some theoretical approaches assert that leadership can be understood only in the context of "followership." But in higher education, there is a strong resistance to leadership as it is generally understood in more traditional and hierarchical organizations; in particular, in most institutions it may be more appropriate to think of faculty as constituents than as followers.

Five basic approaches to studying organizational leadership are found in the literature (for summaries, see, for example, Yukl, 1981; Bass, 1981; Hollander, 1985). They include *trait theories*, which identify specific characteristics that are believed to contribute to a person's ability to assume and successfully function in a leadership position; *power and influence theories*, which attempt to understand leadership in terms of the source and amount of power available to leaders and the manner in which leaders exercise influence over followers through either unilateral or reciprocal interactions with them; *behavioral theories*, which study leadership by examining activity patterns, managerial roles, and behavioral categories of leaders—that is, considering what it is that leaders actually do; *contingency theories*, which emphasize the importance of situational factors such as the nature of the task or the external environment in understanding effective leadership; and *symbolic and cultural theories*, which assume that leadership is a social attribution that permits people to cognitively connect outcomes to causes and thereby make sense of an equivocal, fluid, and complex world.

Social Exchange Theory. One orientation to leadership particularly suited to higher education is known as social exchange theory. The theory posits that there is a reciprocal relationship whereby leaders provide needed services to a group in exchange for the group's approval and compliance with the leader's demands. In essence, the group agrees to collectively reduce its own autonomy and to accept the authority of the leader in exchange for the rewards and benefits (social approval, financial benefits, competitive advantage) the leader can bring them. Leaders are as dependent on followers as followers are on leaders.

Leaders accumulate power through their offices and their own personalities to the extent that they produce the expected rewards and fairly distribute them and lose power to the extent that they do not. This suggests that effectiveness as a leader depends on either fulfilling the expectations of followers by being a transactional leader or changing those expectations by being a transformational leader (Burns, 1978; Bennis and Nanus, 1985). The transactional leader meets the needs of followers and emphasizes means; the transformational leader emphasizes ends and taps the motivations of followers to lead them to new and better values in the support of intended change. Neither form, says Burns, should be confused with what commonly passes for leadership—"acts of oratory, manipulation, sheer self-advancement, brute coercion, . . . conspicuous position-taking without followers or follow through, posturing on various stages, . . . authoritarianism" (Burns, 1978, p. 427).

This caveat is important. It illuminates a common cognitive bias that leads us to base judgments about leaders on the extent to which they have characteristics that make them *look* like leaders. The old joke states the qualifications for college president as "white hair for that look of experience and hemorrhoids for that look of concern." As is true of many jokes, there is an important core of reality in this one that suggests that the effects of leadership may rely as much on our preconceptions and biases as on the observed outcomes that are clearly the consequences of leadership behavior.

Leadership as Symbol. Symbolic, cognitive, or cultural theories (see, for example, Deal and Kennedy, 1982; Cohen and March, 1974; Schein, 1985; Sergiovanni and Corbally, 1984; Weick, 1979) view organizations as systems of belief and perception in which reality is invented, not discovered. From this perspective, the role of leaders in business organizations is to "manage" the organizational culture. But the professional nature of colleges and universities may make the management of culture difficult if not impossible, and the role of leaders may therefore be more symbolic than real. Presidents may have relatively little influence over outcomes when compared with other forces that affect organizational functioning.

The possibility that leadership in its traditional sense may play only a minor role in the life of most colleges and universities most of the time is difficult to accept. We have developed highly romanticized, heroic views of leadership—what leaders do, what they are able to accomplish, and the general effects they have on our lives. One of the principal elements in this romanticized conception is the view that leadership is a central organizational process and the premier force in the scheme of organizational events and activities. It amounts to what might be considered a faith in the potential if not in the actual efficacy of people identified as leaders (Meindl, Ehrlich, and Dukerich, 1985). Cognitive biases allow us to see the "evidence" of the effects of leadership even when it does not exist. For example, work groups that are arbitrarily told that they have been successful at a task are more likely to perceive that they have had good leadership than groups that have been arbitrarily told that they have failed (Staw, 1975). Extreme (good or bad) performance of an organization is likely to lead to a preference to use leadership as an explanation even in the absence of any supporting data (Meindl, Ehrlich, and Dukerich, 1985). And it has been proposed that merely focusing someone's attention on a potential cause (and who is more likely to be visible and thought of than the president?) will affect the extent to which it is perceived as the cause (Nisbett and Ross, 1980). Findings such as these suggest that administrative leadership may be in part a product of social attributions. By creating roles that we declare will provide leadership to an organization, we construct the attribution that organizational effects are due to leadership behavior (Pfeffer, 1977). This allows us to simplify and make sense of complex organizational processes that would otherwise be impossible to comprehend (Meindl, Ehrlich, and Dukerich, 1985). In some ways, it is perhaps as sensible to say that successful organizational events "cause" effective administrators as it is to say that effective administrators "cause" successful events.

In many situations, presidential leadership may not be real but rather may be a social attribution. This can happen because of the tendency of campus constituents to assign to a president the responsibility for unusual institutional outcomes because the leader fills a role identified as that of leader, because presidents are very visible and prominent, because presidents spend a great deal of time doing leaderlike things (such as engaging in ceremonial and symbolic activities), and because we

all have the need to believe in the effectiveness of individual
control. Leaders, then, are people believed by followers to have
caused events. "Successful leaders," says Pfeffer (1977, p. 110),
"are those who can separate themselves from organizational failures and associate themselves with organizational successes."

    Leadership and Environments. Comparing traditional no-
tions of leadership to those that come out of the symbolic or
cognitive approach puts us in a rather difficult situation. Those
who call for the strengthening of presidential leadership recognize the high quality of current presidents (Commission on
Strengthening Presidential Leadership, 1984), and yet the best
appear not to be good enough. The primary factors affecting
leadership may be found not in the presidents themselves but
rather in the constraints that exist in the environment within
which administrators function. Good times seem to call forth
strong leaders. The late nineteenth century is seen now as a time
of giants who founded or expanded great institutions (although
it might have been difficult in 1890 to predict exactly who
these giants would appear to have been in 1990). Similarly, the
early 1960s saw an extraordinary number of campus leaders
who were skillful in directing new construction and burgeoning
enrollments. But, as has been pointed out, administrators then
had an easy job, and "by traditional standards, administrative
effectiveness was almost universal. Enrollments were increasing,
revenues were growing, innovations in the form of new and ex-
perimental programs were common. . . . Of course, the problem
with traditional standards of administrator effectiveness is that
criteria such as those listed above are largely a product of environmental forces and beyond administrative control" (Whetten
and Cameron, 1985, p. 35).

    Unfortunately, leadership appears in short supply in bad
times, such as during eras of decline or of student unrest. In the
late 1960s, for example, presidents faced with campus disruptions were criticized for not calling in the police as frequently as
they were for calling them, and for calling them either too soon
or too late. Presidents were castigated for ineffective leadership
even though post hoc suggestions proposing how one president

could have succeeded were precisely the explanations given on another campus for why a president failed.

Presidential influence is constrained by many factors, and many aspects of institutional functioning do not appear to depend on who the president happens to be (Birnbaum, forthcoming c). But this does not mean that presidents are unimportant. Complex social organizations cannot function effectively over the long term without leaders to coordinate their activities, represent them to their various publics, and symbolize the embodiment of institutional purpose. Moreover, if these leaders are to avoid conspicuous failure, they must have a high level of technical competence, an understanding of the nature of higher education in general and the culture of the individual institution in particular, and skills required to effectively interact with external constituencies. These are uncommon traits, but the processes of presidential selection function in a manner that makes it likely that successful candidates by and large will usually possess them (Birnbaum, forthcoming b). There may be little relationship between institutional functioning and presidential actions, but this does not necessarily mean that presidents are too weak; it could equally well be used to argue that presidents in general are quite good but that they are generally homogeneous in their effectiveness. This may in part be because the training and socialization of a new president are likely to be similar to those of the predecessor president, as well as to those of other persons who could plausibly have been considered for that specific vacancy. In general, most presidents do the right things, and do them right, most of the time; they properly fulfill the requirements of their roles even if they are unlikely to leave a distinctive mark on their institution.

The Nature of Academic Organization—A Summary

Because most institutions of higher education lack a clear and unambiguous mission whose achievement can be assessed through agreed upon quantifiable measures such as "profits," the processes, structures, and systems for accountability commonly used in business firms are not always sensible for them.

Many college and university managers do not exercise primary control over the curriculum, faculty recruitment or promotion, or the methods of teaching, major processes of production that in business firms would be fundamental managerial prerogatives. Issues of governance are clouded at least in part because "there is no center of authority analogous to the owners of the corporation, to the cabinet member, governor or mayor" (Corson, 1979, p. 7). The authority of various constituencies to participate in or make decisions is often unclear and frequently contested.

Although it is tempting to consider a college or university, in view of its corporate existence, as being comparable in many ways to a business corporation, the differences between the two are striking. In addition to matters already discussed, it has been noted (Kerr and Gade, 1986) that business firms, unlike institutions of higher education, have no tenured faculty members, face no criticisms from employees shielded by the principles of academic freedom, and have no alumni. The boards of business firms are likely to include large numbers of corporate officers and to be controlled by the corporate administration. The business firm can make and remake decisions constantly without the need for full consultation. In short, as Baldridge, Curtis, Ecker, and Riley (1978, p. 9) have put it, "the organizational characteristics of academic institutions are so different from other institutions that traditional management theories do not apply to them. Their goals are more ambiguous and diverse. They serve clients instead of processing materials. Their key employees are highly professionalized. They have unclear technologies based more on professional skills than on standard operating procedures. They have 'fluid participation' with amateur decision makers who wander in and out of the decision process. As a result, traditional management theories cannot be applied to educational institutions without carefully considering whether they will work well in that unique academic setting."

Common ideas about the efficacy of strong and decisive leadership may have some validity in business firms that are hierarchical and goal directed and in which subordinates expect to receive directives from superiors. But leaders in higher education are subject to internal and external constraints that limit their effectiveness and may make their roles highly symbolic rather than instrumental.

If traditional management theories are not applicable in higher education—at least in many institutions much of the time—people interested in exercising constructive influence on colleges and universities need other conceptual orientations to guide their interpretations and behaviors. A number of such orientations are presented in the models discussed in the second section of this book. These models will be easier to understand if first we can determine how colleges and universities operate as systems and how people come to act sensibly within them. In the next two chapters, we will look at these two questions using Huxley College, a fictitious institution, as a case in point.

Chapter 2

Thinking in
Systems and Circles:
The Structure and Dynamics
of Academic Organizations

Institutions differ in many ways, including their enrollments, programs, structures, and resource bases. In most of this book, I emphasize these differences in describing various organizational systems. But in introducing some basic systems concepts in this chapter, I present a fictitious generic institution named Huxley College and its president, Quincey Wagstaff. The ideas presented about Huxley are generally applicable to all colleges and universities, and they provide much of the conceptual base on which later chapters rely.

Huxley College is a complex institution, and its many structures and participants make it difficult to study. Understanding Huxley may be simplified by ignoring some of its specific characteristics and instead analyzing it as an abstraction called a "system." A system is an organized whole that has two or more interdependent parts (or subsystems) and is separated from its environment by a boundary (Kast and Rosenzweig, 1973). A lot is known about systems of various kinds, and this knowledge can help us understand how Huxley works. Systems are hierarchical; they are made up of smaller systems and are themselves parts of larger systems. For example, department

Chairperson Chippendale and department Professor Branch represent a subsystem of the urban ecology program area at Huxley, which is a subsystem of the sociology department, which in turn is a subsystem of the college, which is itself a subsystem of an informal statewide network of institutions. Each of these could be studied as a system in which the smaller units were the subsystems and the larger ones the supersystem.

The Nature of Systems

To clarify the system concept, I will describe two different systems, one relatively simple and one relatively complex, and compare their characteristics in terms of three elements common to all systems. In Figure 1, I have depicted the simple Pool System, representing a common recreational pastime, and the more complex School System, representing Huxley College.

The Pool System consists of a table surrounded by resilient borders within which are colored balls arranged in a triangle form. The School System can be depicted in a number of ways, but for this example I have shown it as consisting of two major components of Huxley College: a technical subsystem and an administrative subsystem. The Pool System and the School System are clearly quite different, and yet they share some common characteristics (Katz and Kahn, 1978).

Interacting Components. Both systems are composed of components that interact. In the Pool System, the movement of any of the balls from its initial position at the start of play affects every other ball on the table. In the School System, the components are not simple and clearly identifiable objects but rather are two complex subsystems. One of these, the technical subsystem, is composed of the elements of the system that turn inputs into outputs. For example, faculty, department chairs, academic freedom policy statements, and research laboratories at Huxley turn inputs such as students, money, prestige, societal expectations, chemicals, and books into outputs such as graduates, knowledge, service, and status. The administrative subsystem includes regulations, department chairs, the dean, budgets,

Figure 1. A Comparison of Two Systems.

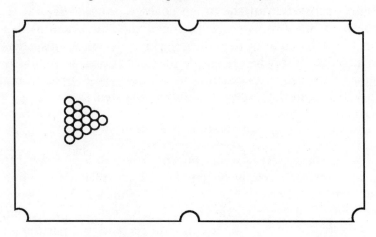

Pool System

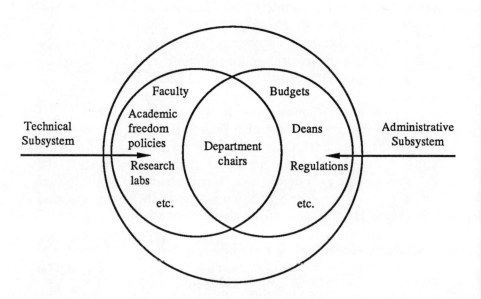

School System

and similar elements that help to coordinate and direct the organization. Although these two subsystems are different, they have some common elements (both include the department chairs, for example), and so they are shown as overlapping. Both the diagram and our everyday organizational experience suggest that these two subsystems interact with and affect each other. A change in the instructional program (for example, the development of a new area of study) may lead to changes in administration (for example, the start of a new department). In turn, the creation of a new department may alter the instructional program.

Boundaries. Both systems have boundaries that delineate them from the larger supersystems of which they are parts. The Pool System boundaries are clearly defined by the pool table itself. The School System boundaries are not as clear-cut, but we are still able for the most part to identify what is part of Huxley College and what is not. In both cases, we can identify everything outside the system boundaries as being a part of that system's environment.

Inputs and Outputs. Systems receive inputs from the environment, transform them in some way, and then return them to the environment. Environmental input into the Pool System is relatively simple. It comes as kinetic energy transferred from the cue stick to the cue ball and then to the other balls, causing them to move. By the time all the balls are again at rest, the kinetic energy from the environment that initiated the process has been transformed by the laws of thermodynamics into heat, which has been dissipated and returned to the environment.

While the Pool System has only one major environmental input, the School System has many. For the present example, consider the students. They enter Huxley College, interact with faculty and each other, and then as graduates or dropouts return to the environment. Both common sense and a considerable body of research (Bowen, 1977; Astin, 1977) indicate that students are likely to be changed in many ways during their involvement with Huxley, so that after the system "processes" them they are different from the way they were initially. Even when they return to the environment as "products," they continue to affect the system as alumni and citizens.

Types of Systems. Both Pool and School meet our definition of a system, but they appear to be quite different in many ways. As administrators, we often ignore our intuitive understanding of these differences and treat School System problems as if they were Pool System problems. We may try to prescribe rigid procedures to be applied in defined ways to produce specified outcomes. We may treat failure to achieve the desired end state as a management deficiency that can be corrected by better measurement or more effective application. Such approaches seldom work. Why is a prescription that works in one system a failure in another?

The answer is that in fact we are dealing with two different kinds of systems: the closed system of the Pool and the open system of the School. Closed systems have boundaries that are relatively rigid and impenetrable and that limit the kinds of interaction that take place with the environment. Input to closed systems tends to be definable, controllable, and relatively simple; processing that input can be systematic and scheduled. Flow charts and formulas can often be used with great precision. Output from closed systems disappears and does not serve to energize the system. Closed systems are linear; the system parts do not change, and cause and effect can be predicted with great accuracy. Success comes from playing by the rules.

In an open system such as Huxley College, the boundaries are relatively permeable, and interactions of many kinds are likely to occur between the environment and many of the system elements. Inputs to open systems are much more complex and may consist of people, ideas, tangible resources, or involvement with other institutions or systems. The characteristics of the input often cannot be accurately assessed or controlled, and processing input can be problematic because it may rely on uncertain interactions between elements. Outputs do not disappear as they do in a closed system but return to the environment, where they may again become inputs. Open systems are dynamic and nonlinear. The system parts are themselves systems; they constantly change as they interact with themselves and with the environment, and the system evolves over time.

Those who write about nonlinear systems use metaphors to suggest their dynamic nature: it is like being in a maze in which the walls change with every step you take; it is like consulting a clock that changes time as a result of being consulted; it is like playing a game in which every move you make changes the rules. Cause and effect in such systems often can be neither predicted nor adequately explained. Dynamic, nonlinear systems such as Huxley College at some times may appear to operate in an orderly manner, and at other times may fluctuate erratically. The complex outcomes that arise from such systems often lead us to infer complicated causes, but in fact the chaotic behavior of nonlinear systems such as Huxley may result from the continued processing and interaction of a small number of relatively simple rules.

Is an open system better than a closed system? No, just different. Each has its place. Consider the difficulty in playing pool if the table were part of an open system affected by many forces inside and outside its boundaries. Suppose, for example, that each ball "learned" from being struck and reacted slightly differently each time it was hit! Recognizing the differences between open and closed systems will turn out to be important in our later considerations of institutional governance and organization. Of course, since we are dealing in this book with social institutions, we will be concerned by definition with open systems. But even open systems can be more or less open, and the effectiveness of some institutions (or parts of institutions) may be enhanced by adjusting the extent to which they are relatively open or closed to influences from the environment.

Tight and Loose Coupling

In order to understand how the various subsystems and elements within a system interact with each other, we must consider how they are connected, or coupled. The coupling be-

tween elements in a system can range from tight to loose. We
can examine two simple systems to see how coupling works.
Both systems are black boxes with an input rotor protruding
from one end and an output rotor from the other. If we turn
the input rotor of the first box one full turn clockwise, the
output rotor turns exactly the same way on a one-to-one basis.
But on the second box, the output rotor appears to move almost randomly. In order to understand why one box is so predictable and the other is so perverse, we open both boxes and
see the elements shown in Figures 2 and 3.

Figure 2. Inside a Predictable Black Box.

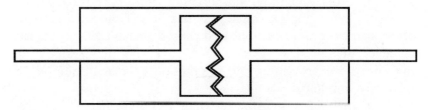

     Seeing inside the predictable box (Figure 2) makes the
reasons for our observations clear. Each rotor is attached to a
gear whose teeth match exactly. This precise correspondence between the two elements is an example of tight coupling. Coupling this tight is common in mechanical structures, but it rarely
occurs in organizations. However, tight coupling is relative, and
even at Huxley College we can observe certain situations in
which changes in one element (actions by the college curriculum committee or President Wagstaff's decisions on administrative salaries, for example) usually produce directly responsive
changes in another (such as new sections in the college catalogue
or revised paychecks).
     Let us turn our attention now to the second black box,
identical in external appearance to the first. We confidently
move the input rotor one full turn clockwise and are startled to
find that the output rotor turns only one-half turn and then
stops. We try it many times and find that sometimes it turns all
the way, sometimes it does not turn at all, and once in a while it

turns a short way in the opposite direction! Sometimes it will run smoothly, and at other times it will go in fits and starts. There just does not seem to be a simple relationship between the two rotors, and when we open this perverse black box and see the internal structure shown in Figure 3, we begin to understand why.

Figure 3. Inside a Perverse Black Box.

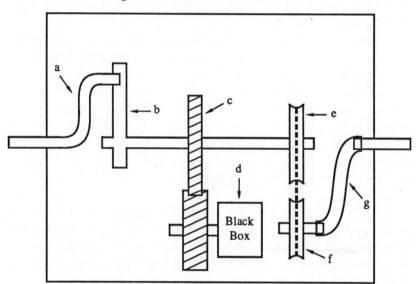

First, the input rotor is offset (*a*), so that sometimes it immediately hits the bar (*b*) when turned, and sometimes it does not. The bar is connected to a gear (*c*), but the connection appears itself to be moderated by another black box (*d*) that we cannot open, so that the motion of large wheel (*e*) cannot always be predicted from the motion of the gear. The large wheel is connected to a smaller wheel (*f*) by a rubber band that sometimes slips, and the big wheel is connected to the output rotor by plastic tubing (*g*) that is semirigid and requires a certain increment of force before it moves. This is a loosely coupled system. The elements of the system are responsive to each other, but they also preserve their own identities and some logical separateness. Describing loose coupling by using this mechanical example oversimplifies the concept. In a social system, not only may there be discontinuities in the way the parts are connected, but the "parts" (participants) themselves have intentions, preconceptions, and wills that change over time. The faculty senate at Huxley, for example, is one "part" of a "perverse" black box. Its members, and their opinions and desires, change over time. Even providing input to the senate alters the senate's configuration.

Our first black box, like the Pool System, can be thought of as *deterministic*. We can accurately predict its future state if we know its present state and the forces that will act on it (Ashby, 1956). The second black box, like the School System, is *probabilistic*. President Wagstaff can say what outcomes are possible if, for example, he rejects a recommendation of the faculty tenure committee and how frequently they will occur *on average*. But no matter how much he knows about Huxley's history or present conditions, he can never predict with certainty the consequences of any future tenure decision, nor can he project Huxley's future state in any specific situation.

The differences between the two black boxes are now clear to us—but only because we have been able to open them. In the real world, the boxes do not open easily, if at all, and we have to make judgments about coupling on the basis of external appearances (remembering that they look the same!) and on what we can learn about the relationship between inputs and outputs. This may be tricky, because sometimes the two boxes will act exactly the same way! There will be times when a loosely coupled system will (by chance) behave consistently, and times when a tightly coupled system (because some connection or part has broken down) will not. The difficulty of distinguishing between deterministic and probabilistic systems causes obvious problems for administrators, who often see only the inputs and outputs and then have to make plausible (but often untestable) inferences about the relationships between them.

We will use the term *loose coupling* to refer to connections between organizational subsystems that may be infrequent, circumscribed, weak in their mutual effects, unimportant, or slow to respond (Weick, 1976). Tight and loose coupling are relative terms. Conceptually they can be differentiated on two criteria: the extent to which subsystems have common variables between them and the extent to which the shared variables are important to the subsystems. If the subsystems have a great many components in common (like the gears on our predictable black box), and if those elements are among the most important in the subsystems, the subsystems are likely to be relatively tightly coupled, and changes in one should produce clear changes in the other.

On the other hand, the instructional and administrative subsystems of the simple School System of Huxley College shown in Figure 1 have only one element in common—the department chair. If the chair is tightly coupled to one subsystem, it is almost certainly loosely coupled to the other (that is, the chair can be completely responsive to either the dean's demands or the faculty's demands but not to both). In addition, the department chair at Huxley is not among the most important elements in either subsystem. Because of this, changes in one subsystem might lead to changes in the other sometimes but not all the time, and the subsystems could be characterized as being loosely coupled. Although this model is highly simplified, it suggests at least one reason why attempts to develop administrative approaches to curriculum reform at Huxley are often unsuccessful. A major frustration of administrative life in loosely coupled systems is the difficulty of getting things to work the way the administrator wants them to.

Functions and Dysfunctions of Loosely Coupled Systems. Loose coupling has often been attacked as merely a slick way to describe waste, inefficiency, or indecisive leadership and as a convenient rationale for the crawling pace of organizational change. It has been argued that if coupling were tighter, institutions would find it easier to communicate, achieve predictability, control their processes, and better achieve their goals (Lutz, 1982). Does loose coupling serve any constructive functions? Should administrators at Huxley try to change loose coupling and run a "tighter ship"?

To be sure, loosely coupled systems have significant

costs. Some subsystems at Huxley may be uncoordinated and in conflict with others. Programs can respond unwisely to environmental stimuli, as happened in the past when the athletic department, without Wagstaff's knowledge, engaged in recruitment violations under pressure from the Huxley Boosters Club. Loose coupling makes it difficult for Huxley to discard bad ideas or to disseminate good ones throughout the institution; the physics department still requires its students to study German despite pressure from the dean to be more flexible, and other programs have been unwilling to consider adopting the "writing through the curriculum" program that has been so successful in the history department. Loose coupling also makes it difficult to repair defective subsystems. Even though the dean knows that there are significant weaknesses in the freshman mathematics program, the number of conflicting internal and external influences on faculty recruitment, curriculum content, and faculty development is so great that the dean despairs of being able to do much about it. In general, loose coupling makes coordination of activities problematic and makes it difficult to use administrative processes to effect change.

But loose coupling has significant benefits as well. Having partially independent and specialized organizational elements increases Huxley's sensitivity to its environment. For example, the college's small continuing education division, which had operated almost independently and invisibly for years, was the first unit at Huxley to sense the growing enrollment potential of the "new learner." The presence of that division also permitted Huxley to respond to the needs of these students without immediately mobilizing all the other programs and subsystems of the college. Over time, many programs were developed, ranging from courses by television to on-campus residential experiences for senior citizens. Loose coupling made it possible for Huxley to create and retain a large number of these novel (and incompatible) solutions to the new situation. It also made it possible for them to seal off ineffective college components so that their failures remained localized. For example, even though the Shakespeare Dinner Theater program for working adults proved to be an academic, fiscal, and culinary disaster, other programs for new learners continued and prospered.

Coupling and Survival. Huxley College is a system composed of subsystems that interact both among themselves and with the environment outside the college's boundaries. Each subsystem is relatively loosely or tightly coupled with each other subsystem, depending on the extent to which common organizational elements are shared and are important to the subsystems. Each subsystem is at the same time relatively loosely or tightly coupled to environmental subsystems, again depending on the extent to which they share common elements. A major change in any subsystem, or in the environment, can be expected to have a marked effect on any other subsystem to which it is relatively tightly coupled and a weaker or less predictable effect if there is loose coupling. In an open system, everything cannot be tightly coupled to everything else, and loose coupling between and within subsystems is more prevalent than tight coupling.

Huxley College has a large number of environmental relationships and demands that are inconsistent with each other. For example, the college is under pressure from one part of the environment to increase the test scores of entering students and from another part to increase student access. Insisting on tight coupling among all the institution's subsystems *and* between those subsystems and the environment would cause Huxley to "freeze" internally. Either it would be unable to respond to any environmental stimuli at all or it would self-destruct in the impossible attempt to simultaneously respond to mutually inconsistent stimuli. Loose coupling makes it possible for Huxley to develop subsystems (for example, an honors program and an equal opportunity program) that respond separately to each of these demands. Loose coupling therefore can be considered not as evidence of organizational pathology or administrative failure to be identified and corrected but rather as an adaptive device essential to the survival of an open system (Weick, 1976). Effective administration may depend not on overcoming it but on accepting and understanding it.

The Contingency Approach

The School System model of Huxley College includes three major parts—the environment, the administrative subsystem, and the technical subsystem. The critical question is how the subsystems (and the smaller subsystems within them, as well as the larger subsystems of which they are a part) are connected together, because it is this pattern of loose and tight coupling that defines the system's organization. The behavior of a college or university as a system depends critically on the details of these connections. A contingency approach to organization suggests that there is no one best pattern but at the same time that not all patterns are equally effective (Galbraith, 1973). In a given situation, some ways of organizing are better than others.

The School System model suggests that at least two things must be considered in designing an effective administrative system—the environment and the technical subsystem. Understanding the environment is critical, because organizations have vital continuing and mutual transactions with elements outside their boundaries. Understanding the technical subsystem is important because it describes the characteristic ways in which colleges and universities transform their inputs into outputs; these processes through which teaching, research, and service are accomplished are the way the organization actually "does" its work. These two elements pose the greatest degree of uncertainty for an organization, and it is the differences in these dimensions that lead to differences in organizations (Thompson, 1967). We would therefore expect that to the extent that colleges and universities have different environments and technologies, they would also find different management and governance systems to be most effective. The key administrative question, therefore, is what administrative and managerial structures and behaviors will most effectively support the organization's technical system, given certain characteristics of the environment.

The Environment of Colleges and Universities. We can understand a great deal about why institutions act as they do if we understand that they are responding to their perception of their environment. This approach has been used recently in a limited way to study how institutions respond to changes in financial and enrollment conditions in the economic sector of their environment. But other environmental sectors, although less studied, are also important. For example, general societal values, political and legal constraints, changes in information and technical processes, and physical and geographical matters are all important elements of the environment with which organizations have to cope (Katz and Kahn, 1978).

Environments can be stable or turbulent, so that some institutions may exist in worlds that look much the same year to year, while others constantly confront new and unexpected problems as enrollments suddenly decline or external agencies demand new and costly programs or reports. Some live in a homogeneous world in which, for example, students have common backgrounds; others face a diverse world of students from different cultures and with different levels of preparation. Institutions may find that necessary resources such as money or students are either scattered randomly throughout the environment or clustered in identifiable areas, and while these resources may be scarce for some colleges, they may be abundant for others. Generalizations are difficult, but it probably can be said that, on average, institutions are becoming less autonomous and more connected into outside systems than in the past. The environment of organizations increasingly consists of other organizations. As environments become increasingly turbulent, they evolve faster than their constituent organizations. Changes in organizations are being caused more by their environments than by internal forces (Terreberry, 1968).

The level of stability, homogeneity, clustering, and munificence of the environment of Huxley College will affect its governance and management systems. Since the environments of other institutions are likely to be different from Huxley's, their governance and management procedures should also differ. Institutions must respond to environments that have different economic, social value, political, informational, and physical characteristics. This is true not only for institutions but for subunits within institutions as well. In order to be effective, the subunits of an organization should parallel the characteristics of the environment with which they must interact (Lawrence and Lorsch, 1967). That is, simple environments call for simple processes and structures, while complex environments call for complex processes and structures. For example, colleges and universities that have generally placid and consistent environments can have internal processes and structures that are reasonably uniform. Since little changes, the coordination of the various subunits to ensure organizational integration is relatively easy and requires little attention. But as institutions become complex and find some or all of their components to be related to environments that are different from each other, each subunit has to specialize and differentiate. As subunits look less alike, integration becomes difficult, and additional resources and attention have to be given to it.

The governance and management of a highly differentiated institution are obviously likely to be significantly different from those of a less differentiated one. Institutions faced with environmental uncertainty and diversity *must* be highly differentiated if they are to be effective. That is why they have so many different kinds of organizational subunits, why their activities pose so many problems of coordination, and why rationalizing and defending their "nonbusinesslike" structure is so difficult.

The Technical Subsystem of Colleges and Universities. Technologies can differ in terms of complexity (the number of diverse elements that the organization must simultaneously deal with), uncertainty or unpredictability (the uniformity of the elements on which work is done and the ability to predict the outcomes of work), and interdependence (whether work processes are interrelated) (Scott, 1981). Colleges and universities are all involved in one way or another with doing the work required for fulfilling their teaching, research, and service missions. But while the technologies of different institutional types may have more elements in common with each other than they do with a bank or a business firm, their technologies are also quite different in many ways. For example:

• Teaching, research, and service are each performed with the use of different technologies. As simple examples, teaching typically involves classroom instruction, student advising, final examinations, and communication with colleagues in the same institution; research may require laboratory investigation, library work, and communication with colleagues in other institutions; service programs utilize workshops, consulting, extension centers, policy analyses, and communications with community agencies.

- Institutions allocate their work effort differently. Some give primary attention to teaching and secondary attention to service; others focus on teaching with particular emphasis on general education and a distinctive model of scholarship (Ruscio, 1987); still others emphasize research, with teaching and service both given secondary emphasis.
- The raw materials to be worked on differ, and they affect the technologies employed. In undergraduate education, for instance, institutions that have an open-door admissions policy may give considerable attention to remedial education technologies that are not utilized at all at selective institutions.
- The people applying the technology at the various institutions differ in terms of their preparation and skills. In some institutions, almost all faculty have doctoral degrees and expertise in highly specialized areas; in others, most faculty have only master's degrees.

Differences such as these create distinctive patterns of technologies (Clark, 1983) at different institutions and, thus, different ways in which people work together. Since the technical and managerial levels of the organization are interdependent, these differences in technologies can be best supported by different management structures and processes (Newman, 1971). When change is infrequent and the problems are precedented, a stable management system may be appropriate. Centralized decision making, coordination by rules and regulations, specific planning with short horizons and limited participation, close supervision, and emphasis on efficiency and dependability may all be effective.

When change is frequent and the problems are precedented, the technology type calls for less centralization, coordination by specialized planning units, planning of interlocking activities with attention to intermediate goals, and emphasis on quality. And when there is frequent need for change and there are few precedents, the technology must be adaptive. Management processes supporting adaptive systems are likely to be decentralized, to be coordinated through face-to-face interaction within the unit, to emphasize general plans that are adjusted according to feedback, and to give attention to learning based on experience.

Differences in Institutional Governance and Management. There is a tendency when discussing institutions of higher education to make general statements concerning the nature of the faculty, the appropriate roles of various constituencies in governance, issues of organization and structure, and even mission and goals, as if all institutions were alike. But in fact, as I have tried to show, colleges and universities may differ from each other in a variety of important ways, and these systemic differences—particularly as they are reflected in the institution's environment and its technology—should significantly influence the ways that institutions are managed and governed. What is good for Huxley College may be ineffectual at another institution. Studies that have compared institutions of various kinds have identified differences in governance and management patterns that might be expected from their environmental and technological differences (Baldridge, Curtis, Ecker, and Riley, 1978).

Institutions with relatively stable technologies and environments should be able to function effectively using closed-system logic and bureaucratic structures. Complex environments and technologies call for open-system logic. Failure to recognize these differences may lead managers to think of all institutions as using closed-system logic, to view their internal operations as confused, and to suggest the application of inappropriate corrective doses of better (that is, tighter) management. However, as a general rule, if a college or university is to be effective, the more uncertain the technical core, the looser must be the linkages to the management subsystem and the tighter the linkages to the environment.

Thinking in Circles

I have discussed colleges and universities as open and dynamic systems composed of patterns of interacting elements and subsystems loosely or tightly coupled to each other and to their environments. What makes things "happen" in such systems, and how can we characterize the relationship between causes and effects? We often think about institutions in a linear fashion ("the faculty shapes the curriculum"). But the curriculum affects the faculty as much as the faculty influences the curriculum; a systems perspective requires us to replace linear thinking with an understanding of how elements and subsystems are connected to each other in nonlinear circles of reciprocal interaction and influence.

As an example, President Wagstaff thinks in circles (Weick, 1979) about the coupling between institutional prestige, student enrollment, and financial resources. The circle in Figure 4 shows

Figure 4. A Circular System That Reinforces and Amplifies Change.

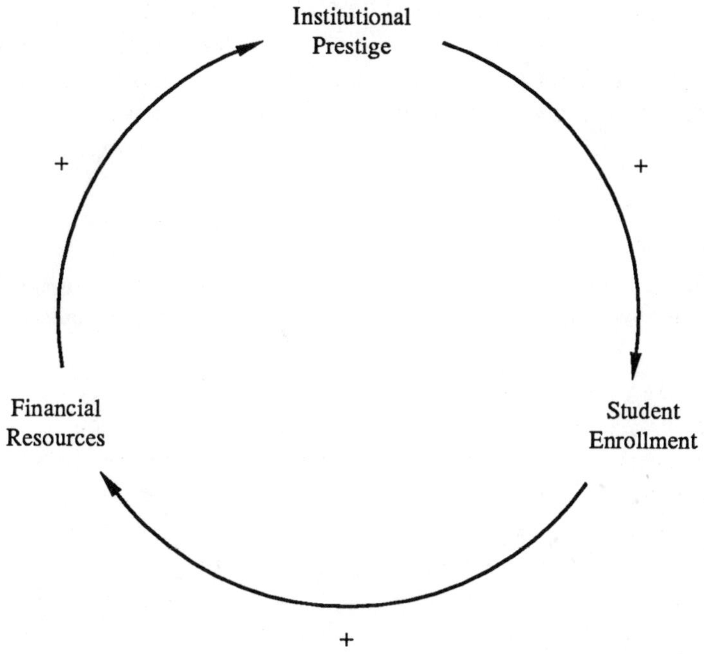

what the president currently believes the important couplings to
be, although these may change over time as the system itself
evolves. The circle suggests that increases in prestige (for example, being named as one of the top twenty-five colleges in the
country) will lead to increased enrollments, which in turn will
increase the financial resources of Huxley and thus raise Huxley's
prestige still further. This kind of map suggests that a change in
any of the elements will be reinforced and amplified as it moves
through the circle. In nonlinear systems such as Huxley, amplifying loops such as this make it possible for small changes in one
part of the system to sometimes have very large effects.

Some circles of interaction are not reinforcing and amplifying but rather are self-correcting and stabilizing. For example,
Figure 5 displays the relationship among institutional prestige,
student enrollment, sense of community, and faculty morale at
Huxley College. When prestige increases, student enrollment in-

Figure 5. A Circular System That Corrects and Stabilizes Change.

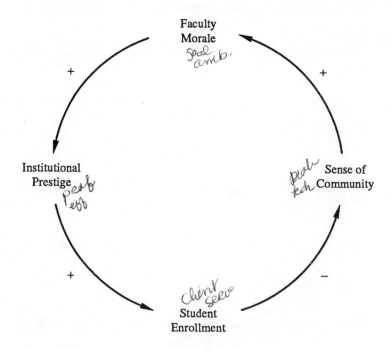

creases as well. Huxley has always prided itself on a sense of community in which faculty and students knew each other well. But if the number of students gets larger, the sense of community on campus decreases. In turn, this reduces faculty morale. As faculty morale declines, so does institutional prestige. Enrollment then also diminishes, so that the sense of community is restored. This kind of circle of interaction corrects and controls changes as they move through the system. Stabilizing loops such as this in nonlinear systems mean that large changes in one element become buffered and can sometimes end up having little effect at all.

These amplifying and stabilizing loops obviously oversimplify the complicated relationships that exist between elements in the circles of interaction. If Huxley consisted only of amplifying loops, any change in prestige or resources would set off a never-ending growth in enrollment. If Huxley consisted only of stabilizing loops, enrollment would eventually return to its previous level regardless of what happened to prestige, resources, or faculty morale. In fact, Huxley contains both types of loop, and the future of the college is dependent not so much on either loop separately but on how these loops are connected.

In Figure 6, for example, the two loops have been combined into what has been called a "cause map" (Weick, 1979) that shows how they share elements that may become loosely or tightly coupled. The complex cause map is still not complete, but it gives a representation of the factors that tie together enrollment, prestige, community, morale, and financial resources at Huxley that is more accurate than that shown by either loop alone. Even if the model was complete and correct, the fact that dynamic systems are always changing and never look exactly the same would still make it impossible to accurately predict the consequences of changing any single element in the system. But by giving President Wagstaff a more complicated sense of the dynamics of Huxley, it may prevent him from making a bad decision on the basis of a simplistic view of how the college works.

Maps such as these can aid understanding to the extent that we can identify the relevant variables, the looseness or tight-

Figure 6. A Cause Map at Huxley College.

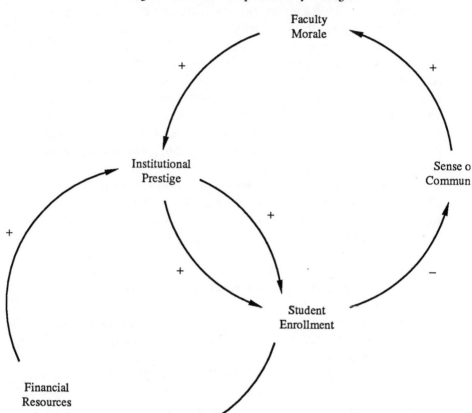

ness of their couplings or interactions, and their relative importance. But even when the critical variables are simple and the relationships clear, predictions of organizational outcomes from administrative behaviors can never be certain. Thinking about systems as loops of interaction therefore is not so much an administrative tool as a way of developing a model of administrative thought. Such models help to suggest that things may be more complex than they appear and prevent us from expecting simplistic solutions to be effective; they can reduce our expectations that the results of administrative actions will necessarily be direct or long lasting and teach us that problems may continually emerge and require attention; they can help us to understand why cause and effect are problematic at best; and they can help administrators think of factors that might influence a proposed action (even though they might not be obviously related to it) and to consider appropriate preventive measures.

Whether consciously or unconsciously, administrators often act on the basis of these kinds of maps. Thinking in circles rather than in straight lines provides a better understanding of organizational dynamics and can make administrators more effective. It often does this not by suggesting what we should do but rather by cautioning us about what not to do. Circular thinking can also lead to administrative indecision and impotence if it is misinterpreted to mean that nothing can be done and that nothing will make a difference. Administrators can make a difference, and consciously attempting to think of circles and other indirect connections will help in determining the potential effectiveness of various strategies and tactics.

Implications for Administrators

In this chapter I have introduced the basic idea of colleges and universities as open systems that are engaged in a number of continuing exchange processes with their environments. These institutions can be thought of as composed of subsystems that are related to each other through shared organizational elements. If these subsystems were tightly connected to each other, a change in one would directly affect them all. Since this often does not happen, it is useful to think of institutions of higher education as consisting of loosely coupled systems. While loose coupling can cause problems for administrators who wish to correct institutional problems or to promote change, it also serves important functions in both preserving institutions and making them adaptable and responsive.

Organizational elements are connected in ways that either intensify or stabilize system responses to environmental pressures. Changes in one part of the organization may affect other parts through a sequence of relationships, rather than directly. Responses to an administrative action may occur long after the action itself has been taken. Small initial actions may have extremely large consequences, and because the interaction is nonlinear, the outcomes may not be predictable and are often quite different from those originally intended.

These basic concepts of systems, loose coupling, and circular maps will be critical in later chapters to a more complete understanding of college and university organization and management. Before exploring their significance in greater depth, however, other more obvious implications for administrators should be considered.

Cause and Effect. Because the elements and subsystems of the organization are coupled (either tightly or loosely) to each other and to the environment with which they are linked in continuous exchange, their relationships are interactive and reciprocal. If cause A leads to effect B, then that effect becomes the new cause that then leads to effect C, which becomes a new cause, and so on. As administrators, we may tend to think in only limited cause-effect chains and to consider the direction of those relationships as linear. Viewing colleges and universities as systems should make us less certain about our assumptions and permit us to realize that the point at which we break into a cause-and-effect loop and separate one from the other is often arbitrary. Sometimes what we see as an effect is really a cause. For example, does increased centralization of decision making in public systems lead to faculty bargaining, or does faculty bargaining lead to increased centralization of decision making? Are institutional research offices started because data needs increase, or do data needs increase because institutional research offices are created? Does disaffection cause faculty to avoid participating in governance activities, or does lack of participation create faculty disaffection? Our often untested assumptions about cause and effect may lead us to act in a manner that unknowingly exacerbates rather than corrects our problems.

Time and Administrative Behavior. Recognition of cause and effect is constrained by the time it takes to see changes made in one part of a loosely coupled system have a measurable effect on another part. The greater the separation in time, the less obvious the cause-and-effect relationship will be. Administrators attempting to understand the impact of their behavior in a specific situation may often have to decide whether their action had no effect, whether their action will have a planned effect that has not yet been felt, whether their action has had an unplanned effect that has not yet been recognized, or whether a planned outcome was actually due to the presumed cause. In each case, the data available to them are likely to be limited and ambiguous, and their conclusions may be based more on their preconceptions and hopes than on careful analysis.

Administrators who often move from one institution to another may be faced with a comparable dilemma. If some positive effects of their behaviors become evident immediately, but due to loose coupling the large-scale negative effects are not visible until after they have left the system, they may "learn" (incorrectly) that their actions have been successful. They may repeat these actions in their new setting, continuing the same cycle of ineffective behavior and uncorrected feedback. A president may develop an undeserved reputation for successfully "turning an institution around" through disruptive activities that lead to short-term accomplishments. Successors may be left to reap the long-term whirlwind. The same problems that may lead administrators to incorrectly assess their successes may also lead them incorrectly to believe that they have failed; they may observe short-term negative consequences but leave before long-term benefits become evident.

Predictability. The relationships between the environment and organizational subsystems, and between the subsystems themselves, are exceptionally complex. We usually cannot specify with assurance precisely what the relevant elements are or how they interact. For that reason, administrative actions may sometimes have a very dramatic and expected effect, but at other times identical actions may appear to have little or no effect (and occasionally may have an effect directly opposite to the one expected). This is what is meant by the "counterintuitive behavior of social systems"; things happen that appear contrary to common sense. We may fail to get what we want not because we have not planned well enough but because many aspects of the system do not operate in a manner that conforms to conventional administrative rationality. One common administrative response is to try to correct this organizational perversity by making the system more rational through tighter controls. Although this often makes the problem worse, much of organizational life is so equivocal that we can easily fool ourselves into believing that things have gotten better. Rather than trying to make colleges more predictable, administrators might be better off learning how to increase their effectiveness under conditions of low predictability.

Differences Between Institutions. Even though institutions of various kinds may be quite different, administrators still tend to discuss issues of college and university faculty, governance, structure, and processes as if that were not true and to support normative ideas such as "shared authority" without regard for organizational differences. For example, the technology employed by an open-admissions college in educating students is likely to be considerably different from the technology utilized by a selective liberal arts college. Systems theory makes it easier to understand why these differences in the technical subsystem are almost certain to be reflected in differences in other subsystems as well. In particular, administrators should be aware that the management subsystems of two different institutions are likely to be different and, indeed, that if their technologies vary, then their management systems *should* vary. We must therefore learn to be wary of any normative statement of administration or management that does not clearly specify the characteristics of the type of organization to which it is to apply.

The Need for Unlearning. Differences in organizational subsystems are reflected in the kinds of loops and cause maps that we develop. Because of our experiences in one kind of organizational setting, we "learn" which organizational elements affect others, and we internalize cause maps on which we act. We usually do not think through these maps, and, because they are often not developed through self-conscious reflection, they tend to be simplistic and to contain many untested assumptions. When administrators move to new institutions, they may bring their old cause maps with them. Whetten and Cameron (1985, p. 41) suggest that administrators who move from one institution to another may be ineffective because of preconceptions "linked to previous personal successes at other universities." Becoming aware of the elements and relationships that form our cause maps permits us in new institutions to recognize the need to unlearn previous maps.

The linear and nonlinear modes of thought discussed in this chapter are related to very different administrative world views. Administrators who see the world as linear believe that their institutions should function in a regular and steady manner. Fluctuations and exceptions are indications of problems that they should attend to and correct. Administrators who appreciate nonlinearity recognize that systems will often exhibit what may appear to be random behavior. They realize that erratic and even bizarre outcomes in the short term may not be an indication of long-term problems, but rather are expected in complex systems. Interventions may make them worse; if allowed to run their course, they will often disappear.

Administrators with linear perspectives are likely to emphasize making rational decisions; administrators with nonlinear perspectives are likely to be concerned with making sense. Linear administrators think they know how the system works and how to change it; nonlinear administrators are more modest in their assumptions and their expectations. The differences in the processes and assumptions of these alternative orientations are the subject of the next chapter.

Chapter 3

Making Decisions
and Making Sense:
The Administrator's Role

Linear administrators view organizations as "hierarchical systems for taking consequential action in a comprehensible world" (March, 1982, p. 1). Such administrators expect to deliberately move an institution toward the effective achievement of its goals, and they advocate complex planning and budgeting systems to assist in making rational and presumably better decisions. Everyone wants to appear rational (particularly considering the alternative!), and deciding on those actions that will maximize the effective achievement of stated goals would probably be seen by many as representing the ideal of how administrators should function. But as reasonable as the idea of rationality might appear, it seems quite elusive in practice at Huxley College. Somehow, many things that happen there do not appear consistent with the analytical principles that appear so "logical" and "correct."

Can this be good? Would Huxley function more effectively if it conformed more closely to rational models? Do some of the unusual organizational characteristics of colleges have an effect on the usefulness of rational models? And if participants in Huxley's organizational and administrative processes are not primarily concerned with being rational, what is it that they *are* concerned with? We explore these questions in this chapter.

Being Rational

Rationality assumes that the purpose of decision making is to create outcomes that maximize the values of the decision maker. An objectively rational administrator is one who knows all the information, considers all the alternatives, evaluates and compares all sets of consequences, and then selects the best alternative. But in the real world of Huxley College, knowledge is never complete. It is always limited or bounded in some way (March and Simon, 1958; Simon, 1961), and therefore rationality must always be bounded as well. There are many reasons why President Wagstaff can never have perfect knowledge. For example: (1) Huxley is exceptionally complex, and there are too many potential variables to permit any single person to give attention to all of them. (2) The information that administrators receive through Huxley's channels of communication is filtered and distorted by the perceptions of those who transmit it. (3) The interactions between and among internal and external variables are intricate and often loosely coupled, and outcomes of alternative courses of action are often uncertain. (4) The number of alternative courses of action that exist in any given situation is so large that they cannot all be examined. Those that are actually considered are always a subset (and usually a rather small subset) of all potential alternatives.

These problems suggest that objective rationality at Huxley is impossible. The best Wagstaff can hope for, given the complexities of the real world, the inherent limitations of human cognitive abilities, and the loose coupling of organizational structures and processes, is subjective rationality. President Wagstaff can try to make the best decisions with what he *does* know. But even this is more difficult than it seems.

Problems of Calculation and Comparison. All but the simplest decisions have many alternative outcomes, each of which requires trade-offs between competing values. These values can be assessed in tangible units, such as dollars or numbers of people, or in intangible units, such as power, relative advantage, or prestige. At Huxley, many decisions are presumed to support desired outcomes such as excellence, equity, participation, access, or choice. Rationality requires calculations and comparisons. Wagstaff can easily compare decisions that rely solely on quantifiable units such as money. But comparing decisions involving intangibles such as "excellence" is much more difficult, since there is no standard unit of value against which all possible outcomes of such a decision can be assessed. As an example, say that Wagstaff, who values both "excellence" and "access," is faced with a choice of accepting plan A, which would produce five units of excellence and three units of access, or plan B, which would result in two units of excellence and six units of access. What is the rational decision? Which plan maximizes his values? Without a standard metric that permits objective weighing of the total value of each alternative, there is no rational answer to these questions.

Satisficing. If rationality were not bounded, Wagstaff could maximize the outcomes of his decisions. But the complexity of the college and his own limited ability to process information make maximizing impossible under most circumstances. Fortunately, there are very few circumstances in which he really has to find the best decision. Most of the time, he need only find an acceptable decision. That is, rather than maximize, he can "satisfice" (March and Simon, 1958).

"Satisficing" means that he establishes criteria for deciding what an outcome would have to achieve to be considered satisfactory, and then he searches for alternatives that meet these criteria. Usually, he searches for alternatives similar to those that have proved successful in the past, and his search ends when a satisfactory alternative is found. The disadvantage to satisficing is that Wagstaff is likely to overlook even better alternatives that might be available. But there are also important advantages. Searching for alternatives in decision making is expensive, and, while there may be "better" solutions available, they may not be so much better as to justify the often considerable costs involved.

Goals and Rationality. "Until you know what goals are being reached for, it is rather difficult to determine what should be done to achieve them" (Richman and Farmer, 1974, p. 135). Statements such as this may appear plausible, but they are based on assumptions that organizations have goals, that individual behaviors are specified and influenced by such goals, and that goal clarity can lead to more rational decisions that improve organizational efficiency and effectiveness. How reasonable are these assumptions?

A goal is a value premise—a statement of what "should" be that is meant to help guide decisions. When the Huxley College catalogue indicates as one of its goals "the preparation of students who will actively participate in civic affairs," it is really stating that this *should* be a major objective. Consensus on this organizational goal presumably should simplify the making of curriculum and budget decisions by telling people at Huxley to follow the rule that, when faced with a decision, they should always select that alternative that maximizes the extent to which students who graduate will be likely to participate in civic affairs.

But things are not that simple. Huxley has a large number of *other* value premises, some overt and some latent, that are also presumed to influence behavior. For example, one additional overt goal is expressed by a catalogue statement that graduates should be "conversant with the great works of Western civilization." An example of a latent goal (not stated in the catalogue or in any other publication but still generally shared by people at Huxley) is that college expenditures should be minimized.

Figure 7 represents some of Huxley's many overt and latent goals. The college cannot optimize the achievement of every goal, but people at Huxley on average would be satisfied if performance for each goal fell within a specified "area of acceptability," shown as a shaded area within the range of each goal. The college cannot make decisions *solely* using the criterion of maximizing student participation in civic affairs, because such decisions are certain to give incomplete attention to other goals, such as being conversant with great works and minimizing costs. In fact, each goal competes with other goals for resources.

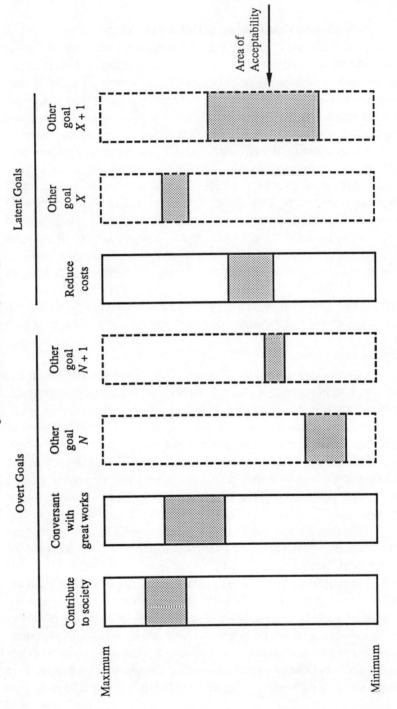

Figure 7. Goals of Huxley College.

People at Huxley would not argue that the goal of minimizing costs means that every effort should be made to avoid incurring *any* costs, even if it prevents preparing students to participate in civic affairs. Instead, they recognize that what it really means is "prevent expenditures from reaching unacceptable levels" or, in other words, prevent expenditure levels from moving outside their area of acceptability. In the same way, the goal of preparing students to participate in civic affairs cannot be allowed to use up all resources so that expenditures are uncontrolled and no funds are available to support other aspects of the programs.

No decision at Huxley can optimize all values, but a decision that emphasizes one value can be acceptable if its outcomes fall within the acceptable *range* for all values. These ranges can be thought of as constraints, since an acceptable decision must at least minimally satisfy all of them. Goals, therefore, can be thought of as systems of constraints that decisions must satisfy. Such constraints at Huxley are usually broad enough that a large number of feasible solutions potentially exist within them. A decision maker may choose to optimize *one* value as long as at least minimal achievement of the others is maintained. We often refer to the value we wish to optimize as "the goal." But, as Simon (1964) points out, since the decision must satisfy a number of constraints, selecting one of them and calling it "the goal" is somewhat arbitrary.

People in different roles will have different ideas about which constraints should be optimized. Whose preferences should be accepted as being the "organizational goals"? We generally use the term "organizational goal" to refer to the constraint sets of upper organizational participants, such as President Wagstaff. These sets in turn are meant to influence the constraints within which people at lower levels behave. Equating organizational goals with those of upper-level participants is often reasonable because of the hierarchical nature of most organizations. In higher education, too, there is a tendency to refer to goals of trustees or presidents or deans as the organization's goals, but this perhaps becomes less defensible at Huxley because much of the college's life is decentralized. Faculty and others have influence on outcomes.

The importance of organizational goals is their presumed effect on individual and group behavior. But even the sharing of goals does not necessarily mean that people will agree either on which goals should be optimized or on how to optimize them. For example, three people at Huxley College may share the goals of transmitting works of Western culture, preparing students for civic leadership, and limiting fiscal expenditures but still make different choices. Dean Artium of the school of letters and science, for example, may wish to select an alternative that optimizes the study of Western culture, as long as civic leadership and budget requirements do not fall below acceptable levels; President Wagstaff may wish to emphasize civic responsibility as long as cultural and financial matters are not unduly compromised; and Dr. Heep, the vice-president for administration, may want to emphasize the limiting of costs assuming that basic program needs are met. In this case, even though each shares the organization's goals (that is, their preferences all fall within the constraints), each would *optimize* a different goal and would therefore have different solutions to many organization problems.

Even if they were all interested in optimizing the *same* goal, their behaviors might not be consistent because of disagreements about the most effective means for doing so. People at Huxley have different views on whether the best way to transmit Western culture is through immersion study in a specific culture, survey courses, or topical seminars, for example. The number of ways of optimizing this goal is practically infinite. Decision makers will embrace different alternatives and have access to different information that would make one alternative appear to be superior to another.

It is common for people to say that organizational goals are important because they direct and coordinate the behavior of individuals. But at Huxley, as at other institutions, "no one can expect such statements to guide choices and steer behavior. Formal goals may help give meaning to the general character of the system, for insiders and outsiders alike. As integrating myths, they can be good for morale and can help keep external groups pacified. But they hardly give you a clue about what to do" (Clark, 1983). Fortunately, people can work in collaboration even when they disagree on what appear to be fundamental questions of goals or values. By and large, coordination of functions at Huxley is achieved because participants agree on means (courses are offered, administrative procedures are followed), rather than because of consensus on ends.

Effectiveness and Rationality. Some people at Huxley believe that more would be achieved if everyone would just work to make the college more effective. But "effectiveness" does not appear to be as useful in directing institutional behavior as might first be thought. That is because people at Huxley have different definitions of effectiveness (for example, reaching goals, running smoothly, gaining resources, or satisfying constituents), and it is difficult to measure any of them (Cameron, 1984). There are different audiences (such as faculty or students) using different criteria (for example, student satisfaction or achievement test scores) over different time periods (this semester or twenty years from now) to make the assessment (Cameron and Whetten, 1983). And finally, achieving effectiveness in one area of institutional functioning may inhibit or prevent effectiveness in another (Cameron, 1978), because optimizing one preferred outcome always comes at the expense of others.

So while people at Huxley College may agree that institutional effectiveness should be increased, "indicators of effectiveness are not obvious, principles for improving and maintaining effectiveness have not been developed, no standards exist against which to judge effectiveness, and ambiguity persists regarding the meaning of the word and its relationship to other similar concepts" (Cameron, 1985, p. 1). Since all definitions of effectiveness reflect subjective biases and values, the criterion of effectiveness does not offer much guidance for institutional behavior.

The Rational Institution. The idea that rational administrators make decisions that maximize the achievement of institutional goals does not fully reflect the Huxley experience.

Decision making there seems to satisfice rather than maximize, and their actual goals are vague and conflicting. Decision makers are limited in the information they have and in their ability to process data. Reasonable people reasonably disagree on what the measures of outcomes and effectiveness should be, and the structures, processes, and resources that improve performance on one measure of effectiveness are likely to inhibit or prevent achievement on others. People at Huxley do indeed share some values. If they did not, there would be no organization at all. But their different roles make some of these values appear to be more important than others, creating conflict in preferences and in assessing outcomes.

Rationality is not unimportant at Huxley, but it is not the driving force and major purpose of administration. And yet, even though rationality and decision making may not serve as the center of institutional life, it is clear that the institution changes and that choices are made. How does this happen?

Being Sensible

"Organizations are in the business of making sense. If they attend to anything with consistency and regularity, it is to their sense-making activities" (Weick, 1979, p. 250). People at Huxley College agree on some things, but because of differences in their background, training, experiences, and roles, they disagree on other things and see them in different ways. What is significant and real for one person may appear trivial and illusory for another. People may have different views of what is most important (academic achievement or moral growth, for example) or of the nature of cause and effect (whether management effectiveness is increased by delegation or by close supervision, for example). They may assess the nature of the coupling between systems differently. They may become sensitive to different stimuli, put data together in different patterns, and derive different meanings from them. People may come to believe that their perceptions are accurate representations of reality, that other perceptions are false, and that those who insist on the truthfulness of those other interpretations are confused, ignorant, or self-serving.

There are many ways in which the environment can be experienced, interpretations made, meanings attributed, and responses selected. But if people are to be able to interact effectively, there must be some agreement on these matters. If Huxley is to function, there must be some degree of consensus about the nature of reality, how certain events are to be interpreted, and to what attention should be paid. For Huxley, reality is what participants agree it is. Reality, therefore, is not waiting to be discovered but is waiting to be invented. The process of negotiating agreements about the nature of reality—of "making sense"—is the process of organizing.

The Meaning of Organizing. The rational view of organization leads us to think of administrative structures, rules, and systems for activities such as planning and decision making. But there is another way to look at the concept of organizing, without explicit reference to organization charts, regulations, or formal procedures (Weick, 1979).

The environment of Huxley College is filled with an indefinite number of ambiguous stimuli. Attention cannot be given to all of them, and different observers may differ about which of these stimuli are important or what they mean. In the absence of objective standards, what is real and important can be decided only by mutual agreement. At some institutions, there is agreement that the SAT scores of entering freshmen are important; at other colleges, the ethnic mix of students is given great weight. Such agreements about what is important are developed over time through the interacting behaviors of organizational participants.

Through their continuing interaction, organizational participants develop agreed-upon rules for identifying institutional elements and for interpreting actions so that they have meaning for organizational members. These meanings and relationships are arbitrary and are not rooted in objective reality. They consist "of recipes for getting things done when one person alone can't do them and recipes for interpreting what has been done" (Weick, 1979, p. 4). If people at Huxley did not share such meanings, they would be faced with a continuous stream of apparently random, conflicting—and therefore meaningless—events.

Equivocality—or uncertainty as to which of two or more possible meanings is correct—is distinctly uncomfortable. People at Huxley are constantly bombarded by information of various kinds, including the activities of other people, written communications, and pages of numbers. Over time, much of the information becomes part of a familiar pattern, and its meaning is clear and unquestioned (although exactly the same pattern may have a different meaning in another institution). But some of the information may be new; it may have more than one meaning, and its importance may be uncertain. When this happens, people have to expend considerable energy to interpret the ambiguous stimulus so that it can be understood. The meanings that organizational participants develop through their interactions reduce equivocality and therefore increase certainty. They enable people at Huxley to organize their interactions into sequences that appear meaningful and that lead to consequences that appear meaningful.

How Organizing Takes Place. Organizing is the process through which groups of people develop similar perceptions of reality and come to share common meanings about their experiences. Individuals and groups within Huxley come to interpret reality through the nonlinear, four-stage process (Weick, 1979) of environmental change, enactment, selection, and retention shown in Figure 8. The stages are connected to each other by causal linkages and by feedback loops. The sequence suggests that people at Huxley identify a specific change in the environment that requires their attention (enactment). The meaning of the change is unclear, and from a number of alternative interpretations, they eventually agree on one (selection) and remember it (retention) so that it can be used when they face a similar situation in the future.

If the environment were static, or if there were a way to create a closed system to provide insulation from the environment, people at Huxley would be able to stabilize their operations. There would be no need for change and no requirement for feedback or for learning. But both people and the college exist as part of open systems. They interact with other elements

Figure 8. Organizing Processes at Huxley College.

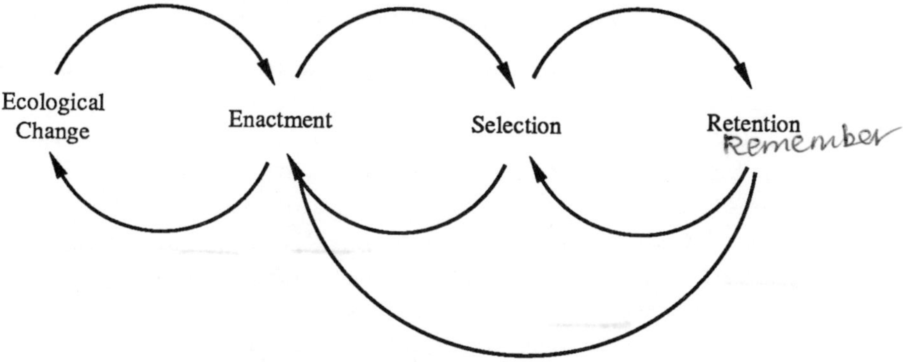

Source: Adapted from Weick, 1979, p. 132.

of those systems and the environment in which they are imbedded.

Enacting the environment is a process of abstraction. It is a way of focusing attention on some aspects of a stream of events while ignoring others, and thereby developing a vocabulary that permits an organization to function through commonly accepted meanings. Their interpretations make them more likely to focus attention on the same environmental elements in the future, to see the same patterns of cause and effect, and to confirm and strengthen their interpretations. Their expectations filter their perceptions so that they come to see what they expect to see. These interlocked cycles explain how people at Huxley "make sense" of newly encountered experiences and how their interpretations then affect what they see and how they act in the future.

At Huxley College, for example, people now talk about "new learners." The college had always enrolled some older students, but no one had ever thought of them as different from other students. Defining and naming specific elements such as new learners have now permitted Huxley to make sense of them, to talk about them, and to make them socially "real." Talking is a critical part of sense making, because it permits people to discover what they are thinking about. After all, "how can I know what I think until I see what I say?" (Weick, 1979, p. 165). It is enactment that provides the way of bringing order out of randomness.

When organizational members confront people or actions that are different from those seen before, they must figure out what they mean. There are usually many possible ways that certain behaviors can be separated from a stream of activity, linkages of cause and effect inferred, and meaningful scenarios developed to explain them. Having enacted a new environmental element, such as new learners, a basic question for Huxley College is what meaning (if any) does this have for us? Are new learners an annoyance? A threat? A drain on scarce resources? An opportunity? The process of selection involves trying out alternative answers to that question. Interpretations that are not found to be meaningful—for example, that new learners are no different from other students—are gradually eliminated; those found useful are stored (retention) to be used again. Since Huxley College turned out to see new learners as an opportunity, and created successful new programs for them, it is more likely in the future that they will be sensitive to additional ways of categorizing students and to respond to these new groups with curriculum changes.

It is through these processes of interpreting its environment to make sense that Huxley College constructs its reality—a reality so intense that people there reject out of hand the idea that reality consists of arbitrary categories that were not discovered but invented and reinforced through their own behaviors. The environment of an organization can be thought of not as a "given" but as a construction of the organization itself.

Sharing Meanings. Systems are composed of subsystems, and understanding the process by which Huxleyites come to share common perceptions of reality begins with considering a subsystem of two people. Figure 9 shows two ways that the perceptions of Dr. Chippendale, a department chair, and Professor Branch, a faculty member, might become more consistent. Chippendale has just said to Branch, "We should offer an honors section of the introductory course." Viewed as a linear interaction,

Figure 9. Two Kinds of Interaction.

Linear Interaction

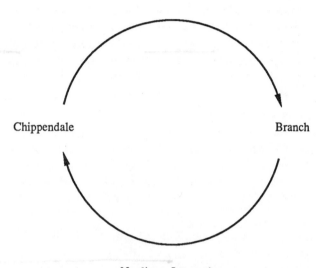

Nonlinear Interaction

Branch's view of reality related to curriculum is presumed to change to become more consistent with Chippendale's.

But a more complex subsystem is formed when the relationship is viewed as looping and nonlinear. When Branch replies, "Do you really think we have enough top students to do that?" prompting in turn a reply from Chippendale, their perceptions of reality related to curriculum are likely to become more consistent, not because just *one* of them changes but because *both* of them do. Perceptions of reality become even more consistent as these interactions are continuously repeated, but with each repetitive cycle, the subsystem has changed and is somewhat different. Neither participant is rigid; they both absorb part of their perception from the other (Wiener, 1964).

Loops such as these compose the basic building blocks of

organizations. In later chapters we will see how different types
of institution are defined by the relative importance of certain
loops and the patterns by which they are connected.

Retrospective Sense Making. The human mind is an inference machine. It is constantly engaged in trying to see patterns
and relationships, to infer cause and effect, or to impose previously retained selections on incoming data in an effort to create order and meaning. When people at Huxley encounter someone's behavior, they attempt to understand what caused it.
When they see organizational outcomes, they try to infer what
policies, decisions, or interests led to them. It is easy for them
to construct reasonable scenarios that account for observed outcomes. They can see on the basis of hindsight that all the cues
that would have permitted them to predict the outcome were in
fact present if only they had paid attention to them. The ease
with which this can be done reinforces their belief that, in fact,
cause and effect can be understood and that the world is predictable. But they can be easily misled in several ways.

There are many reasonable ways that cause-and-effect inferences can be constructed in an equivocal situation. People
observing the situation from two different organizational perspectives might see different sets of "facts." Different facts will
lead to different interpretations of reality. Each interpretation
might be plausible, each might be "wrong," and persons holding
each might be equally convinced of the accuracy of their interpretation.

People can also be fooled by predictable biases in their
thinking processes. Because making judgments in organizational
settings is so complex, people at Huxley commonly simplify the
required calculations through the application of heuristics—that
is, shortcuts, rules of thumb, or guiding principles—that assist
them in making judgments under conditions of uncertainty.
These heuristic principles enable them to generalize, to make
judgments, and to function in an equivocal environment. But
these principles can also lead Huxleyites to erroneously believe
that two unrelated factors are in fact correlated, or that an outcome was caused by a specific activity even when in fact they
were independent.

Two heuristics that often lead to biased judgments of this kind are known as representativeness and availability (Tversky and Kahneman, 1982). Representativeness relies in part on stereotypes that lead people to make judgments of relationships on the basis of whether things *resemble* each other in some way. For example, representativeness biases Huxley search committees to believe that faculty candidates who have good interviews are likely to be better teachers than those with weaker interviews. Representativeness also biases administrators to believe that apparently rational processes such as management by objectives increase organizational effectiveness. These beliefs appear reasonable, and they are widely held even in the absence of empirical evidence that supports their validity.

The second heuristic, availability, leads people to make judgments of relationships on the basis of the ease with which examples can be imagined or brought to mind and are therefore cognitively "available" (Nisbett and Ross, 1980). Things or events may become available to a person for reasons other than their importance—for example, when they are vivid or when a certain outcome was expected.

It is impossible as activities and events are unfolding (only some of which are accessible to any single person) to know which will affect the future. It is only in hindsight that events at Huxley clearly can be identified as important or unimportant to eventual outcomes. Cause and effect are difficult to predict or determine because of loose coupling, the existence of nonlinear amplifying systems, and cognitive biases. Loose coupling implies that the source of an effect may be located at a considerable distance in time or organizational structure from the effect itself. For example, an action by the director of public relations last year may have an impact on the admissions director next year. Amplifying nonlinear cycles make it possible for an apparently insignificant action to become more pronounced and have a major effect as it moves through the system over time. Meteorologists at Huxley know this as the "butterfly effect," because it has been suggested that the movement of a butterfly's wings in Beijing can influence the weather in New York a month later (Gleick, 1987). The same effect can be seen at Huxley College when a casual comment by a faculty member alters a student's career goals, or when a trivial difference in merit salary awards causes an expensive class-action lawsuit, or when the televised reports of a distant sporting event lead to ugly campus confrontations between black and white students. Such incidents make accurate learning difficult. Since sometimes the same "causes" have completely different effects, and people see what they expect to see, incorrect inferences about what "works" at Huxley and what does not can be made. And once people become convinced of one explanation, they are likely to find it difficult to accept the possibility of others. Their interpretation of history also influences what they will see in the future.

As people at Huxley continually interact with each other and with their environment, their interpretations of reality become more consistent in many ways. They develop common understandings, a common language, and a common history. They create a culture.

Institutional Culture:
Efficiency, Ceremony, and Management

Through what they do and how they think, people at Huxley have developed a culture that, in turn, influences what people do and what they think. Organizational culture is a powerful way of looking at how people in institutions create social reality through their interactions and interpretations. Culture reflects the processes through which Huxley reconciles the tensions between rationality and sense making.

Culture is the "social or normative glue that holds an organization together. It expresses the values or social ideals and the beliefs that organizational members come to share. These values or patterns of belief are manifested by symbolic devices such as myths, rituals, stories, legends, and specialized language" (Smircich, 1983, p. 344). Culture influences what people at Huxley perceive and how they behave. It "induces purpose, commitment, and order; provides meaning and social cohesion; and clarifies and explains behavioral expectations. Culture influences an organization through the people within it" (Masland, 1985, p. 158).

Culture provides the "central tendencies" that make it possible to generalize about the character of nonlinear systems such as Huxley. It establishes an "envelope" or range of possible behaviors within which the organization usually functions. All organizations by definition have a culture, but the culture can be strong or weak, consistent or inconsistent, and it can inhibit, as well as facilitate, institutional development and effectiveness. When a culture is very strong and consistent, it can take the form of an "organizational saga," the collective understandings of uniqueness and accomplishment held by participants in a small number of distinctive institutions (Clark, 1972). Such sagas are usually initiated by charismatic leaders with strong values who either founded an institution or arrived at the institution during a time of crisis or dramatic change. Comparable stories apparently appear in many organizations, although in each they may be considered unique (Martin, Feldman, Hatch, and Sitkin, 1983). This suggests that organizational cultures may have sources other than simply the organizations themselves.

Since systems are hierarchical, Huxley is a subsystem of other systems, and its culture is therefore influenced by the cultures of those supersystems. For example, some aspects of Huxley's culture are rooted in the culture of the national educational system, in the culture of the academic profession, and in the culture of the disciplines, as well as in the culture of Huxley itself (Clark, 1983). Institutional cultures can also be influenced by the culture of the peer system composed of comparable institutions, such as community colleges, state universities, or small liberal arts colleges. Some of these forces make all colleges and universities look alike in some ways, while others make them look quite different.

Forces for Cultural Similarity. Many cultural forces affect Huxley as they do most other colleges and universities in this country. The culture of the national educational system leads institutions to share understandings of such concepts as excellence and access, to agree that an education is valuable not only for intrinsic reasons but also because of its importance in preparing graduates for employment, and to accept the principle that institutional policy is under the control of lay boards of trustees.

The professional culture gives importance to autonomy, symbols of professional preparation such as academic degrees, and belief in the altruistic commitment of faculty and administration. It leads faculty to believe in serving the cause of knowledge and understanding, in intellectual honesty, and in the critical importance of academic freedom. These are ideas that help to bind together the academic professions. The strength of these values is demonstrated by their apparent consistency across institutions of various types (Bowen and Schuster, 1986).

Cultures based on academic disciplines have the potential to differentiate campuses, but this potential is infrequently realized. Academic disciplines have varying cultures that are based on differences in their research techniques and methodologies, common vocabularies, membership in learned societies, membership requirements, codes of ethics, and similar substantive and symbolic perspectives (Ladd and Lipset, 1975; Clark, 1983). These differences are significant enough that a campus composed primarily of a liberal arts faculty and their students would be expected to have a very different culture from that of one inhabited primarily by engineers. But as institutions programmatically become more alike (Birnbaum, 1983), major differences in campus cultures become less prominent.

These three cultural systems—the national educational system, the academic profession, and the academic discipline—have had a major effect on Huxley, as they have on most other institutions as well.

Forces for Cultural Differences. The most obvious source of cultural differentiation comes from within the individual institution itself. At every institution, myths, legends, stories, and symbols over time begin to assume meaning, help to create a sense of community, and seem to inspire loyalty. Yet the strength of these cultures varies widely. Strong cultures are more likely to be found at campuses that are small, have interdependent parts, are older, have experienced a dramatic birth or significant transformation, and have successfully engaged in a struggle for survival and status (Clark, 1983; Masland, 1985).

Another major source of cultural differentiation occurs between subsets of institutions, such as community colleges, research universities, or liberal arts colleges. Their trustees and administrators are apt to use different vocabularies, belong to different associations, read different journals, and emphasize the importance of different missions and purposes, and their faculties are likely to have different interests and training.

Cultural Distinctiveness. Every college, including Huxley, has unique characteristics. At one level, organizational cultures, like individual personalities, are all distinctive. But not all of these distinctions really make a difference. Cultural differences among colleges and universities derive from basic assumptions and beliefs, and not from superficial differences in administrative structure or academic program (Schein, 1985). To a great extent, institutions are likely to share these core values with others in their peer groups, even though these values may be reflected through somewhat different procedures. For Huxley College, as for other organizations (Wilkins and Ouchi, 1983), the shared background cultures of peer groups are likely to exert more influence than institutional differences in most cases.

Culture and Environment. In previous chapters, the environment has been discussed as something "outside" the organization. But it can also be said that "beliefs, norms, rules, and understandings are not just 'out there' but additionally are 'in here.' Participants, clients, constituents all participate in and are carriers of the culture. Thus, institutional environments are notoriously invasive. To paraphrase Pogo, We have met the environment and it is us!" (Scott, 1983, p. 16). The culture of Huxley College influences, and is influenced by, the cultures of the larger systems of which it is a part. The tendency for institutions to adapt to their environments means that the culture at Huxley will be similar in many ways to the cultures of other campuses.

There is another major aspect which locates the environment inside as well as outside of Huxley. In the process of sense making, organizations interact with their environments. But the environment to which they respond is not the "real" environment, but rather the enacted environment—that is, the one sensed by the organization through processes that affect perception and meaning. In a very real sense, then, "organizations select their environments from ranges of alternatives, then they selectively perceive the environments they inhabit" (Starbuck, 1976, p. 1069). Organizational environments are in large measure invented by organizations themselves!

Myths and Management. In a rational world, colleges and universities would be organized and managed in the manner that most effectively supported their activities or achieved their goals. They would have structures to guide their processes and rules and procedures to meet stated objectives. Indeed, institutions *do* have structures, rules, and stated goals. But these may not determine how institutions actually function. Some see this discrepancy as a sign of weakness in leadership or management. But there is another perspective—one rooted in the cultural context that we have been discussing—which views the discrepancy as often necessary and functional (Meyer and Rowan, 1983).

Societies develop expectations about how their institutions should be structured and function. These expectations, which are part of the shared culture, are enforced in many ways; for example, through legal requirements, through the actions and opinions of important constituents, or through the granting or withholding of social prestige. This shared social reality binds organizations to develop procedures, structures, and programs consistent with it. When social expectations influence the shape of formal organization structure, they can be thought of as "rationalized myths" (Meyer and Rowan, 1983, p. 25). They are "rationalized" because they are defined as necessary to meet the technical requirements of the organization; they are "myths" because they are generally accepted as legitimate social constructions that need no proof.

Examples of rationalized myths that affect colleges are legion. Huxley College, for example, has developed goal statements (in order to increase organizational effectiveness), has required SAT scores in the admissions office (to ensure academic quality), has developed job descriptions (to prevent duplication of effort), and has prepared organization charts (to facilitate communication and delegation of authority). Almost everyone at the college agrees that each of these is "necessary." But very few can point to specific incidents in which the "necessary" process or rule was actually instrumental in leading to the presumed outcomes. In fact, Huxley often ignores its own rules in order to carry out its business effectively and efficiently.

Huxley can be seen publicly as legitimate and prudent and can protect itself against claims of negligence, irrationality, or ineffectiveness to the extent that it can point to the existence of the long-range plans, mission statements, and accountability systems that legitimate and prudent institutions are presumed to have. Such plans, statements, and systems may come to have symbolic and ceremonial, rather than instrumental, significance. It may be more important for Huxley to be able to say "we *have* a strategic plan," for example, than it is for Huxley to actually implement one.

Huxley College conforms to social expectations of what a college should be. It emphasizes credentials and accreditation, ceremony and ritual, and the satisfaction of participants and reputation—all measures of success that can stand in lieu of more objective output measures. The more the college is seen as conforming to societal expectations about what it should be doing and how it should be doing it, the more successful it will be (Meyer and Rowan, 1983). Sometimes these societal expectations are consistent with the technical requirements of the college, but sometimes they are antithetical. Huxley administrators therefore must structure portions of the institution to accommodate the activities and outputs expected by rationalized myths. When these activities and outputs are antagonistic to effective institutional work, President Wagstaff tries to find ways to formally comply with them in a way that does not interfere with the activities of the faculty. The existence of loose coupling at Huxley makes it possible to often meet simultaneously the incompatible demands of ceremony and of effectiveness. Huxley has discovered the rewards of doing what its constituents see as important, so long as the real work of the college remains protected.

Implications for the Administrator as
Decision Maker or Sense Maker

The linear rational decision maker inhabits a discoverable world of objective reality. This administrator selects from among many available alternatives the one that is most likely to maximize organizational goals. The selected alternative may then be imposed on the organization and structures and procedures developed to support it. Rational administrators give particular attention to collecting and analyzing data, calculating cost-benefit ratios, establishing systems for communicating directives to those who will implement the decision, collecting information from others to ensure accountability, and constantly comparing outcomes to objectives.

The administrator as nonlinear sense maker lives in an invented world of subjective interpretation. The role of an administrator in this setting is obviously quite different. Emphasis must be placed on assisting organization members in their activity of "spending time trying to make their views of the world more similar" (Weick, 1979, p. 149). This means providing forums for interaction in which the "negotiations" that determine reality can be carried out, making more explicit the assumptions behind present rules and ongoing processes so that they can be accepted or challenged, and giving prominence to certain activities that can serve as attention cues for others in the institution. Leadership of this kind can be thought of as "the management of meaning" (Smircich and Morgan, 1982), and leaders emerge because of "their role in framing experience in a way that provides the basis for action, e.g. by mobilizing meaning, articulating and defining what has previously remained implicit or unsaid, by inventing images and meanings that provide a focus for new attention, and by consolidating, confronting, or changing prevailing wisdom" (p. 258).

From a cultural perspective, then, administration may to a great extent consist of symbolic action. For example, President Wagstaff typically collects more information than he needs or can use, often collects it *after* the decision has been made, ignores available information, complains that the information he has is not useful, and always asks for more information (Feldman and March, 1981). The collection and analysis of information in such cases serve as a symbol that Wagstaff and Huxley are committed to the cultural value of intelligent and rational decision making. Administrators who regularly collect data and show their command of it are viewed as being more competent, and this inspires the confidence of constituents. Decisions for which large quantities of data have been collected can be considered as more legitimate, even though the information has served only a ritualistic purpose. The data are useful for managing the impressions that people have about the college, even if they are not helpful in actual college management (Rourke and Brooks, 1964). The importance of using diligence in data collection as a proxy for the quality of a decision probably increases as the actual effects of the decision itself become more difficult to evaluate. Developing a computerized management information system tends "to give at least the appearance of efficiency" (Diran, 1978, p. 273) and so responds to charges of inefficient operation that sometimes have been leveled at Huxley.

But clearly there are other, perhaps more important purposes of such management processes. In the development of an institutional culture, the kinds of data collected and the ways they are interpreted also serve to construct common perceptions of reality, to identify what is important, and to establish a common vocabulary. All these can help organizational participants "make sense" of what they are doing and verify the legitimacy of the organization.

Data can help meet the sense-making needs of President Wagstaff as well. In the absence of data or clear cause-and-effect relationships that permit him to reliably determine how his activity affects outcomes, the smooth functioning of administrative efficacy. Wagstaff can believe himself to be effective—and be seen as effective by others—to the extent that the five-year plan for which he is responsible gets published on time. Administrators can sustain self-assessments of high effectiveness by doing those things, such as setting up computerized data bases, that they believe are signs of progressive administration. When they cannot really evaluate program effectiveness, external agencies such as legislative budget committees or accrediting associations can fulfill their oversight responsibilities by assessing instead the degree to which administrators are doing what it is that good administrators are supposed to do.

When it is difficult to tell whether an organization is being effective, symbolic actions taken by administrators become particularly important. For example, a rational budgeting process can be important because of its symbolic value even when it has only marginal effects on resource allocations (Chaffee, 1983). Because scholars value objectivity, they are more likely to accept unequal budgets among departments when they believe rational processes have been used to make the decisions. Why is discontent minimized when decisions are thought to be rational? In part, it may be because so many scholars have written that administration is a science, leadership is important, and rational design can achieve specific ends (Pfeffer, 1981a). When such ideas are repeatedly put forth, and when public opposition to them is muted, they take on added standing almost automatically. We have created our own reality!

Symbolic administrative action may be important in all organizations but is perhaps of even greater significance in "process cultures" (Deal and Kennedy, 1982). Such cultures are characteristic of organizations, such as Huxley College, where feedback on the effect of decisions is delayed, sometimes for years. Participants give particular attention to *how* something is done because it is difficult or impossible to obtain direct feedback on the effectiveness of their activities.

In sum, organizational cultures establish the boundaries within which various behaviors and processes take place. By helping to create shared symbols, myths, and perceptions of reality, they allow participants to make sense of an equivocal world and to establish a consensus on appropriate behavior. Unlike explicit mechanisms for controlling the behavior of organizational participants, such as rules, regulations, job descriptions, or chains of command, cultures are implicit, unobtrusive, and for the most part not subject to purposeful manipulation by administrators.

This is not to say that administrators can have no effect

upon culture but rather that in most settings their role is probably not so much to create it as to sustain it once it is created. In most settings, presidents cannot generate a new culture merely by continued and insistent reference to new ideas, goals, or symbols. However, they can strengthen and protect the existing culture by constantly articulating it, screening out personnel who challenge it, and in other ways continually rebuilding it. Culture, like other aspects of organizations and all other systems, constantly loses energy and moves toward entropy and disorder. A major function of the energy of administrators is to prevent the organization's culture from falling apart. In the next part of this book, we investigate different ways in which leaders fulfill that role at four different types of institution.

role

Part Two

Models of Organizational Functioning

A model is an abstraction of reality that, if it is good enough, allows us to understand (and sometimes to predict) some of the dynamics of the system that it represents. Models are seldom right or wrong; they are just more or less useful for examining different aspects of organizational functioning. A model serves as a conceptual lens that focuses our attention on some particular organizational dimensions; but in the process of doing so it inevitably obscures or obliterates other dimensions. Models create perceptual frames, or "windows on the world. Frames filter out some things while allowing others to pass through easily. Frames help us to order the world and decide what action to take. Every manager uses a personal frame, or image, of organizations to gather information, make judgments, and get things done" (Bolman and Deal, 1984, p. 4). No model of a complex system such as a college or university can be a perfect representation of that system, but some models appear to reflect what usually happens in some parts of some institutions and therefore suggest useful courses of action. The use of alternative models leads to differing—yet complementary—perceptions of reality (Allison, 1971; Bolman and Deal, 1984; Morgan, 1986).

In the next four chapters, I describe four fictitious institutions to illustrate different models of college and university governance, organization, and leadership. In each case, the model and the institutional type have been matched because, *on average*, the concepts often fit that type in the real world. For example, People's Community College is the setting for analyzing bureaucratic organizational models because public two-year institutions are generally considered more hierarchically structured and their management more rationally focused than other institutional types, such as liberal arts colleges (Bensimon, 1984; Richardson and Rhodes, 1983). However, it is important to avoid the error of totally equating models with particular types of institutions; one message this book carries is that no model illuminates all aspects of any institution all of the time, and every model illuminates some aspects of every institution some of the time. Just as a person who is familiar with only one institution does not understand any institution, so a person familiar with only one model does not really understand any model.

Each model represents an idealized version of an institution as seen through the lens of a specific cognitive frame. Anyone experienced in higher education will immediately note that while each model is familiar, none of the descriptions fully captures the richness of a real institution. This purposeful simplification serves two purposes: it allows the salient aspects of that frame to be placed in uncluttered and bold relief, and it also shows the essential limitation faced by any administrator or researcher who takes a single frame approach to understanding higher education. Because each frame emphasizes some parts of reality while ignoring others, no frame by itself provides a truly complete sense of how any campus really works.

After briefly presenting the fictitious institution, each chapter begins with a discussion of the characteristics of the model it represents. It then examines the patterns of interaction that reflect its properties as a system. Each chapter concludes with a discussion of the implications of the model for effective leadership.

Chapter 4

The Collegial Institution: Sharing Power and Values in a Community of Equals

The 150-year-old campus of Heritage College sits on a wooded hilltop several miles outside a large town. Older buildings are interspersed with a new science building and a new gymnasium, both donated by grateful alumni. Several new residence halls were built a decade ago, when, after years of discussion, the college decided to expand to its current enrollment of 1,150 students. Heritage offers a wide range of baccalaureate programs in the arts and sciences, all built on a general education core curriculum. The Heritage catalogue, its graduation speakers, and its funding appeals all emphasize a liberating education in the Judeo-Christian tradition as preparation for a life of individual meaning and social purpose.

The students, most from the top quarter of their high school classes, attend full time, and few fall outside the traditional eighteen- to twenty-one-year-old age group. Students are required to live in residence halls unless they are "townies." In many students' families, an older relative has had a previous association with the college; some families can trace students back over three generations.

All but a few of the seventy-four faculty have doctorates. Faculty are expected to be scholars and to keep current in their disciplines, but there is no pressure for research or publication. Classroom teaching and student advisement are emphasized, and faculty prestige and promotions are largely based on demonstrated expertise and commitment to these activities. There is an active college senate, run as a town meeting with the president presiding.

President Harold Henderson had been a popular faculty member at Heritage who left to accept the deanship of a similar institution and was asked to "come home" to Heritage as president several years later by a unanimous search committee. His inauguration was as much a community celebration as an academic ceremony.

The campus serves as the center of an active if somewhat subdued social life. The many clubs and activities include a number concerned with political and social causes, but even a casual campus visitor can sense that academic pursuits are the primary concern of students and faculty alike. Most faculty live close to campus, and many commute by bicycle in good weather. They often attend campus functions, and some regularly invite their students to their homes for dinner.

Current issues on campus include the pending report of a joint campus committee studying divestiture in companies doing business in South Africa, continuing discussions in the senate about modifications to the core curriculum, a student government investigation of the food service, and initiation of a new capital campaign among alumni.

Heritage College as a Collegial System

It is useful to study the organization and management of Heritage as a collegial system. An emphasis on consensus, shared power, common commitments and aspirations, and leadership that emphasizes consultation and collective responsibilities are clearly important factors at Heritage. It is a community in which status differences are deemphasized and people interact as equals, making it possible to consider the college as a community of colleagues—in other words, as a collegium. Hierarchical bureaucracies are so ubiquitous in our society that we often overlook the many examples of egalitarian collegial bodies, such as corporate boards of directors, the United States Senate, town meetings, the College of Cardinals, and some institutions of higher education.

The terms *collegium* and *collegiality* are often used in higher education. A recent study of college and university faculty (Bowen and Schuster, 1986) suggested that collegiality has three major components: the right to participate in institutional affairs, membership in "a congenial and sympathetic company of scholars in which friendships, good conversation, and mutual aid can flourish," and the equal worth of knowledge in various fields that precludes preferential treatment of faculty in different disciplines (p. 55). Sanders (1973), in like vein, identified collegiality as "marked by a sense of mutual respect for the opinions of others, by agreement about the canons of good scholarship, and by a willingness to be judged by one's peers" (p. 65).

Since conceptions of collegiality sometimes vary (see, for example, Baldridge, Curtis, Ecker, and Riley, 1978; Zimmerman, 1969), it will be useful to develop a more expanded understanding of the term as we shall use it in this book. We shall do so by examining the ways in which the faculty and administration of Heritage College work together to form what has been called a community of scholars (Millett, 1962).

Characteristics of Collegial Systems

The organization of Heritage College reflects certain characteristics that collegial groups of all kinds share to some degree (Anderson, 1963). For example, just as members of collegial groups usually have undergone some specialized training or have other identifying qualifications that set them apart from nonmembers, almost all faculty and administrators at Heritage have advanced academic or professional degrees.

Heritage is not an institution in which hierarchy is considered to be very important, and much of the interaction among members of the collegium is informal in nature. The college is egalitarian and democratic, and members of the administration and faculty consider each other as equals, all of whom have the right and opportunity for discussion and influence as issues come up. Like some other collegial bodies, the faculty and administration of Heritage are concerned about the views of nonmembers such as staff and students, but the right of these others to participation is severely circumscribed and often only token in nature.

The hierarchical structure and rational administrative procedures seen at many institutions, which emphasize precision and efficiency in decision making, are absent at Heritage. Instead, because all members have equal standing, there is an emphasis on thoroughness and deliberation. It often takes a long time to reach major decisions, such as whether the college should divest the stock it holds in businesses operating in South Africa. Decisions are ultimately to be made by consensus, and not by fiat, so everyone must have an opportunity to speak and to consider carefully the views of colleagues. Certainly, some members are more influential and persuasive than others, but these differences arise from the norms of Heritage itself and from the personal characteristics of members, rather than from their official or legal status. For example, it is generally believed that the views of senior faculty are more influential than those of their juniors and that positions advanced by faculty who are regarded as among the best teachers are given special weight. These characteristics are quite conspicuous at Heritage, but they are not completely unique to this kind of institution. Clark Kerr (1982), for example, has noted in the faculties of research universities "the tendency to rely on consensus and on the opinions of the older members of any academic group in making decisions" (p. 27).

Consensus does not require unanimity. In fact, at some other institutions under some circumstances (for example, when the cabinet of an authoritarian president "votes" on a proposal on which the president has clearly already reached a decision), one can find unanimity even when consensus is absent. Real consensus, by contrast, arises when open discussion is possible and expected, when participants feel that they have had a fair chance to state their position and to influence the outcome, and when people are comfortable about supporting the chosen alternative even if it was not their first view (Schein, 1969). When the faculty at Heritage attempt to reach consensus, they allow sufficient time in their deliberations to make it possible for participants to state their reservations or opposition and to feel that they have been heard and understood. If they do not have this opportunity, frustrated critics may later withdraw their support at crucial times or engage in other disruptive activities.

Heritage, as does any collegial group, has an administration to provide support services and to represent the college's interests to its various publics, but the administration is understood to be subordinate to the collegium and carries out the collegium's will. Administrators are often members of the faculty who agree to serve for a limited time and then return to their classroom responsibilities. Administrators therefore tend to be "amateurs," rather than professionals.

Since members of a collegial body are presumed to be equals, their leader is not appointed. The faculty tend to think of President Henderson as having been elected, since he was recommended to the Heritage trustees by a unanimous faculty search committee. Although his faculty colleagues expect that the president will make decisions about ordinary problems as they come along, they see him as their agent rather than as an independent actor. They concede that he has some extraordinary powers not available to other members (and in fact they understand that it is important to them that these differences exist), but he is seen by them not as a "boss" but rather as serving as *primus inter pares*, or "first among equals." In that capacity, he is thought of as the group's servant as well as its master. At larger and more highly structured institutions, the faculty may refer to the president, vice-presidents, and deans as "them" or as "central administration." Heritage faculty refer to the president by his preferred nickname, "Bud," when they meet with him alone or with other faculty members. When outsiders are present, however, they speak of him as "Mr. President" to enhance his standing with external audiences.

In many ways, Henderson at Heritage reflects the romance of the collegial tradition and its implications for the relationship of faculty and administration, as articulated by Veblen ([1918] 1957, p. 182) in discussing the proper role of the president as:

> the senior member of the faculty, its confidential spokesman in official and corporate concerns, and the moderator of its town meeting-like deliberative assemblies. As chairman of its meetings he is, by tradition, presumed to exercise no particular control, beyond such guidance as the superior experience of the senior member may be presumed to afford his colleagues. As a spokesman for the faculty he is, by tradition, presumed to be a scholar of such erudition, breadth, and maturity as may fairly command something of filial respect and affection from his associates in the corporation of learning; and it is by virtue of these qualities of scholarly wisdom, which give him his place as senior member of a corporation of scholars, that he is, by tradition, competent to serve as their spokesman and to occupy the chair in their deliberative assembly.

Sustaining a sense of community that permits collegial organization requires shared sentiments and values on such matters as the general purposes of the organization, loyalty to the collectivity, and agreement about institutional character as reflected in the shared understanding of members, rather than necessarily by a written document, and this is evident at Heritage. Problems related to dualism of control or differences in values between trustees, faculty, and administrators that cause conflict on many other campuses are generally absent here. Board members tend to be alumni, administrators tend to be faculty, and there is general agreement on the expected and accepted relationships among and between the groups. Faculty are predominantly locals who are loyal to the institution; they derive their greatest satisfactions and rewards from their activities within the college, rather than from groups outside it.

An important condition for the maintenance of a true collegial form is that it be comparatively small. Although some believe that the tradition of an academic community could be maintained only in institutions with no more than ten teachers and 150 students (Goodman, 1962), these are probably unduly restrictive limits. Heritage, with fewer than eighty faculty and a handful of administrators, has little difficulty in supporting a collegial culture. Even though the faculty as a whole meets only once a month, they interact with each other constantly, at lunch in the faculty dining room, in meetings of the many committees that oversee important aspects of college life, and in their neighborhoods near the campus. There is little doubt, however, that if the college were to grow much larger, maintaining collegiality would be increasingly difficult.

Common backgrounds, continuing interaction, and a long tradition have made it possible for Heritage to develop a strong and coherent culture with distinctive symbols, rites, and myths. Consider, for example, The Teas, one of the first programs renewed by President Henderson when he took over the underfinanced and somewhat dispirited campus eleven years ago. Now a tradition, The Teas are open houses for students held every evening of final examination week featuring home-baked cookies and pastries (but never tea) served by faculty members and their spouses. More than just an opportunity for calming frayed nerves, The Teas have over the years become a ritual and a metaphor, symbolizing the campus ideal of teaching as service, the nurturing and supportive role of the faculty, and the importance attached to achievement in examinations, as well as reinforcing the sense of Heritage as a total community. When Heritage faculty end the last class of the semester with "See you at The Teas," its meaning is understood to be "good luck," rather than a statement of their intention to attend (although most do).

The usefulness of The Teas sometimes transcends the mere opportunity for meaningful interaction, as important as that is. For example, when The Teas were held even during a campuswide student demonstration on endowment policy, much of the tension between faculty, administrators, and students dissipated. The story is still told that President Henderson and his wife brought and served cupcakes to students who were conducting a nonnegotiable sit-in in his office. Henderson refused to cancel final exams but said that if students wanted to go home and study, they could return unimpeded and continue their sit-in when exams were over. At nearby Darwin College, in contrast, exams were cancelled, and six demonstrators were suspended.

The Teas are a symbol of enduring values and relationships that helps to stabilize the campus when transient issues are occasionally the subject of contention. Those who are not effectively socialized into the Heritage culture may misinterpret the importance of The Teas, believing them to be merely social gatherings. The recent dean, for example, who was the first ever appointed from outside the faculty, spent end-of-semester evenings catching up on critical administrative office work. He did not understand that his absence from The Teas was perceived as reflecting an antipathy to college values and a lack of sensitivity to the unique programs and stellar achievements of the college. The dean's replacement, to no one's surprise, was a senior Heritage faculty member.

The collegial model does not completely describe Heritage College. The model ignores the fact that there are differences in legal authority between various participants that are spelled out in the college's charter and in civil law; it overlooks the importance of some standard procedures that have been codified and no longer appear under the control of any individual or group; and it assumes general agreement on values when in fact many matters are the subject of great contention.

Still, much (but not all) of what happens at Heritage on a daily basis can be understood by thinking of it as a self-governing collegial body. The civil discourse with which faculty on opposite sides of an issue refute the arguments of "my learned colleague," the formation of elected faculty search committees that usually select deans from the faculty itself, the traditional refusal of deans to serve more than two five-year terms in order that they may return to the classroom or laboratory, the rotation of department chairs, and references to shared authority are all familiar examples of the processes that characterize much of Heritage College most of the time.

Of course, not all small liberal arts colleges can be reasonably characterized as collegiums. Many cannot be. On the other hand, some colleges and universities of other types might occasionally be appropriately described as collegiums, and collegial structures and processes can almost certainly be seen at least some of the time in at least some of the parts of most institutions.

Collegiality, seen as a community of individuals with shared interests, can probably be maintained only where regular face-to-face contact provides the necessary coordinating mechanisms and where programs and traditions are integrated enough to permit the development of a coherent culture. Size is probably thus a necessary but not sufficient condition of a collegium, and this limits the possibility of the development of collegiality on an institutional level to relatively small campuses.

As organizations grew, there would eventually come a point at which the probabilities of interaction between any two randomly selected members would be comparatively low. Increased size and numbers would lead toward specialization, which would tend to decrease communications and interaction. However, the traditional concept of community would still be viable in *subgroups* within institutions (such as departments). On some campuses, collections of these subgroups may share common interests and institutional commitments that, at least on some major issues, would override parochial concerns. These colleges might be thought of as "loosely coupled communities." But at other institutions, still greater size, complexity, and cosmopolitanism might create departments with tighter coupling to external groups (such as disciplinary associations) than to campus colleagues. Such situations present the ultimate irony—that under certain conditions, strong subunit collegiality inhibits or prevents the development of collegial governance in the institution as a whole.

This discussion of collegiums is based on analyses of small groups—that is, groups of people who communicate with each other frequently on a face-to-face basis over a period of time. The social forces that develop common attitudes, activities, and norms are not available to a large institution in the same way as they are to a small one. But even if many colleges and universities are not truly communities governed through collegial structures, the concept of the collegial model as an ideal type may have significant consequences for the ways in which these institutions are controlled.

As is true of other organizational forms, there is nothing innately effective or ineffective in the collegium. Cohesiveness and the development of powerful norms may reduce effectiveness if the norms emphasize the maintenance of interpersonal rewards. However, if norms emphasize commitment to task performance, then cohesiveness can be used to improve organizational performance.

Loops of Interaction in Collegial Systems

Collegium members interact and influence each other through a network of continuous personal exchanges based on social attraction, value consensus, and reciprocity. Through these processes, the subsystems of Heritage have been integrated into an enduring institution whose ideals and beliefs transcend individual faculty members and are transmitted from generation to generation (Blau, 1964). Communities or collegiums such as Heritage College are sustained and reinforced by nonlinear loops that control the behavior of their members. These loops permit the faculty and administration of Heritage College to form a coherent and effective working group, even in the absence of an obvious hierarchical control system.

People who interact with each other in groups tend to like each other (Homans, 1950, 1961). As interaction increases, so does liking. The relationship between these factors is illustrated by the loop shown in Figure 10. It is a nonlinear interaction whose relationships are reciprocal (liking leads to interaction, and interaction leads to liking) and reversible (decreased interaction leads to decreased liking). The relationship does not hold under certain conditions; when the interaction is involuntary, when there is an authority relationship between the persons involved, when one of the persons engages in irritating behavior, or when the organization itself is not successful, increased interaction may not lead to increased liking. For example, if

Figure 10. The Relationship Between Interaction and Liking.

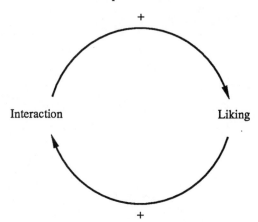

there were large status differences between them, a dean and a department chair might not come to like each other even as they spent more time together. Much of their contact would not be voluntary, and the relationship would consist in large measure of one person giving orders to, monitoring activities of, and controlling the behavior of the other. Interaction of this kind is more likely to produce alienation than liking.

But at Heritage, little attention is given to orders, monitoring, or controlling, and interaction sustains the liking that people have for each other. Because people like and are friendly to each other, they interact with each other frequently, as might be expected in a group whose members have similar backgrounds and interests. The relatively small differences in status between members mean that the chances of interaction are increased, because people are more likely to interact when they are of equal status and less likely to interact as status differences between them increase. And the increased interaction in turn reduces status differences still further.

As people at Heritage like each other more, they tend to spend more time together in both work and nonwork situations. This means that their activities increasingly become more alike, which further increases their interactions and thus their mutual liking. Interaction also increases the sharing of sentiments or attitudes. The causal loops relating interaction, activities, and attitudes are shown in Figure 11.

Figure 11. Relationships Between Interaction, Attitudes, and Activities.

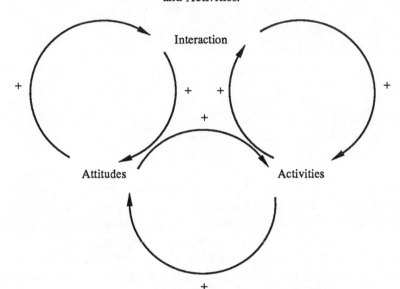

Obviously, spending more time with people who share the same values reinforces those values. When Heritage recruits new personnel, it gives a great deal of attention to appointing people whose values appear to be compatible with those of people already on campus. Applicants, in turn, usually base their continued interest in an appointment on whether they are intrigued or turned off by the Heritage environment. Because of the attention given to making good "matches" between people and the organization, Heritage appointments usually work out well, and new people tend to become closely integrated into the community. But if the values or behavior of the newcomer deviate from those of the group, certain things are likely to happen.

Members of the community will respond in a manner that indicates their disapproval—sometimes by overt attempts to correct the behavior ("We missed you at The Teas last night, John") and sometimes by decreasing interaction (and thus withholding the reward of friendship). If the newcomer changes behavior to conform to Heritage's culture, interaction with colleagues will increase. If not, interactions between colleagues and the newcomer are likely to continue to diminish. They will not seek each other out as frequently on campus or socialize as much afterward. The recruit eventually will feel like an outsider and leave after a year or so. The mutual effects of liking, interaction, values, and activities are therefore strengthened both by the self-selection of candidates to the collegium and by the strong pressures for conformity found in a cohesive community. Members of such groups find the positive feelings of other group members to be particularly rewarding and do not wish to risk their diminution or loss.

As people in a group interact, share activities, and develop common values, the group develops norms—expectations about what people are supposed to do in given situations. Examples of norms at Heritage College are that it is wrong to criticize a colleague in public, that faculty members should not wear jeans to class, that administrators and faculty should address each other by first name, and that courses in the general education core should emphasize original sources. Informal norms control behavior even more powerfully than do written rules and regulations. Such shared understandings arise gradually and covertly through the interaction of group members, and for the most part are not even consciously considered by the group. Since norms often indicate a range of acceptable behavior, deviations from them can often bring group disapproval (Hackman, 1976). For example, faculty meetings are of the "town hall" variety at Heritage, and members are expected to participate at an appropriate level. A member who speaks too much is as likely to experience expressions of disapproval from colleagues as one who speaks too little.

The strength and clarity of norms are directly related to the frequency with which group members interact and the extent to which they participate in common activities. Since interaction and common activities decrease as group size increases (March and Simon, 1958), it would be expected that norms would be a more powerful influence on behavior at small Heritage College than at a larger institution.

Tight and Loose Coupling in Collegial Systems

Heritage College, while not a wealthy institution, is fiscally stable. The existence of an established clientele enables it to perceive a reasonably placid, clustered, and munificent environment. Heritage's applicant pool is stable, comes from a small number of identifiable sources, and is large enough to permit the college to be moderately selective. Through continuing interaction with the alumni association and with counselors in certain "feeder" high schools, the administration is tightly coupled to the interests of this core clientele, and student support programs and administrative processes are likely to respond quickly as student interests change. But for the most part, the institution is only loosely coupled with other environmental elements. It pays little attention to national reports criticizing higher education, to federal policy on research and development, or to the politics of the local community. Changes considered important by some other institutions, such as the increase in secondary school enrollments of minority students or the provision of educational services to business corporations, have had no effect on Heritage.

The faculty are locals and loosely coupled to the academic guilds, so that the curriculum changes only slowly and subtly. Heritage students are generally not exposed to "cutting edge" material and esoteric specializations created by the latest research findings. However, there is tight coupling within the faculty itself. Changes in the content of the core curriculum are likely to lead to changes in other courses as well.

Values that guide the administrative and instructional subsystems at Heritage are tightly coupled and therefore consistent because of the significant overlap in their personnel. But these same values, such as autonomy and academic freedom, lead to loose coupling within the administrative systems, because giving directives challenges the assumption of equality. The dean is more likely to give the registrar a suggestion than an order; therefore some record-keeping changes that the dean would like to see never happen. Similarly, procedures to follow up and assess the consequences of decisions are often lacking, so that once decisions have been reached, they may not be implemented, or, if implemented, they may not be evaluated. As a consequence, many agreements reached on campus are never reduced to writing; if they are, they get buried in files. The degree to which the campus relies on an oral tradition increases the potential for inaccuracy and misinterpretation. Some administrative operations at Heritage have not changed for many years even though the situations for which they were created have long since passed. There is little accountability in the system, because decisions are made by consensus, and no specific person is responsible. Moreover, even if responsibility for improper behavior could be fixed, campus norms resist the imposition of official sanctions, and informal sanctions (such as withdrawal of interaction) can have only a cumulative effect over an extended period of time.

Loose coupling at Heritage often makes the college look very inefficient, but there are benefits as well. The collegium's emphasis on thoroughness and deliberation makes it likely that a greater number of approaches to a problem will be explored, and in greater depth, than would be true if greater attention were paid to efficiency and precision. The willingness of members to themselves be influenced in exchange for the opportunity to influence others leads to the development of compromises that most people on campus can support. Through this process of extended discussion, campus members can ensure the eventual adoption of workable solutions rather than engaging only in idealistic and unachievable rhetoric. Full participation also means that members will be likely to understand the implications of their deliberations and to be committed to them. As understanding increases, the need for interpretative rules and regulations decreases, and as commitment rises, the need for systems of monitoring and control that inevitably lead to alienation diminishes. While attention to maintaining and strengthening the social ties that bind the collegium together has many advantages as a means of coordination, it may also lead to over-

looking deficiencies in performance. The term "community of
scholars" may itself be self-contradictory. Good scholarship requires the critical assessment of colleagues' work, so that
strengthening scholarship may weaken the sense of community
(Weick, 1983a).

Effective Leadership in Collegial Systems

President Henderson and the other members of the collegial body are constantly engaged in processes of social exchange (Blau, 1964). For Henderson, serving in the presidential
role provides rewards of status, of service, and of support; for
the other members, having a competent, sensible, and supportive
person such as Henderson as president is seen as providing benefits to the group. Because of the expectation that Henderson
will have more influence over individual members than they will
have over him, the existence of a president somewhat diminishes
the individual autonomy of every other member. But the president's activities also provide the group with increased prestige
and resources. The satisfactory exchange of these benefits over
time leads to mutual feelings of obligation, gratitude, and trust.

Henderson is more influential than the other group members and is accorded higher status. He is a leader partly because
he is seen as having expertise in activities the group considers to
be important and partly because he is seen as conforming to the
group's norms. He relies on expert and referent power to exert
his influence. Reward power and coercive power have no place
at the college, and even legitimate power is suspect. Both the
president and the faculty realize that reliance on legal authority
is an admission of weakness. Henderson knows that while he
could probably win any campus battle because of his superior
status, the long-term consequences of doing so would be to lose,
rather than gain, power.

But, in fact, there are few situations in which the president's interests are different from those of the faculty. At Heritage, as in other groups, the higher the rank of a person in a
group, the more nearly that person's activities will conform to
the expectations of the group. The group creates its own lead-

ers, who are typically drawn from the group itself and who remain members of it in spirit. President Henderson was selected by his colleagues because they believed him to exemplify the norms of Heritage College—they saw him as "the most of us and the best of us." His perceived effectiveness at Heritage is likely to depend on his fulfilling the presidential role—that is, behaving as the collegium's members believe he ought to. Among other things, this means making decisions that are "right"—that is, decisions that prove to be acceptable to the group.

President Henderson is believed by his colleagues to make major contributions to the welfare of the collegium, and they receive his suggestions with considerable respect. However, if he were to make demands on the group that they considered unfair, their respect and liking for him (and their willingness to accede to his suggestions) would decrease. His leadership therefore is based on mutual influence, and Henderson's ability to influence other people depends on his willingness in turn to be influenced by them (Homans, 1961). While Henderson must follow the college's norms, because of his high status he can exercise disproportionate influence over the development of those norms. Indeed, because he has demonstrated his adherence to college values in the past, he has also earned the privilege of engaging in a limited amount of deviant behavior (Hackman, 1976; Hollander, 1985). It is in this sense that Henderson is "part creature and part creator of the organization in which he works" (Demerath, Stephens, and Taylor, 1967, p. 41).

President Henderson's attitudes and activities, and the norms in which he believes, are influenced whenever he interacts with others. But because he enjoys higher rank, his influence on them is likely to be even more important. If Heritage were to grow much larger, Henderson would be able to spend less time on average with individuals and therefore would be less influential. With the decline in interaction would also come a parallel decline in common attitudes and activities and the clarity of norms at Heritage. Social control would be reduced. Henderson might feel the need to introduce rules and regulations in an effort to regain influence and in doing so would still further reduce interaction and increase status differences. This is one way in which collegial structures may become transformed into bureaucratic ones.

Persons in leadership positions in collegial systems are expected to influence without coercion, to direct without sanctions, and to control without inducing alienation. They must provide benefits that other participants see as a fair exchange for yielding some degree of their autonomy. Their selection as leaders provides them significant leverage to influence their communities, their new status has been legitimated by the participation of their constituencies, and these constituents have certified, at least initially, both their competence and their commitment to group values. Leaders in collegial settings should follow certain rules if they wish to retain their effectiveness.

Live Up to the Norms of the Group. Leaders exemplify the values of the group to an exceptional degree. They are able to exert disproportionate influence because they serve as role models, and their perceived conformity even allows them some freedom to engage in occasional deviant behavior. Conforming to group norms engenders trust, and this trust (and the leverage it confers) can be lost if a leader is seen as persistently acting in a manner at odds with the values of the group.

Conform to Group Expectations of Leadership. Conforming to group norms need not require collegial leaders to be passive; indeed, groups expect their leaders to be aggressive and to initiate action in some circumstances. If a group expects a leader to make certain decisions, they must be made or the leader will lose status. This is particularly true in an emergency, when "any failure on his part to initiate interaction, to take the initiative . . . will make him that much less the leader" (Homans, 1950, p. 428). The student takeover of the president's office during the divestiture demonstrations at Heritage was just such a crisis. As it was unprecedented, there was no consensus on the "right thing to do." Henderson's actions were immediate and decisive, but because they were clearly consistent with Heritage norms and traditions, faculty were not at all upset that they had not been consulted. To the contrary, his actions reconfirmed their judgments about his expertise.

Use Established Channels of Communication. Since a collegial group has established understandings of what is appropriate, members come to expect that both formal and informal communications will follow certain customs. Deviating from these customs is apt to create confusion. Leaders may also create confusion when they praise or blame members in front of others. Doing so raises or lowers their social rank and thus may change group interaction in unpredictable ways.

Do Not Give an Order That Will Not Be Obeyed. Collegial leaders can give orders, as long as those receiving the orders see them as fair and appropriate. To give an order that will be obeyed is to confirm the tacit understanding of an exchange; to give an order that is questioned is to question the relationship and the position of the leader.

Listen. The essence of leadership in a collegial group is displaying marked conformity to group expectations. The leader can best do this when there is a clear understanding of group norms and values. The leader is at the center of a communications web. The leader may initiate the interaction but then must listen and overcome the tendency of leaders to talk. The leader should acknowledge the importance and relevance of the group values that are expressed and accept them without taking a moral or judgmental stand. Influence requires interaction; to influence, one must allow oneself to be influenced. In permitting others to talk or argue, the leader is not abrogating responsibility, because in any social exchange the leader's values will ultimately carry more weight than those of others.

Reduce Status Differences. Open communication is critical to the maintenance of a collegial body whose members are viewed as equals. Since status differentials inhibit communication, people who wish to be influential in a collegium should attempt to reduce such differences where they exist. That is why President Henderson encourages all faculty to call him Bud, why in public pronouncements he always identifies himself as a spokesperson and agent for the faculty and emphasizes their good works, and why he is often self-deprecating about his own abilities (Blau, 1964) and apologetic about conspicuous status symbols (such as his large office and chauffeur-driven college car, which "are just to impress the donors so we can get more from them"). The president often visits faculty in their offices rather than his, and makes frequent opportunities to socialize with them.

Encourage Self-Control. The leader in a collegium has the ultimate responsibility for controlling behavior but little authority to do so. Moreover, uses of traditional organizational sanctions are likely to be considered illegitimate by the group; recourse to them will be taken as a sign of weakness and will increase alienation, thereby reducing still further the leader's effectiveness. Good leaders create the conditions in which the group will discipline itself (Homans, 1950) by appealing to relevant group norms and values and by making deviations more publicly visible to activate controls exercised by other group members. Leaders remove the onus of others' admissions of error (thereby making the detection and correction of errors easier) by treating errors as useful learning experiences that contribute to personal and institutional growth.

Chapter 5

The Bureaucratic Institution: Rationalizing Structure and Decision Making

People's Community College is a two-year public institution in a middle- and working-class suburb of a large metropolitan area. The college opened in an urban storefront in 1962, and in 1975 it finally moved into a large, attractive megastructure on a permanent twenty-five-acre site. The contemporary concrete-and-glass facade gives the appearance of a successful corporation's headquarters. People's offers transfer programs that parallel the first two years of a baccalaureate program, as well as a wide range of career programs in technical, business, and health science areas. Its mission statement emphasizes access, low cost, career preparation, and meeting community needs.

There are 5,700 degree students, many of them studying part time in the evening. Many students are working, married, or both. Their average age is twenty-eight, and most graduated near the middle of their high school class. Additional students are enrolled in nondegree certificate programs and adult education courses. All students reside in the city and commute. Minority enrollment peaked at 21 percent in 1982 and is declining.

All the faculty in the transfer programs have master's degrees, usually from a nearby university. Half have a year of addi-

tional graduate work, and 10 percent have doctorates. Most of
the faculty in the career programs have baccalaureate degrees,
and half have master's degrees. The faculty is represented by a
local chapter of a national union. There is a faculty senate, but
its membership overlaps the union leadership, and the senate's
role is unclear. People's was originally part of the municipal
school system, and many faculty and administrators have had
some secondary school teaching experience.

President Peter Potter came to People's from the administrative vice-presidency of a similar institution. As the third
president of People's, he followed the extended term of a be-
nign but paternalistic founding president and the tumultuous
and disastrous three-year tenure of his successor, which included
a bitter two-week faculty strike. Potter's expertise is in management and community relations.

Students view their educational experience primarily in
practical terms, and most have clear vocational objectives. Few
students participate in campus organizations, and many maintain closer ties with high school friends than with fellow students. Faculty are dispersed throughout the metropolitan area
and spend little nonteaching time on campus.

Current issues on campus include state pressure for student assessment examinations, the intrusiveness of some local
trustees who think the college should be run "more like a business," transfer articulation disagreements with local four-year
colleges, implementation by the new academic vice-president of
a management-by-objectives program, and negotiations with
local firms over the expansion of contract training activities.

People's Community College as a Bureaucratic System

We have seen how activities at Heritage College are coordinated by internally generated norms that are continually reinforced by face-to-face interactions of participants. In general,
the larger the organization, the greater the number of positions
between the top leader and the ordinary member (Homans,
1950). As organizations grow, the number of subunits (such as
departments) increases, these subunits become increasingly specialized, and administrative structures become more complex

(Blau, 1973). Interaction decreases, and norms become confused and no longer serve to control behavior. More structured means of interaction are required, and the institution becomes bureaucratized. The same processes that create bureaucracies in other settings do so in colleges and universities as well (Stroup, 1966).

Collegial interaction may still exist, but it becomes a characteristic of subgroups rather than the total group. To a great degree, campus constituencies find themselves isolated from each other, with neither a consistent culture of belief nor face-to-face communication through which to coordinate activity. Rules and regulations become the important mediators of interaction, and administrators become specialists in distinctive areas. Administrators spend little time with faculty and talk instead to other administrators and to external nonfaculty audiences in state legislatures, professional associations, and boardrooms.

The word *bureaucracy* is so burdened by connotations of rigidity, waste, and lack of human concern that merely mentioning it in the context of college life almost always provokes responses ranging from helpless shrugs to cries of outrage. A useful discussion of the college as a bureaucracy must therefore begin by using the word in a descriptive and analytical rather than a pejorative sense. In this chapter, we will consider *bureaucracy* to refer to "the type of organization designed to accomplish large-scale administrative tasks by systematically coordinating the work of many individuals" (Blau, 1956). Bureaucratic structures are established to efficiently relate organizational programs to the achievement of specified goals. When behavior is standardized, the activities and processes of organizations are made more predictable, so that the organization can become more efficient and effective.

Characteristics of Bureaucratic Systems

People's Community College can be most clearly described within the context of that icon of all bureaucracies, the organizational chart. The chart of People's shown in Figure 12 has been greatly simplified; there are many more people employed

Figure 12. Organization Chart of People's Community College.

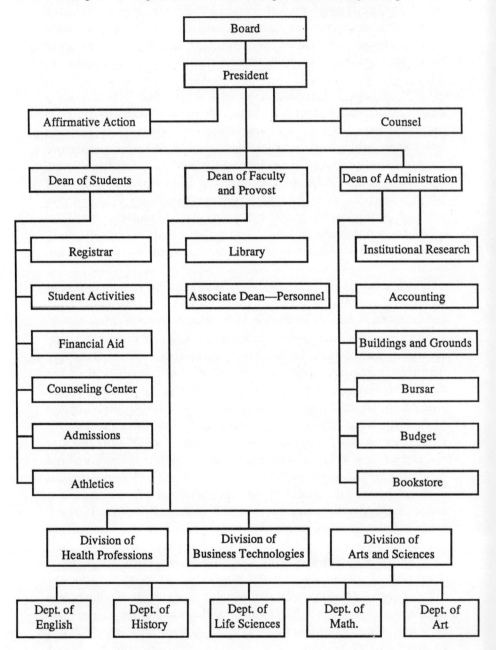

at People's than indicated here, and a complete chart would list every existing office.

The vertical lines connecting the offices are referred to as "lines of authority" or "lines of communication." They represent the way work is supposed to flow through the college; information and reports are presumed to flow up the chart to President Potter and through him to the board, and their directives are to flow downward. Organizational structures make a difference, and the organization chart of People's Community College contains important information that might be overlooked by the casual observer. For example, the number of levels between the highest and the lowest offices on the chart can be counted. Organizations with relatively few levels are considered to be "flat," and those with more levels are considered to be "tall." Fewer levels lead to less distortion in communications as information flows through the system. At the same time, it means that more people report to each supervisor, and therefore they cannot be as closely monitored. Higher education organizations are typically much flatter than business organizations of comparable size. At People's, there are only two levels between the highest supervisory office (President Potter) and the lowest (department chairs). A business firm of comparable size might have many more levels between them.

The existence (or nonexistence) of an office on the chart and its location in the hierarchy are a signal both inside and outside the campus of the importance of the substantive area. Location on the chart has a practical effect as well. People located near each other on the chart are more likely to interact with—and therefore to mutually influence—each other than people who are distant on the chart. People's is large, and the attention of senior administrators is limited. Those who report directly to senior people are more likely to be able to bring things to their attention—for example, requests for resources—than those who do not. At People's, it is not likely that President Potter believes intercollegiate athletics (which reports to the dean of students) to be as important as does the president of nearby Darwin College, to whom the athletic director reports directly. And since the values of senior officers are likely to differ because of their roles, the fortunes of programs will often depend on the office to which they report. It is likely, for example, that more attention is paid to the fiscal aspects and less to the academic aspects of the bookstore at People's, which reports to the dean of administration, than would be the case if the bookstore reported to the dean of faculty. The structure of the college thus affects how offices will interact and influence each other. Structure has a major effect on the patterns of loose and tight coupling between offices.

Organizational structure also affects who will be responsible for gathering certain kinds of information, an important issue because whoever collects information also determines how it is to be communicated and evaluated (Cyert and March, 1963). Since data are often equivocal, and since many data potentially available are filtered out by the expectations and experiences of the person encountering them, the assignment of responsibility for data gathering is really an assignment to define the environment for the organization. It makes a difference whether the collection, analysis, and dissemination of student outcomes data, for example, are a responsibility of the dean of students, the director of institutional research, or the director of admissions.

People's as an organization has been consciously structured to facilitate certain organizational processes. But since it is not possible to optimize all values, structures that increase communication between two specific units are likely to decrease communication with other units. Putting the budget office and the bookstore at the same organizational level under the dean of administration makes it more likely that their work will be closely coordinated and that the financial viability of auxiliary enterprises will be protected. At the same time, it makes coordination between the bookstore and the library more difficult because they are supervised by different administrators. Every structure not only provides certain benefits to the organization but at the same time makes other benefits more difficult to achieve. There is no perfect structure, and the creation of structure is therefore a matter of trade-offs.

In addition to the organization chart, there are a number of other specific attributes of People's that would be expected in a bureaucracy (Anderson, 1963; Weber, 1969). For example, the functions of each office are codified in rules and regulations, and officers are expected to respond to each other in terms of their roles, not their personalities. A new directive on financial aid policy issued by President Potter should elicit the same response even if someone else had been president. In the same way, the new rule would be expected to be administered at People's in the same way by each of the financial aid officers, and all students to whom the rule applied to be treated identically.

The emphasis on written job descriptions and on rules and regulations that guide behavior increases organizational certainty and efficiency at People's. Deans, registrars, and financial aid officers fill specific roles, but the role and the person are not identical. People filling roles can be replaced by others (as long as they are technically competent) without having a noticeable impact on the functioning of the college. Rules and regulations have been created at People's to deal with situations that occur on a regular basis. Rules are one way in which People's coordinates its activities and ensures an acceptable level of predictability in the actions of various offices. Rules also serve as a means by which the college transmits to present personnel what has been learned about appropriate solutions to problems in the past. This means that each problem does not have to be considered as unique, and each new employee does not confront the problem with a blank slate (Cyert and March, 1963). Although college administrators and faculty often become frustrated with rules, rules serve many functions, and by themselves they are neither good nor bad. As Perrow (1979) comments, "they protect as well as restrict; coordinate as well as block; channel effort as well as limit it; permit universalism as well as provide sanctuary for the inept; maintain stability as well as retard change; permit diversity as well as restrict it. They constitute the organizational memory and the means for change" (p. 30).

People's has developed a systematic division of labor, rights, and responsibilities and enforces it through a hierarchical control system. Individuals know what their jobs are, and they understand the limits of their own responsibilities and those of others. This formal division of labor serves many functions. It prevents duplicating activities, it minimizes the possibility of things "falling between the cracks," and it makes it possible for people to specialize and to develop high levels of expertise in specific areas. In the financial aid office, for example, one professional specializes in federal and state grants and entitlements, while another focuses on bank loans and work-study packages. Together they know more and are more efficient in dealing with issues within their specific spheres of interest than would be two people who shared the same general knowledge about both areas.

Effective and efficient operation of the college depends on compliance with rules and regulations, and compliance at People's is not left to chance or to goodwill. Instead, the organization is organized as a hierarchy. The activities of every lower office are supervised by the next higher office on the organization chart. Administrative rules, actions, and decisions at the college are formulated in writing. The issues with which People's must deal are complex, and the incumbents filling various roles change over time. If rules are to be applied uniformly, there has to be a written record of their interpretation that can serve as precedent for implementation in the future. At People's, written records are kept of trustee resolutions, faculty senate actions, presidential decisions, registrar interpretations, union contracts, and every other facet of institutional functioning. Not everything known by anyone in the college can be codified, and no one in the college can know everything there is to be known. Therefore, rules must also be developed for determining what information is to be available in different offices, and for identifying the channels through which such information will move. These have been codified at People's through procedures such as the use of preprinted "buck slips" by which a single check mark sends copies of a document through any one of six different distribution systems. The information that People's collects and retains, the forms on which it is stored, and the conventions by which they analyze their data affect the college's perception of its environment (Pfeffer, 1981b) and suggest what alternative actions the college may consider (Cyert and March, 1963).

Administrative promotions at People's are based on merit. In some social systems, promotion in rank is based on birth; in others, it depends on personality or other attributes. But in bureaucracies, technical competence and performance are what count. The higher one is on the organizational chart, the greater competence and expertise one is assumed to have. This is why bureaucrats are appointed by their presumably more expert superiors, and not elected. This relationship between organizational status and merit is important, since it reinforces the willingness of subordinates to accept the directives of superiors by associating rank with expertise.

Bureaucracies such as People's are rational organizations. This does not necessarily mean that People's always makes good decisions, or even necessarily efficient ones. Rather, it implies that at People's there is some conscious attempt to link means to ends, resources to objectives, and intentions to activities. "Rationality refers to consistent, value-maximizing choice within specified constraints" (Allison, 1971, p. 30). The hierarchical nature of People's presumes that much of this process of determining goals and deciding on how to achieve them will occur in the senior levels of administration and in particular gives a preeminent role to President Potter.

Rationality requires as a first step the articulation of objectives. The more precise and measurable these objectives can be made, the more accurate will be the calculations of costs and benefits of alternative courses of action. People's emphasizes long-range planning and develops definable subgoals and schedules for their completion. The new vice-president for academic affairs was selected in good part because of having had experience in this type of activity. Administrators give attention to the collection and analysis of data that permits the selection of alternatives that maximize the achievement of stated organizational goals. The development of specific offices (such as institutional research) and procedures (such as management information systems) for this purpose is an important organizational priority.

Faculty and administrators at People's often grumble about bureaucratic procedures and red tape, and it is easy for them to overlook some of the advantages of their system. For example, existence of written rules and regulations that seem to pose barriers to faculty or student interests in fact also have the complementary function of limiting administrative discretion. Administrators and faculty who function within their roles must apply the same criteria to everyone, ensuring fairness and equity rather than personal favoritism, and subordinates are less subject to administrative caprice. The emphasis on rationality, performance, and expertise also limits the extent to which incompetent people can move into higher positions and reduces reliance on extraneous factors such as social status, sex, or religion in personnel decisions. But perhaps the greatest benefits of bureaucratic systems are those explained by Max Weber: "Experience tends universally to show that the purely bureaucratic type of administrative organization . . . is . . . the most rational known means of carrying out imperative control over human beings. It is superior to any other form in precision, in stability, in the stringency of its discipline, and in its reliability. . . . However much people may complain about the 'evils' of bureaucracy, it would be sheer illusion to think for a moment that continuous administrative work can be carried out in any field except by means of officials working in offices. . . . The choice is only between bureaucracy and dilettantism in the field of administration" (Weber, 1952, p. 24).

The legitimacy of colleges and universities and their support by society depend at least as much on the appearance of regularity and stability as on the quality of their technical performance. As long as this continues to be true, bureaucratic structures and patterns may be expected to be an essential component of institutional life at People's Community College.

Loops of Interaction in Bureaucratic Systems

People's, like any organization, is constructed of interacting subsystems. The characteristic that identifies People's as a bureaucracy, however, is the expectation that these interactions will be influenced primarily by legitimated hierarchical relationships. People's can be considered as composed of hierarchically arranged relationships between superiors and subordinates. In such relationships, as depicted in Figure 13, a superior gives directions to a subordinate, who complies and submits a report to the superior. On the basis of the report, the superior then prepares new directives. Each event as it takes place provides feedback that affects its successor as the superior discovers the consequences of the directive and the subordinate is informed of the extent to which performance was acceptable. The inter-action not only gets work done but also reinforces the control structure of the organization itself. A decisive statement by President Potter, once accepted and acted on by the dean of faculty, increases the president's tendency to make decisive statements and in turn the dean's willingness to accept them.

Figure 13. Relationship of Superior and Subordinate
at People's Community College.

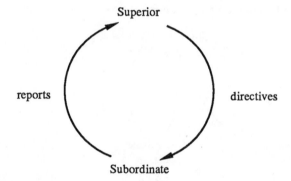

The horizontal relationships between equals that control behavior at Heritage are much less effective at People's. When personal interaction occurs outside the superior-subordinate relationship, it often conflicts with, rather than reinforces, the processes desired by institutional management. President Potter, for example, likes to communicate certain information to staff members through the weekly *People's News and Views* newslet-ter. But most people find out about really interesting happen-ings (many of which never make *News and Views*) through the informal grapevine.

Because of the hierarchical nature of People's, superiors

at one organizational level are subordinates at the next lower level, and so the organization can be depicted as a continuous linkage of levels, as shown in Figure 14. Superiors give directives to subordinates as problems are encountered for the first time, but some problems are encountered so frequently that they become part of standard operating procedures (SOPs). SOPs are the systematic processes guided by rules and regulations through which reports are prepared, forms are processed, budgets are developed, and the other work of People's gets done. For example, the processing of class selections by students, the preparation of class rosters, and the determination of student academic eligibility are all incorporated into separate SOPs at People's that permit each process to run smoothly and allow other parts of the college to predict those processes.

Figure 14. Linking Vertical Loops at People's Community College.

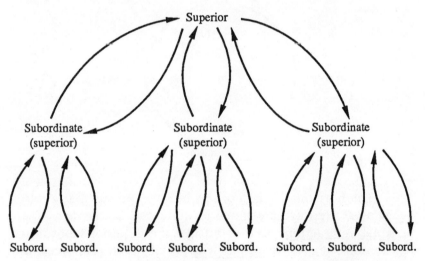

SOPs are in turn grouped into sets, or programs (Allison, 1971) that permit coordinated action in specific situations. The SOPs previously mentioned, for example, are part of a program at People's that might be thought of as "class enrollment." Among other programs at People's are those that direct the activities of "annual budgeting," "degree approval," and "faculty appointment." Clusters of programs initiated under certain conditions can be considered in the aggregate as organizational repertoires. People's, for example, has a "fall registration" repertoire that includes not only the class enrollment program mentioned earlier but also other, related programs, such as those for fee payments and academic advisement. It also has budget and personnel repertoires that are regularly implemented.

SOPs, programs, and repertoires make certain interactions more likely than others, and these eventually come to be considered as a "given" by the organization. They all help to establish a consistency of organizational perception and functioning through the creation of precedents that then direct future behavior. Once budgets are determined, decisions are reached, or responsibilities allocated at People's, they tend not to change (Cyert and March, 1963; Perrow, 1979).

Vertical bureaucratic loops can make some aspects of institutional functioning more effective. But they can cause ineffectiveness as well. For example, they can lead to "vicious circles" (Masuch, 1985) similar to those created at People's when the academic dean announced new work-load rules to increase faculty office hours. The resulting alienation of faculty actually reduced rather than increased the time faculty spent in their offices, leading to the creation of additional rules and further alienation. In the same way, vicious circles can create self-reinforcing ideas that take on a life of their own. Processes initially set up to support goals may become goals in themselves; perpetuating the means may become the ends. At People's, for example, the development of management information systems created large quantities of data that then required further interpretation and explanation. This led to a need for more data and the hiring of people who believed in the importance of collecting and analyzing information (Feldman and March, 1981). As a result, People's allocates significant resources to its management information system, although the system itself is now so complex that managers find it virtually useless for their daily needs. The importance of such information is one of the rational myths of the college. The availability of computerized data is considered by internal administrative groups and by external political groups to be a sign of managerial effectiveness and efficiency, even though there is little evidence these data have much impact on what actually happens at People's.

The very programs created by People's to enable it to repeat its successes ironically may inhibit its perception of new problems (Starbuck, 1976), and the assurances of reliability that are made possible by SOPs, programs, and repertoires may prove to be the greatest barriers to organizational effectiveness, particularly during times of rapid environmental change. Systems of accountability may lead to "red tape" so that perfectly reasonable actions and rules generated in one part of the organization are thwarted by perfectly reasonable actions and rules created in another. Situations encountered for the first time may create confusion and "buck passing" to higher levels. Heads of organizations of all kinds, from presidents of the United States to academic department chairs at People's, have bemoaned their inability to overcome the inertia of the bureaucratic system. Ongoing processes are difficult to stop and new ones often impossible to start. As a consequence, the ability of leaders to engage in strategic decision making is severely circumscribed, and bureaucracies often go on doing what they have always done and paying relatively little attention to what their participants (sometimes even their most powerful participants) want them to do.

Bureaucratic elements are present to some extent in all parts of all institutions (even the philosophy faculty at Heritage College are on personnel "lines," teach courses at times listed in the class schedule, and keep records of student achievement). Some offices at People's are more bureaucratic than others (compare, for example, the registrar's office, whose activities occur in regular cycles and are guided by extensive procedure and policy documents, with the public relations office, which seems to function in a state of constant disorder as it responds daily to unanticipated events). Some types of institutions appear in general to be more bureaucratic than others (People's has more departments, more regulations, more planning systems, more formal evaluation, and less subunit autonomy, and is therefore more bureaucratic than Heritage). In general, public institu-

tions are likely to be more bureaucratic than independent institutions, because they are often embedded in bureaucratic systems of local and state government. This may often require that
certain aspects of personnel processes and administrative procedures in higher education institutions be consistent with those
of other public agencies.

Are bureaucratic systems effective at People's? The board
of trustees (composed mainly of local businesspeople) and the
administration believe that they permit them to be efficient and
responsive to emerging needs. Many of the faculty had previously taught in public school systems. They accept administrative
dominance as long as it is not oppressive. The environment provides clusters of acceptable if not overabundant resources. The
technology of People's, restricted to introductory liberal arts
courses and semiprofessional training, is relatively clear. Students
differ in level of preparation, but the college has developed bat-
teries of placement examinations so that faculty face few unprecedented problems.

The essence of contingency theory is that different forms
of organization and administration prove to be the most effective under different conditions. People's has responded to its
particular environmental and technical problems by creating a
relatively mechanistic organization that appears to work and
that in general is accepted by the participants. The problem of
dualism of controls exists at People's, as it does at Heritage, but
in both institutions, conflict between them is muted because
one control system so clearly dominates the other. At People's,
administrative authority is supreme. It is reflected not only in
the way decisions are made but also in the culture of the institution. Adherence to rules has created a coherent but in many
ways superficial culture that engages the activities but not the
full devotion of many participants. People work hard, and many
are committed to educating less advantaged youth. But most
have a calculative involvement with the college, arriving and
leaving at times dictated by the union contract and cautiously
assessing changes that might lead to personal disadvantage or in-
convenience.

Other institutions, facing more turbulent environments or

complex technologies, would not find the system at People's acceptable, although they would almost certainly adopt bureaucratic structures and processes in some subunits of the organization. We would expect, therefore, that while bureaucratic systems may not be effective in some parts of some institutions all the time, they would reflect a significant aspect of reality at almost all institutions at some times. While bureaucracies have many significant weaknesses, bureaucratic structure and processes are ubiquitous in colleges and universities. Much of what happens in most institutions is influenced by the SOPs, programs, and scenarios created by the legitimacy of hierarchy and reinforced by structures and rules. This is what allows colleges and universities to continue to perform their functions even as goals are disputed, crises occur, and the external environment becomes more turbulent.

Nonroutine tasks are difficult to bureaucratize. But in general, "when the tasks people perform are well understood, predictable, routine, and repetitive, a bureaucratic structure is the most efficient" (Perrow, 1979, p. 162). It may also be that under these same conditions of relative certainty, bureaucratic structures and processes also lead to greater satisfaction of participants (Morse, 1970). When structure and technology "fit," an organization may be more productive and its members may have a greater feeling of competence and accomplishment.

Tight and Loose Coupling in Bureaucratic Systems

Relating the idea of a bureaucracy to the concept of loose coupling may initially appear contradictory. After all, bureaucratic structure emphasizes precisely the directive and control functions that appear to most tightly couple administrative and instructional subsystems. Tight linkages are certainly not unusual in nonacademic institutions: in many, "managers decide, performers implement; managers command, performers obey; managers coordinate, performers carry out special tasks" (Scott, 1981, p. 254). The administrative and instructional subsystems of People's are by no means as tightly coupled internally as they are in many business organizations, but they are much more tightly coupled than at Heritage.

Tight coupling in one part of an organization leads to loose coupling in another. The various SOPs that make up a program, for example, are more tightly coupled than those in unrelated programs. The close alignment between management structure and institutional production at People's is possible because of loose coupling between the technical subsystem and the environment. As work and management become more tightly coupled, work and environment become more loosely coupled and the institution becomes more of a closed system. Most of the environmental input into People's comes through President Potter, and the curriculum of People's is much more administratively controlled than that at Heritage. Although departmental faculty design courses, new programs are more likely to emerge as a result of the interaction of the president, academic vice-president, deans, and department chairs than as a consequence of faculty debate. This is not necessarily dysfunctional, since President Potter is more tightly coupled to community needs than the faculty. Faculty are locals, rather than cosmopolitans, and the president and senior members of his academic administrative staff are more "professional" than the faculty (they on average have higher credentials). In addition, the purpose of major parts of the educational program is primarily administrative and technical (to articulate most efficiently with programs of four-year institutions) rather than educational (reaching consensus on the knowledge of greatest worth). The degree of professional autonomy involved is relatively small.

To a limited extent, People's can affect the degree to which organizational elements will be tightly or loosely coupled by the way it designs its own structure. There is a tendency to see both problems and solutions in structural terms. When the system does not appear to be functioning effectively, or the quality of performance is declining, President Potter's typical response is to reorganize. Sometimes the change is primarily a symbolic act that indicates that "something is being done," even though it has no instrumental consequences. But at other times, reorganizing severs existing connections between units, thereby loosening the coupling between them, and creates new connections that tighten coupling.

Even though coupling between administration and instruction is tighter at People's than in many other institutions, achievements based on plans are still elusive for many reasons. For example, the status differences created by the hierarchy at People's inhibit the full transmission of information between levels. Subordinates, aware of the consequences to them of passing negative information upward, tend to withhold data that might reflect poorly on their own performance or that might anger their superior. The very information for which Potter has the greatest need, because it indicates organizational problems, is precisely the information that is most likely to be either distorted or withheld. In addition, while Potter may tell subordinates what they need to know to do their jobs, he often does not provide them with operating discretion or enough background information to place a directive in organizational context. When subordinates encounter equivocal situations, they must therefore respond according to the directives, even when carrying out the directive in that specific situation might be adverse to larger organizational interests. The distortion or blocking of communications means that it is difficult for subordinates to clarify confusing or ambiguous directives. In response, subordinates may minimally comply by observing only the letter of the law (Katz and Kahn, 1978, p. 444).

Effective Leadership in Bureaucratic Systems

The work of individuals can be coordinated and controlled by having them follow the directives of a superior. The most effective organizations are those in which the processes through which coordination is attempted are accepted as legitimate. Attempts to exercise control by a person not seen as having the right to do so can lead to alienation and refusal to comply.

There are several different ways in which legitimation can be achieved. One way is through tradition, whereby activities may be coordinated by accepting orders from someone because "it's always been done that way." Work can also be coordinated when people follow the directives of a charismatic leader whose personal authority they accept. Traditional or charismatic legitimation can coordinate work, but there are costs to organizational functioning and stability that become particularly apparent when changes in leadership take place. The boss's daughter or the chief's son may initially be accepted because of tradition, but they may not be as effective as their fathers. The charismatic leader's lieutenant may take over but may lack that magical ability to keep the organization together. An alternative to control by tradition or charisma is to create a system in which people accept directives from others as legitimate because they are consistent with rules or norms that all accept. Bureaucratic authority at People's rests on a common agreement about rules, including an understanding of what the legitimate range of activities and behaviors of a president is and of the appropriate responses of faculty, students, and other administrators.

This acceptance has profound effects, not only on how people make sense of the college but also on how people behave. For example, before President Potter took office, he was somewhat unsure about his judgments and decisions and often hesitant in his statements. When he became president, people seemed more willing to accept his decisions. He consequently became more confident in his judgment and more able to make authoritative statements, which in turn led people to have increased confidence in him. The acceptance of decisions by subordinates changed Potter's behavior, which made subordinate acceptance of decisions (as well as further changes in Potter's behavior) even more likely in the future. In the absence of the legitimate authority to make decisions conferred by his role, the opposite reaction might have occurred and Potter could have become more hesitant to make judgments as his previous decisions were ignored or rejected.

On the organizational chart, President Potter can be seen as at the apex of a pyramid—the ultimate recipient of all information that flows from the bottom of the organization to the top, and the ultimate decision maker and initiator of all directives that flow down from the top through channels of communication and authority. Deans and other senior executives have similar status in their own organizational subunits. The bureaucratic ethos of competence-based mobility suggests that since those who are more rational get promoted, deans are more rational than department chairs, vice-presidents more rational than deans, and the person who becomes president the most rational of all. Potter's main source of power is the legitimation conferred by the legal and organizational system, but this can be reinforced by the expertise he demonstrates through the performance of his role. Potter believes in utilizing the resources of his office to motivate others, and he often influences their performance through his power to reward and much less frequently through his power to punish. As a consequence, he has little referent power at People's; he is respected, but few things at the college happen because others identify with him and eagerly embrace his latest projects.

The core of bureaucratic management is seen to be decision making, and Potter is expected to be a rational analyst who can not only calculate the most efficient means by which goals can be achieved but also design the systems of control and coordination that direct the activities of others. He is also cast as a heroic leader, able to articulate noble values and goals, to solve the most complex problems, to energize and motivate people, and to direct an efficient and effective organization. "Much of the organization's power is held by the hero, and great expectations are raised because people trust him to solve problems and fend off threats from the environment" (Baldridge, Curtis, Ecker, and Riley, 1978, p. 44). Bureaucratic structures rationalize the hero role. By legitimating leaders, they give them some of the aura of heroes, so that merely by the nature of their office they have more influence. As heroic leader, President Potter can justifiably accept credit for significant institutional advances whether or not he caused them, but at the same time he risks being blamed for failures that cannot be otherwise explained. The image of the heroic leader can be seen in many higher education processes and arenas. Examples include:

- the advertisement prepared by the trustee committee for the search that ended with Potter's appointment, which listed almost superhuman qualities and competencies expected of candidates
- reports of national task forces and commissions that call for

"stronger presidential leadership," either to arrest significant decline or to forge brave new worlds
- touting of successive management systems (program planning and budgeting system, zero-based budgeting, management by objectives, strategic planning) that will increase rationality and finally permit presidents to "take charge" of their institutions
- calling for presidents not only to clarify institutional goals and objectives as the first step toward increasing effectiveness but to create better goals and objectives

Almost any book on management will contain lengthy lists prescribing presumably effective leader behaviors. Bureaucrats are concerned with planning, directing, organizing, staffing, controlling, and evaluating. They "control activity by making decisions, resolving conflicts, solving problems, evaluating performances and output, and distributing rewards and penalties" (Bolman and Deal, 1984, p. 39). Good bureaucrats collect and analyze the right data in the right amount, follow organizational processes and systems, and follow the orders of their superiors. Better bureaucrats even anticipate these orders, thus making giving directives less necessary.

The distinctive value of a bureaucracy is that Potter and other administrators need not do all the work of the institution themselves. They may empower others to do it through the concept of delegation of authority. In the academic bureaucracy, the right to make authoritative decisions stems initially from a charter or legislation approved by civil government. In the case of People's, the charter gives the board of trustees "the powers, rights, and privileges that are incident to the proper government, conduct, and management of the college, and they may make and ordain, as occasion may require, reasonable rules, orders, and by-laws not repugnant to the Constitution and Laws of the State." The legal authority given to the trustees then serves as the basis for the delegation of specific authority by them to President Potter. If President Potter could do everything himself, then good trusteeship would require only one rule—"Hire the right president"—and good administration only one corollary—"Do the right thing." But Potter has neither the time nor the expertise to do everything, and the bureaucratic structure is designed specifically to enable him to expand the influence of his leadership by delegating some of his authority to subordinates.

Potter's predecessor talked constantly about delegation but in fact never practiced it. Instead, he exercised close supervision over his subordinates and reviewed their decisions before giving final approval. To delegate in the full sense, responsibilities have to be assigned, the right to make decisions or expend funds has to be granted, and the person to whom authority has been delegated must be held accountable by the authorizing agent. President Potter's effectiveness as a leader depends on his ability to delegate. His delegations usually follow the "lines of authority" on the organizational chart, which flow in an unbroken chain from the civil government granting the charter to the person exercising authority in a specific instance.

As long as the person receiving an order from a superior believes in the legitimacy of the rule of law that provided for the delegation, that person is likely to expect to receive such orders and to be predisposed to accept them. But we know through our experiences that not all orders are obeyed. To understand why, it is necessary to examine the idea of authority from an organizational, rather than a legal, perspective: "a subordinate is said to accept authority whenever he permits his behavior to be guided by the decision of a superior, without independently examining the merits of that decision. When exercising authority, the superior does not seek to convince the subordinate, but only to obtain his acquiescence" (Simon, 1961, p. 11).

This remarkable definition may superficially sound similar to the legal concept of authority, but in fact it is quite different. Authority is no longer defined by the power of the person giving an order but instead by the willingness of the person receiving it to accept it. It is the subordinate at People's, not the superior, who establishes an authority relationship. In essence, the subordinate defines the area in which orders will be accepted without concern for what those orders are, and the authority relationship exists only within that area and not outside it. This area in which the subordinate will accept orders has been called the "zone of indifference" (that is, the subordinate is indifferent as to whether the superior orders A or B). At People's, for example, faculty accept the right of administrators to call meetings, and they are usually indifferent to when they are scheduled. But a dean who called weekly meetings on Friday afternoons would quickly discover that few would attend. It is the faculty, not the dean, who would decide which directives would be obeyed.

This understanding of the nature of authority has significant implications for the application of the bureaucratic model to colleges and universities, since professionals have relatively narrow zones of acceptance (Simon, 1961). This means that the greater the professional level of institutional staff members, the less effective bureaucratic controls will be in coordinating their behavior. It suggests why bureaucratic controls are usually less influential in dealing with faculty than in dealing with administrators. It also suggests why bureaucratic controls may be more effective at People's than they would be at Heritage. Fewer faculty at People's have the doctorate, and they are therefore less professional. They are also more likely to have had experience in secondary school systems and therefore to have been socialized to expect less involvement in decision making. As long as Potter is seen as equitably administering institutional processes, as consulting with faculty even though reserving to himself the right to make final decisions, as maintaining or expanding institutional resources, and as providing for the faculty's own economic interests through fair dealings with their union representatives, his leadership at People's is likely to be accepted.

Chapter 6

The Political Institution: Competing for Power and Resources

Over the past seventy-five years, Regional State University (RSU) has been transformed successively from a state normal school to a state teachers' college, to a state college, and finally in 1972 (when it had enrolled 3,000 students), into one of five comprehensive public universities controlled by a statewide board of regents. The university includes five colleges—arts and sciences, education, business, health sciences, and technology—and an evening division. Its mission statement is over a page in length and includes extended references to teaching, research, and service and to almost every campus program.

The present enrollment of about 13,500 students represents a decline of about 10 percent in the past five years. Almost all of the undergraduates come from the northwest portion of the state; half commute, a quarter live in residence hall apartments, and the rest rent dilapidated houses in the community. About 1,550 part-time commuting graduate students are in master's degree programs, in education, in computer technology, and in an M.B.A. program that is now seeking professional accreditation.

Most faculty who were at RSU before 1972 received their

doctorates (often in education) from in-state institutions; they have strong commitments to RSU and deep roots in the small city in which it is located. More recently hired faculty tend to have doctorates from national universities and to focus more attention on their discipline or profession than on the institution. Many came to RSU after unsuccessfully seeking appointment at a research university. The elected senate, now dominated by disaffected associate professors who are unlikely to be promoted, spends most of its time opposing actions by the administration—actions often taken without formal consultation with faculty representatives.

President Rita Robinson came to RSU from a career as a campus dean and a state coordinating board officer. Knowledgeable, innovative, and impatient, she is strongly supported by the regents and some segments of the faculty. Her relationships with the senate, as well as with some deans and chairs, are often contentious.

Most students come from the top two-fifths of their high school class, and while a good number are interested in academic matters, most are pursuing vocational interests or are giving primary attention to the active social scene. Fewer than half stay to graduate. Faculty work hard at teaching but tend to focus attention on the more able students. Pressures for publication have increased, and achieving tenure is now more difficult.

Current issues on campus include a request to the regents for authorization to award the doctorate, complaints about faculty work load and lack of faculty research support, debates on salary levels for scarce faculty in some fields, effects on faculty reappointments of midyear state budget rescissions, and a National Collegiate Athletics Association investigation into the recruitment of athletes.

Regional State University as a Political System

People familiar with colleges and universities have often observed that they have many political characteristics. As far back as the turn of the century, an Oxford don turned his wicked wit to writing a set of instructions for aspiring academic politicians. His comments remind us that now, as then, there are ways to get things done in academic institutions even in the absence of collegial agreement or bureaucratic directives.

> This most important branch of political activity is, of course, closely connected with *Jobs.* . . . When you and I have, each of us, a Job on hand, we shall proceed to go on the Square. . . . The proper course to pursue is to walk, between 2 and 4 p.m., up and down the King's Parade. . . . When we have succeeded in meeting accidently, it is etiquette to talk about indifferent matters for ten minutes and then part. After walking five paces in the opposite direction you should call me back, and begin with the words "Oh, by the way, if you should happen. . . ." The nature of your Job must then be vaguely indicated. . . . Then we shall part as before, and I shall call you back and introduce the subject of My Job, in the same formula. By observing this procedure we shall emphasize the fact that there is *no connection whatever* between my supporting your Job and your supporting mine [Cornford, (1908) 1964, p. 30].

At RSU, as at Oxford long ago, individuals or groups with different interests can go "on the Square" and interact by forming coalitions, bargaining, compromising, and reaching agreements that they believe to be to their advantage. These processes of interaction, in which the power to get one's way comes neither from norms nor from rules but is negotiated, identify Regional State University as a political system.

We have already seen how social processes lead the faculty and administration of Heritage College to like each other, interact with each other, engage in common activities, and in doing so share and sustain important values. This is possible because the relatively small size of Heritage and its coherent program permit and encourage frequent face-to-face communication between its members. As a consequence, Heritage possesses a sense of community in which those inside the college's boundaries are thought of as "us," and those outside are considered "they." "We" become more and more alike, and increasingly different from "them."

In a more complex institution, member groups tend to be more specialized and heterogeneous, with divergent interests and preferences. Subgroups may have their own perceptions of community, but the institution as a whole seldom does. Sometimes these subgroups are work groups, such as academic departments or administrative offices, and sometimes they are based on social factors such as sex, age, ethnicity, or ideology. Those who identify strongly with any of these groups think of each other as "we," and "they" can come to refer not just to groups outside the institution but to other groups *inside* as well.

That is what has happened at Regional State University. The institution grew, became more diverse, added new missions, increasingly received resources from external agencies, and appointed new staff with values different from those of older staff. For example, it has one group of administrators who were hired when RSU was still a state college emphasizing teacher education and who remain interested in developing closer ties with school systems in the region, and another group of "fast-track" younger administrators pushing for a state-of-the-art program in robotics. Older faculty have formed an alliance to challenge retirement policies that are being advocated by younger faculty concerned with the possibility of layoffs, and a group of scientists connected to an "old boys' network" has coalesced to defend recruiting practices that are being questioned by the Women's Caucus. The interests of different groups are reflected even in the seating patterns in the faculty dining room, where members of a small but close-knit set of European émigrés in the social sciences are likely to be found at one table, while issues of campus racism are being debated at another.

Resources at RSU are no longer under the sole control of a small group of administrators, decision making has become diffused and decentralized, and the organization is too complex to control activities through bureaucratic systems such as those at People's Community College. As centralized authority has

weak

weakened, consensus for preferred goals has diminished. RSU has become fragmented into special interest groups, each competing for influence and resources. The influence of any group is limited by the interests and activities of other groups; in order to obtain desired outcomes, groups have to join with other groups, to compromise their positions, and to bargain.

To consider a college as a political system is to consider it as a supercoalition of subcoalitions with diverse interests, preferences, and goals (Cyert and March, 1963). Each of the subcoalitions is composed of interest groups that see at least some commonality in their goals and work together to attempt to achieve them (Bacharach and Lawler, 1980). If the collegium can be metaphorically described as a family, and the bureaucracy as a machine, then the political college or university can be seen as a shifting kaleidoscope of interest groups and coalitions. The patterns in the kaleidoscope are not static, and group membership, participation, and interests constantly change with emerging issues.

Characteristics of Political Systems

Organizational politics involves acquiring, developing, and using power to obtain preferred outcomes in situations in which groups disagree (Pfeffer, 1981b). To consider RSU as a political system is to focus attention on uncertainty, dissension, and conflict. RSU is composed of a large number of individuals and groups that in some ways operate autonomously but in other ways remain interdependent. Without interdependence, there can be no politics, and no power; it is only when individuals must rely on others for some of their necessary resources that they become concerned about or interested in the activities or behaviors of others. Political systems depend on social exchange and, therefore, on mutual dependence. The power of any party depends to some extent on the value of that party's contribution to the political community and the extent to which such a contribution is available from other sources (Bacharach and Lawler, 1980). For example, academic departments at RSU that bring in highly valued external resources such as research grants, or that have high prestige and increasing graduate enrollments, have more power and influence over the allocation of internal budgets than do other departments (Salancik and Pfeffer, 1974; Hills and Mahoney, 1978).

Power at RSU is diffused rather than concentrated, and many individuals and groups have power of different kinds in different situations. The vice-president for academic affairs is believed to have considerable influence on campus, but the business school at RSU often appears more responsive to its professional accrediting body than to the vice-president; President Robinson has more power than any other individual on campus, but she has been unable to fire a popular but ineffective dean of students; and the Women's Caucus, a group with no official standing whatever, exerts a powerful influence on the actions of the Faculty Personnel Committee. Under most circumstances, neither the accrediting association, the Women's Caucus, President Robinson, nor any single person or group can impose its will unilaterally on the others.

RSU has an organizational culture, as do Heritage College and People's Community College. The culture at Heritage is supported by norms that are pervasive in all parts of the institution; the culture at People's is made coherent through structure and the ethos of rationality. But at RSU, development of a pervasive or coherent culture is inhibited by the various and competing interests of different groups. To be sure, there is widespread public agreement that the teaching, service, and research missions are all important. But agreement in the abstract conceals the fact that people have different ideas about which programs are the *most* important. When resources are plentiful, so that everyone gets what they want, these ambiguities and disagreements cause no problems. But when resources are scarce, their specific allocation becomes vigorously contested, and conflict is inevitable. Last year, for example, various groups had sharply different views on whether a $50,000 budget windfall should be used to begin a freshman honors program, to support released time for faculty research, or to develop a regional natural resources institute to do research and provide consultation to local governments on water quality and environmental safety.

The three programs were all consistent with the institutional mission, but the mission statement provided no guidance for choosing among them.

In this situation, as in many others at RSU, choices have to be made not between good and bad things but rather between competing goods. People in the institution differ about which objective is most important, and even those who agree on the objective often disagree on how it can be achieved. There are no data that can "prove" that supporting freshman honors is "better" than supporting faculty research, and there are no rational calculations, laws, or rules to help decide what to do. In a collegial system such as Heritage, such decisions can be made by consensus, and in a bureaucratic system such as People's by fiat. But these processes are either unavailable or unacceptable in the complex and decentralized social system of RSU. The institution is too large and the interests of various groups are too diverse to achieve consensus, and the socialization and expectations of the various participants make authoritarian decrees unacceptable and therefore unenforceable. If they are to be able to make a decision at all, they must rely on politics.

Subgroups wish to exert influence so that their preferences are reflected in the allocation of institutional resources such as money, prestige, or influence. Since the board of trustees legally *is* the institution, and all legal authority resides in the board, some might say that the preferences of the trustees and the president as their executive officer should always dominate choice processes at a college or university. But at RSU, as at other institutions, legal delegation is not the sole source of authority, and many groups are able to exercise power in different ways. Administrators have power through their access to budget and personnel procedures, to sources of information, and to internal and external legal authority; faculty and other professionals have power related to their specialized expertise, to tradition, and to external guilds (Baldridge, 1971; Clark, 1983). Clerical and blue-collar groups may invoke the power of their unions in order to influence policies. And, as the example of the Women's Caucus demonstrates, it is possible for groups to obtain power through informal contacts and through appeals based on moral or ethical principles, such as equity.

The problems caused by the dualism of controls are manifest at RSU, and there are constant conflicts between administrative and professional authority. Because of this, it is tempting to view RSU as composed of monolithic groups, and to refer to the battles as being between "the administration and others" or "the faculty and others." This view may occasionally be valid, but it is more often misleading. The president and the deans can have conflicting interests, trustees (particularly in public institutions such as RSU) can disagree on many issues, not all students share the same concerns, and faculty in different disciplines and departments are as much divided by their professionalism as united by it (Clark, 1963). Academics are highly ideological, and the ideologies of different academic departments—and therefore the preferences they might have in institutional decision making—are quite disparate (Ladd and Lipset, 1975). RSU "is not one community, but several—the community of the undergraduate and the community of the graduate; the community of the humanist, the community of the social scientist, and the community of the scientist; the communities of the professional schools; the community of all the nonacademic personnel; the community of the administrators" (Kerr, 1963, p. 19). But, of course, the communities are far more complex even than that on a contemporary campus. On any issue, for example, subgroups of faculty transcending department or discipline bring young and old, male and female, minority and white, tenured and nontenured, local and cosmopolitan, into arenas in which their conflicting interests must be addressed. We commonly think of the president as the institutional leader, and it is true that President Robinson plays a part in decision making in many areas of governance. But in each, she is opposed by countervailing forces of different groups (Corson, 1960).

Some groups are stronger than others and have more power, but no group is strong enough to dominate all the others all the time. Those who desire certain outcomes must spend time building positions that are supported by other groups as well. This requires the development of coalitions among various groups, and trade-offs and compromises are often among the costs that must be paid. For example, the faculty senate finally approved President Robinson's proposal for a freshman honors program after she successfully persuaded the humanities division to also support it. Their support, in turn, required her to agree to have the program reviewed after two years and to express willingness to appoint its director from among the existing faculty.

The idea that political processes in academic institutions are somehow "dirty" reflects the misunderstanding that if people would only act in the best interests of the institution, they would agree on what to do. It assumes that the institution's best interests are either known or knowable, rather than that different people, especially committed to what they believe to be the institution's welfare, can, in good faith, have completely different ideas of what that means and how it should be accomplished. The allocation decision is primarily a political one of who gets what, when, and how, and in a democratic and pluralistic organization, political processes are appropriate means for resolving such political issues.

It might be expected that, because groups contend for power and there are differences in their preferred outcomes, RSU would be typified by constant turmoil and instability. There are several reasons why this is usually not the case. First, organizations tend to develop continuing and quasi-stable dominant coalitions (Thompson, 1967) whose established power serves to inhibit overt conflict. At RSU, the president, senior administrators, and board have for a decade been the dominant coalition; they agree on policies most (but not all) of the time, and general campus recognition of their power inhibits those who would otherwise challenge it.

In addition, individuals belong to more than one group, and they participate in many political processes, each of which involves different people. The existence of a large number of small cross-cutting disagreements provides checks and balances against major disruptions, so that the agitation of political processes can ironically lead to system stability. At RSU, people who engage in total conflict are generally referred to as "crazies." Most people on campuses are not crazies; they participate in conflict segmentally—for example, supporting the administration on one issue and disagreeing with them on another. Even within the faculty senate itself, which has quasi-stable pro-administration and antiadministration voting blocs, the balance of power is held by a third, "unaffiliated" coalition, whose members align themselves with one or another bloc on the basis of specific issues (Bowen, 1987). As a result, deep cleavages dividing major groups at RSU on many issues are unlikely (Coser, 1956). By permitting groups to assess their relative power, and by encouraging the development of associations and coalitions, political conflict may increase the cohesiveness of RSU.

A central characteristic of most political communities is indifference. Most people at RSU are not concerned about most issues most of the time. Even during the last great budget crisis, which had the potential for faculty layoffs, only a small percentage of the faculty actively participated in governance activities, while another small group looked on with interest; the majority were apathetic (Baldridge, 1971). Most of the time, most of what happens at RSU is routine and guided by existing procedures and informal understandings. But at irregular intervals, and for reasons that are not at all clear, a specific issue emerges and becomes contentious on campus. Sometimes the issue is one of great substance, such as whether RSU should offer doctoral programs. And sometimes, as in the case of whether RSU deans should have reserved spaces in the faculty parking lot, it is primarily symbolic. Similar situations have occurred in the past without activating political interest, and President Robinson has found it impossible to accurately predict campus responses to her initiatives. Political processes at RSU may sometimes be initiated by new issues, or sometimes by the loss of an old coalition or consensus.

Finally, disruptive conflict is inhibited because power in higher education tends to be issue specific. Different groups develop spheres of influence around issues of concern to them (Baldridge, Curtis, Ecker, and Riley, 1978). Deans at RSU leave course development to faculty most of the time, faculty leave fund raising to the president most of the time, and President Robinson leaves faculty recruiting to the deans most of the time. As long as these tacit agreements are maintained, contention is unlikely. All parties recognize that intrusion into tacitly approved spheres of influence is usually costly, and they ordinarily go to unusual lengths to avoid it.

The political processes at RSU have organizational advantages and disadvantages. If there were institutional consensus about preferences and agreement on how to achieve them, political processes would be wasteful and unnecessary. The costs and benefits of any proposed program could be specified, and calculations would give unequivocal direction to the participants. But since at RSU such a consensus does not exist, decisions can be made only through the exercise of power (Pfeffer, 1981b). A major advantage of political systems, therefore, is that they permit decisions to be made even in the absence of clear goals. Political systems also simplify the influence process, since it need not involve the active participation of everyone in the organization but only their representatives (Weick, 1979). They also simplify budgeting processes. If politics is a game in which power is used to influence resource allocation in support of one's preferences, then the budget is the document on which the yearly score at RSU is kept. "Rational" approaches to budgeting would suggest that the funding of all programs be reassessed each year, with the costs and benefits of each compared to each other, and decisions based on the optimization of stated objectives. Political processes in budget formulation, on the other hand, simplify calculations and usually lead to outcomes acceptable to a majority of stakeholders. Among other things, only those issues raised by specific groups need be addressed (most programs approved in the past are continued, so that budgets next year are likely to be similar to budgets this year), only politically feasible alternatives need to be considered (so that time is not wasted on alternatives that could not be supported), and participants need consider only their own preferences without worrying about others (since other groups will have representation somewhere in the process) (Wildavsky, 1974).

Political systems have another great advantage: their inefficiency provides institutional stability. There is a lot of consistency at Heritage College because people tend to think alike; there is consistency at People's Community College as well because people follow the same rules. In both cases, having similar data and sharing uniformity of opinion or action make it possible for small changes to be amplified as they move through the system. Everyone knows what is going on, an unexpected situation may become volatile, and balance becomes precarious. But at RSU, people have access to different data from different sources on which they place different interpretations. No one knows the totality of what is happening, and their activities often resemble random movements that cancel each other out and provide stability.

There are, of course, disadvantages to political systems as well. Some groups at RSU attempt to control information as a source of power to achieve their own ends, and this may weaken other organizational functions. Competing for resources means that groups have to present the reasons why their claims are stronger than those of other groups. This ensures that the best arguments are given, but at the same time it may lead to advocacy, the hardening of positions, and difficulty in developing reasonable compromises. Since not all programs get reviewed all the time, programs that are no longer effective may be allowed to continue if no one challenges them. The system therefore has little accountability. In addition, coalitions can arise that are not concerned about protecting the weak. Too, political processes may sometimes be used in situations in which more rational approaches are feasible and could be more effective.

While the instrumental activities associated with obtaining benefits at RSU are one side of politics, there is another side as well. Political processes and structures also have important symbolic elements and outcomes (Edelman, 1967). They permit interest groups at RSU to display or confirm their status, provide individuals with rituals and enjoyable pastimes, protect organizations from disruption by deviant members, and confirm important institutional values and myths (Birnbaum, 1987a, 1987b). It is the constant involvement of various constituents in campus political activity that permits both change and stability. The existence of political instruments for change, and the potential of influencing policy, rather than merely getting one's way, permit people at RSU to work together even as they have disparate objectives.

Loops of Interaction in Political Systems

In the previous chapters, we have described how collegial or bureaucratic systems are coordinated through the development of stable vertical or horizontal interactions. Considering RSU as a political system focuses on coordination through conflict. Formal and informal groups change, overlap, are created, and fall apart, as they search for the power to induce outcomes consistent with their preferences. Senior tenured science faculty may comprise a group for the purpose of one policy decision, but it may be fragmented into life science and physical sciences, or gender or age groups, on another issue. There are at least two important processes through which groups are created and develop their positions: one is the formation of coalitions, and the other is the process of negotiations.

Coalitions. If politics is the pursuit and exercise of power to achieve desired objectives, then the purpose of forming coalitions is to join with other individuals or groups in order to achieve a level of power and influence that cannot be achieved by acting alone. Coalitions can involve any number of parties, but the triadic structure is the one about which the most is known. A current conflict at RSU over faculty work load, for example, involves three parties: the dean of the College of Business, who wants to reduce the teaching load of faculty in the M.B.A. program; the faculty senate, which wants to establish precedents for reducing teaching loads in general; and the president, who does not wish to support a policy with such substantial fiscal implications. None of the parties has the power to impose its will if the other two disagree. Normally, President Robinson and the dean are part of the dominant coalition, but in this case the issue is business faculty work load, and the dean disagrees with the president's position.

Coalitions are theoretically possible between any two of the three parties; in Figure 15, I show a coalition between the dean and the senate on this issue. The *actual* coalition that will form in cases such as this will depend on the relative strength of the three parties and whether the relationships between them

Figure 15. Parties to Coalitions in a Triad.

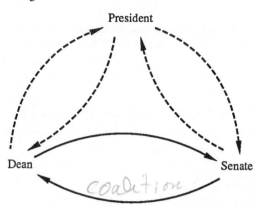

are continuous or episodic (Caplow, 1968). The opportunity to form coalitions serves to balance power in an organization because even relatively weak parties can swing the balance of power and can exact a price for doing so. Particularly in continuous relationships, coalitions tend to be stable over time, but that does not mean that the same coalitions will inevitably form in the same way as issues change. Coalitions can preserve ongoing balances of power (the fact that the president and the dean are both members of the dominant coalition increased the probability that they would support each other on this issue as well), or they can change balances (in this case, the senate and the dean, both weaker members of the triad, formed a coalition that was stronger than the president, who is the most powerful member). Coalitions challenging the formal authority structure are more likely to form in decentralized organizations such as RSU than in others; it seldom happens at People's Community College, where centralized administrative power is considered strong enough to overwhelm any conceivable coalition, or at Heritage College, where power is accessible to all and people believe that their interests will receive due consideration in all decisions.

The formation of coalitions can be extended throughout entire organizations by linking triads together. Although the bureaucratic model suggests that the power of higher-level officers will always prevail over lower-level ones (and therefore that no coalitions are necessary), a political system makes it possible for lower-level participants to form coalitions that can be stronger than their superiors. At RSU, for example, the dean of the School of Education felt threatened by the possibility that the school's two associate deans were working together to curtail the dean's influence over academic policy. To prevent this, the dean gave special recognition and program support to one of them. The development of this new dean-associate dean coalition effectively ended any possibility that the two subordinates would work collectively to undermine the dean's authority.

Negotiations. Coalitions do not just "happen." Before parties can decide whether to join forces with others, they must try to assess their own power, the power of potential coalition partners, the degree to which the interests of the parties coincide, and the potential costs and benefits of forming alliances. Bargaining processes are often carried on by identifiable people who fill roles spanning the boundaries between institutional subsystems. They interact with each other as representatives of a group rather than as individuals. Negotiators in these boundary-spanning roles must engage in two sequential and continuing processes. In one process, they have to negotiate with representatives of the other group to discover the most advantageous outcomes or compromises that can be achieved. In the other process, they have to negotiate with the members of their own group in order to understand their desires, clarify their willingness to accept potential outcomes, and help them to adjust their aspirations as the political process unfolds. Often, the negotiations with members of one's own group prove to be more difficult than those with representatives of the other side! These interactions are shown in Figure 16, which depicts the interaction of President Robinson and the chairperson of the faculty senate as they negotiate an issue of faculty salaries.

Political processes often involve the interaction of two people who are the representatives of different interests. For example, President Robinson often meets with the chairperson of the faculty senate to bargain over issues of mutual concern, such as the president's proposal (opposed by the senate) to give

Figure 16. Representatives Negotiating in a Political System.

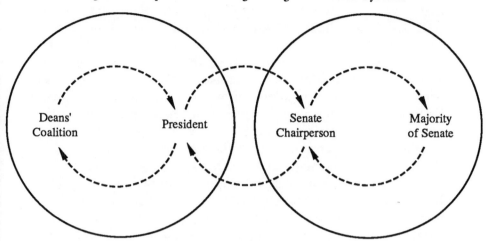

higher salaries to faculty in scarce areas. The president's position was developed in consultation with a coalition that included most of the deans and the faculties of several departments in business and computer science that are unable to successfully recruit; the chairperson's position was endorsed by a majority of the senate, by several humanities departments, and by the Women's Caucus, which wishes to see sex-related salary inequities rectified before paying higher salaries in fields dominated by men. Both sides see their positions as justified and reasonable, and each tends to identify the other's position as self-serving and inconsistent with institutional effectiveness. President Robinson thinks that she can obtain approval from the trustees for her own position even over the objections of others, but she is unwilling to pay the probable cost in terms of campus disruption. The alternative is negotiation.

President Robinson and the senate chairperson meet to argue their cases, and each tries to change the attitudes and behaviors of the other. The processes through which they interact have probably been best described in terms of labor negotiations (Walton and McKersie, 1965), but they are applicable in any social negotiation setting. To some extent, the relationship between these two people is governed by the same interpersonal processes that govern all interpersonal exchanges. All other things being equal, feelings of liking should increase and values become more consistent as they interact and engage in common activities. If only the two of them were involved, they might find common ground that they could both endorse. But as coalition spokespersons, their ability to alter their positions is constrained; they are not just individuals but representatives of groups with different interests. Yielding to the other could be seen as betrayal by their constituencies, and to the extent that they are persuaded by the arguments of the other side, they must return to their constituents and engage in negotiations with them as well. Both representatives find themselves engaged simultaneously in boundary roles in which they are negotiating with both their own constituencies and the opposing negotiator. They are simultaneously part of two dynamic, nonlinear systems in which every action changes the situation and the state of both systems.

Tight and Loose Coupling in Political Systems

The parties to political processes have different preferences. As they interact through negotiations, compromises, and coalition formation, their original objectives change. Since the groups with which they interact are also modifying their positions, the social environment in which they are functioning changes more quickly than they can respond to it. It is impossible to predict in advance which of many alternative outcomes will in fact take place. The actual outcome is likely to be the resultant by-product of many forces and may be neither intended nor preferred by any of the participants (Steinbruner, 1974).

Not only are the outcomes of political processes often not consistent with the preferences of any of the actors, but because they represent compromises and are embedded in ongoing organizational processes, they are usually not as radical as the rhetoric of debate might suggest. Most change at RSU is incremental rather than comprehensive, and while some of the battles may be revolutionary in intent, the changes they provoke are usually neither radical nor dramatic (Baldridge, 1971). In the political arena of RSU, loose coupling between what is said and what is done is the rule rather than the exception. Since participants in the process know that the final result is likely to be compromise, they usually ask for much more than they expect to get in order to increase the chances of their getting at least a minimum of what they want.

Political outcomes are difficult to predict also because they may depend greatly on the forums in which they are discussed and the timing with which alternatives are considered. What happens in a particular case at RSU may be related to whether the issue is discussed first in the faculty senate or the administrative council, and the conflict related to where an issue is properly to be discussed may at times be as contentious as the issue itself. In addition, when there are a large number of alternatives, the sequence in which they are considered is critical; depending on these sequences, it is possible for an alternative desired by fewer participants to be selected over one desired by many more (Plott, 1982). President Robinson has become aware of this possibility because of two versions of a bill recently introduced in the state legislature that would permit faculty members to join unions and bargain collectively. One bill calls for two sequential elections. In the first, faculty would vote whether or not to unionize, and if the second vote is needed, they would select their bargaining agent. The other bill calls for one election in which faculty could vote for any contending bargaining representative or for "no agent." There are two contending union groups on campus. If the first bill passes, President Robinson thinks the faculty would reject bargaining. But if the second passes, some faculty opposed to unionization might vote for one union in order to prevent the other, less desirable union from winning, and the campus might unionize even though a majority opposed it.

Leadership in Political Systems

President Robinson acts like a political leader much of the time. She gives high priority to informally learning about the concerns and attitudes of the many institutional constituents and low priority to data and analytical reports (Dill, 1984). She knows that leadership depends in good measure on presence and timing; influence is exerted by people who are present when compromises are being effected and coalitions are being negotiated. "Being there" is critical, and part of Robinson's influence as a political leader comes from knowing where to be. It has also been said that in politics, "timing is everything." Timing refers to the understanding that a political leader brings to the questions of the positions of other campus groups, the possible linkages between one issue and another, and one's own power at a particular moment. Leaders must decide whether to do something now or to wait.

The heavy reliance of political leaders on intuition, experience, and a sense of the particular situation at hand makes it difficult to generalize about what works in specific circumstances. Practitioners and scholars from the time of Machiavelli have offered their counsel on gaining political advantage. College presidents who see politics merely as the exercise of raw power might wish to heed the advice said to have been offered by a former master at Oxford: Never retract. Never Explain. Get the thing done and let them howl! But President Robinson sees the campus as a democratic community whose leaders depend on the consent of the governed (Walker, 1979). She believes that persuasion and diplomacy are her most reliable administrative tools. She sees conflict and disagreement as normal rather than as an indication of organizational pathology, and she recognizes that others may hold different views in good faith. She tries not to attack opposing opinions but to use them creatively. The president believes that there are many ways that objectives (for example, excellence or access) can be achieved, and she tries not to become irrevocably committed to any single proposal or program. She strives for "flexible rigidity"; she is willing to compromise on means but unwilling to compromise on ends. Most of all, she is a realist, and tries to understand the dynamics of the institution not as she would like it to be but as it really is. She appreciates the need to bring a degree of rationality to management processes, but she tries to balance this in her judgment with an understanding of the values of others. In her previous position, for example, she was surprised by the vehemence with which her attempts to "improve budgeting" through apparently neutral technical reforms provoked criticism and anger. Now she realizes that management systems such as budgeting are not merely technical; in fact, they significantly change the balance of campus power and the processes through which individuals and groups express their preferences.

Political systems have many sources of power. President Robinson is certainly *a* leader, but only the naive on campus think of her as the *only* leader. Many groups attempt to exercise influence, and leadership at RSU of necessity must be referred to in the plural rather than the singular. Representatives of each of the various coalitions and subgroups must all be leaders in the sense of representing or altering the interests of their constituencies, entering into negotiations with other representatives, and seeking outcomes acceptable both to their constituencies and to their coalition partners. Of course, not all groups, and therefore not all representatives, have equal power, and the central power figure is the one who can manage the coalition (Thompson, 1967). At most colleges and universities, as at RSU, that individual is the president.

President Robinson's major leadership role is to help the community manage its own affairs, to assist in the process by which issues are deliberated and judgments reached, and to take the actions necessary to implement decisions (Tucker, 1981). This emphasis on giving direction to a community suggests that President Robinson does not rule—she serves. Since a college or university consists of different groups with legitimate interests, she tries to find solutions to problems in a manner that constituencies find acceptable (Walker, 1979). Probably the most famous statement of this political role of the president was Clark Kerr's characterization of the president as "leader, educator, creator, initiator, wielder of power, pump; he is also officeholder, caretaker, inheritor, consensus-seeker, persuader, bottleneck. But he is mostly a mediator. The first task of the mediator is peace . . . peace within the student body, the faculty, the trustees; and peace between and among them" (Kerr, 1963, p. 36).

The responsibilities of mediation as Kerr defined them

transcend merely the institutional and personal survival that peace might bring—they include institutional progress as well. The political leader, therefore, is a person who practices the art of the possible. President Robinson has learned that she cannot always get everything she wants. But she can usually get something. She has become an expert in analyzing differences in the stated preferences of different campus groups, designing alternatives that find a common ground between them, and persuading the conflicting parties that their own interests are furthered by accepting these compromise alternatives (Lindblom, 1980). She tries to develop positions that can be endorsed by the dominant coalition to minimize disruption and maximize satisfaction, while at the same time moving RSU—even if only in an incremental way—toward her own objectives.

In addition to providing what might be thought of as "mediated progress," President Robinson performs many other important services that are often not given appropriate recognition by the constituent community. Two of these are the design of programs that help clarify group values and the facilitation of constituent involvement in governance by reducing the cost of participation.

Clarifying Group Values. The rational model suggests that leaders should first seek agreement on values, and then design programs consistent with these values. It is easy to agree on many of these values, and at RSU, as at most institutions, consensus could be found that values such as "excellence" and "diversity" are good. But the meanings of these terms, and the relative value that they have in any specific situation, cannot be assessed in the abstract. Values can be clarified only by inventing alternative policies and programs, and then selecting between them (Lindblom, 1959). The relative importance of excellence or diversity in a specific situation at RSU can therefore be determined only by designing policies whose various outcomes differ in terms of these values. It is through the selection process that relevant values are disclosed. President Robinson functions as a political leader by having alternatives designed or designing them personally and by developing systems that de-

liver relevant information concerning them to participants in
the political community (Wildavsky, 1979). She minimizes conflict by ensuring that the alternatives she designs are plausible
and fall within the constraints of important constituents and by
focusing attention during debate on common bonds between
participants. She does this so that, while constituencies may
struggle to achieve their objectives, at the same time they recognize that they do not wish to destroy the other side or wreck
the organization.

Reducing the Cost of Participation. In a political community, mere dissatisfaction with the state of affairs is not enough
to activate political interest. Without special incentives (or a degree of coercion), members of a group often will not act to
achieve the interests of the group (Olson, 1982). The reason for
this is that individual participation is costly (in terms of time
and energy, as well as money), and each member will get the
benefits of the group activity even without participating. It is
particularly difficult to obtain participation when past participation has not been successful. In general, when the chances for
success are low and the benefits can be achieved without participating, the rational self-interested person will not participate.
Faculty apathy at RSU turns out to be rational!

One of President Robinson's roles as a political leader is
to identify the issues that political groups should deal with, to
reduce the cost of participation to elicit support, and to provide added incentives or coercion when necessary to induce involvement. This is true not only for President Robinson but for
the leaders of other campus groups as well. As an example, one
of the contending union organizations at RSU is the Faculty
Association of Regional State University (FARSU). Their elected
chairperson has developed systems of internal communication
and influence within RSU so that faculty members need do
nothing more than sign a card and pay a nominal fee to "participate" in the union and through their representatives to influence institutional policy. When faculty are not motivated to join
the union by economic incentives, the union may try to provide
added incentives by giving only members access to certain bene-

fits or through coercion by bringing social pressure to bear against "freeloaders."

A consideration of leadership in political systems can conclude in no better fashion than by returning to the sage advice of Cornford, our Oxford don, directed toward persons who, like President Robinson, wish to be influential in academic institutions: "Remember this: *the men who get things done are the men who walk up and down King's Parade, from 2 to 4, every day of their lives.* You can either join them, and become a powerful person; or you can join the great throng of those who spend their time in preventing them from getting things done, and in the larger task of preventing one another from doing anything whatever" (Cornford, [1908] 1964, p. 31).

Chapter 7

The Anarchical Institution: Finding Meaning in a Community of Autonomous Actors

Flagship University is a complex institution with two undergraduate colleges, a graduate school, six professional schools, and many research centers and institutes, occupying an attractive, sprawling campus near the state capital. Flagship ranks among the top twenty-five universities in the nation in its level of federal research support, and many of its graduate and professional programs enjoy national and even international reputations. A brief statement of purpose in its bulletin emphasizes the university's search for knowledge and service to the state.

Of the 27,500 students, two-thirds are undergraduates. All in-state students in the top half of their high school class are admitted, but performance expectations are rigorous, and attrition is high in the freshman year. Faculty pay close attention to departmental courses and major sequences, but general education commands little interest and is defined by distribution requirements only. Undergraduate life is not closely monitored, and students live where and how they please. Graduate programs are highly selective.

Almost all faculty have doctorates, many from institutions as prestigious as or more prestigious than Flagship. Teaching loads are low, and much undergraduate teaching is done in

large lectures or by teaching assistants. Scholarly productivity
is the key to promotion, tenure, salary increases, and individual prestige. Most issues of faculty interest are resolved through
the interaction of deans and faculty at the college level. There
is a large academic senate, whose major activities seem to be
"pointing with pride" or "viewing with alarm," but the president does consult regularly with an elected faculty advisory
committee composed of five senior and respected faculty. While
the president does not always take their counsel, he is unlikely
to act contrary to it.

President Franklin Foster served as a professor, and then
dean, of one of the professional schools at Flagship before being
recommended for the presidency to the trustees by a faculty-
dominated search committee. He is polished and urbane—equally at home addressing a colloquium of visiting scholars, solicit-
ing alumni contributions, or standing his ground at a legislative
budget hearing. He is as proud of the football team's bowl vic-
tory last New Year's Day as he is of the number of members of
the National Academy of Sciences who grace the faculty. Not an
acclaimed scholar himself, his commitment to rigorous standards
when he became dean of a weak school is legendary.

Jocks, grinds, radicals, partygoers, student government
politicians, esthetes, and groups identified by ethnic, religious,
or other factors all form subcultures on the campus. Faculty are
likely to associate with colleagues sharing common disciplinary
or research interests, and, except at the doctoral level, there is
little faculty-student interaction outside formal class settings.
Current issues on campus include efforts to influence federal
policy to limit the monitoring of grant activity, a campaign to
make faculty salaries more competitive, an effort to convince
the legislature to support development of a high-technology research park, and a debate about the role of the campus in urban
education.

Flagship University as an Anarchical System

"Imagine that you're either the referee, coach, player, or
spectator at an unconventional soccer match: the field for the
game is round; there are several goals scattered haphazardly

around the circular field; people can enter and leave the game whenever they want to; they can throw balls in whenever they want; they can say 'that's my goal' whenever they want to, and for as many goals as they want to; the entire game takes place on a sloped field; and the game is played as if it makes sense" (March, cited in Weick, 1976, p. 1). This soccer-field image may strike a resonant note for administrators and faculty at Flagship. It depicts a setting that to the observer appears chaotic and in which people appear to do what they feel like doing. Yet there is structure to it. Roles are specified, the players stay on an officially designated field (by and large), and they usually throw balls rather than bricks or marshmallows. Moreover, the participants can make sense of what is happening (although their versions may differ) even if the observer cannot.

People at Flagship must constantly deal with issues of attention and meaning. But their rationality is bounded, or limited, and they cannot give attention to the infinite number of elements that exist in the organization's environment. How can they decide which of these elements are the most important? And given the equivocal nature of events, how can they interpret the relationships between the selected elements so that they make sense? Since these questions have no objective answers, observers may come to the conclusion that "processes of campus governance are dictated largely by intuition, irrational precedent, and from-the-hip responses" (Hodgkinson, 1971, p. 1). The model developed to describe this system where everyone does what they wish has been referred to as an organized anarchy. In it, "teachers decide if, when, and what to teach. Students decide if, when, and what to learn. Legislators and donors decide if, when, and what to support. Neither coordination (except the spontaneous mutual adaptation of decision) nor control are practiced. Resources are allocated by whatever process emerges but without explicit accommodation and without explicit reference to some superordinate goals. The 'decisions' of the system are a consequence produced by the system but intended by no one and decisively controlled by no one" (Cohen and March, 1974, pp. 33–34).

The concepts of the organized anarchy are counterintuitive. They defy the common expectations that are part of the

more familiar ideas of organizations as communities, as bureaucracies, or as political systems. To understand them requires sus-
pension of some commonsense ideas about organizations that
we "know" are correct—ideas that we have internalized and that
are potent enough to filter and distort our perceptions. Among
these ideas are that organizational leaders play critical roles in
institutional processes, that institutions have goals, that individuals can specify their preferences, that chains of cause and effect
lead individuals and organizations to take certain actions in
order to effectuate outcomes they consider desirable, that problems are solved by decisions, and that decision making is a primary occupation of organizational participants. In other words,
they question common understandings of organizational rationality that presuppose that thinking precedes action, action
serves a purpose, purposes are related to consistent sets of goals,
and choice is based on logical relationships between actions and
consequences.

What might the dynamics of an institution look like if
these ideas were not true—at least not all of the time? How
might such an institution function if cause-and-effect relationships were equivocal, and autonomous and essentially unpredictable behavior operated within invented yet accepted boundaries and rules? The ideas of open systems, loose coupling,
bounded rationality, and sense making discussed in earlier chapters can provide an alternative lens for viewing Flagship University as an organized anarchy.

Characteristics of Anarchical Systems

An organized anarchy exhibits three characteristics: problematic goals, an unclear technology, and fluid participation.
When goals are vague, no one knows exactly how the technology
works, and decision-making processes are unclear, describing and
understanding how Flagship University works becomes extremely
difficult (Cohen and March, 1974). Let us take each of these
properties and discuss the extent to which they apply to Flagship
University, using as our example the teaching activities of its
undergraduate College of Liberal Arts and Science (CLAS).

Problematic Goals. The *CLAS Bulletin* states that its goal is to prepare students who are "liberally educated." Within the college, however, there is wide disagreement about what liberal education means; consequently, the college finds itself unable to define this goal more clearly or assess the extent to which it is being achieved. Within the ambiguous framework of the idea of a liberal education, the curriculum in actuality often reflects primarily the interests of individual departments and faculty members. Specific college goals are often stated after, rather than before, programs have been developed. For example, several years after enrollments burgeoned in a new computer course developed by interested mathematics faculty, the college added "computer literacy" to its list of objectives. At Flagship, "goals" are typically a loose collection of changing ideas rather than a coherent educational philosophy. The curriculum at Flagship is not so much a reflection of thoughtful consideration by scholars of the knowledge most worth knowing as it is a beanbag. New faculty enter the institution and drop in their own beans as they begin their careers. The institution discovers what it prefers by seeing what it has already done, rather than by acting on the basis of preferences.

Unclear Technology. We have defined technology as the characteristic processes through which organizations convert inputs to outputs. For example, CLAS employs a number of technologies in its efforts to convert new students into educated graduates, the most familiar of which include large lecture sections, small discussion classes, laboratory sessions, seminars, remedial instruction, and independent study. Each of these technologies has been used over an extended period of time, and all of them appear to be effective. However, no one knows why they are effective. It is not clear specifically what processes in a lecture promote student change and what processes do not. In one recent experiment at Flagship, for example, students seemed to learn equally well if they were taught with a lecture and a book, only read the book, or also discussed the book in small groups. Without strong evidence that one method is more effective than another, choices about technology tend to be based on trial and error, previous experiences, imitation, and inventions born of necessity (Cohen and March, 1974).

Fluid Participation. There are various formal and informal groups at the program, departmental, and college level at CLAS that deal with curriculum. In some cases, participants are elected so that committee membership changes regularly. Any curriculum issue might go through one, two, or all three levels of review, depending on the topic, the committee work load, the desires of the committee chairs, and the interest shown in particular situations by individual committee members. The attendance of some faculty members is often sporadic, depending on their teaching schedules, the specific days of the week they work at home, and related factors. The dean is an ex officio member of the collegewide committee and may attend except when there are meetings of the college budget committee or of the president's cabinet. Faculty who are not committee members but who have an interest in the agenda may attend meetings, and they often actively participate in discussions. There are probably few, if any, occasions on which decisions on two related issues are made by the same people. People tend to move in and out of various parts of the organization, and their involvement in any issue depends to a great extent on what other opportunities for their attention happen to be available at the same time.

If we looked at other parts of Flagship University, we would find that many of them also have these key characteristics of an organized anarchy. The reasons why colleges and universities often find it difficult to make "rational" decisions should now be somewhat clearer: common understandings of organizational decision making assume agreed-upon goals, a clear technology, and stable levels of participation—and none of these conditions is present at Flagship. But their absence does not mean that there are no patterns. The image that the word *anarchy* creates of an inchoate formless entity must be tempered. *Both* words in the concept of organized anarchy have meaning. Flagship *is* organized. It has a structure, roles, and rules and regulations. Organizational status is related to influ-

ence. There are standardized procedures for information flow
and communication that direct people's attention, and many
decisions follow prescribed processes. In addition, the institution has a culture and exists within a still larger culture, both of
which increase the probability that certain behaviors will take
place and decrease the probability of other behaviors. Unlike
Heritage College, where major aspects of the culture are rooted
in some of the unique history of the institution, Flagship has a
culture that is driven by national meritocratic standards based
on the professional and expert authority of the faculty. These
features of organizational life all constrain the behavior of participants and officeholders, and much—perhaps most—of what
happens at Flagship is routine.

Loops of Interaction in Anarchical Systems

In a rational world, people learn about cause and effect
by taking actions consistent with their beliefs, observing the
consequences of these actions, and then modifying their future
actions as necessary to more closely achieve desired outcomes.
The cycle through which this learning takes place (March and
Olsen, 1979, p. 57) is shown in Figure 17.

In a simple world, the cycle suggests a readily comprehensible sequence permitting the learning of cause and effect
through observation. But in a complex world, there are too
many variables and potential interactions to permit complete
understanding, and the bounds of rationality interfere both
with observation and with interpretation. In particular, errors
in thinking caused by organizational constraints or systematic
psychological biases, or both, may break the continuity of the
loop and lead people to make incorrect inferences and judgments. These breaks may occur between any of the elements of
the loop, and four of the problem areas that may lead to incorrect learning have been identified with a question mark (?).

At Flagship, for example, President Foster believes that
the physics department is weak and that "something ought to
be done" about it. However, his individual belief concerning the
marginal quality of the physics department may not lead to ac-

Figure 17. The Organization Learning Cycle.

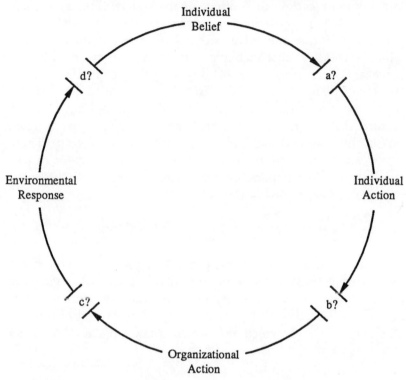

Source: Adapted from March and Olsen, 1979, p. 57.

tion on his part (*a?*) because of role definitions (presidents at
Flagship do not interfere in departmental business), the existence of organizational standard operating procedures (program
reviews are a responsibility of the dean, who has them con-
ducted on a five-year cycle), and the fact that Foster has many
such beliefs but does not have time to act on all of them. Even
if Foster were to act by telling the dean to "do something about
physics," it would be difficult to say with certainty (*b?*) whether the dean's subsequent behavior was due to the president's
comments. In addition to the president, many persons and
groups both inside and outside Flagship influence what the dean
does. For example, the dean has also been exposed to accrediting reports, internal data summaries, and informal lunchroom

discussions with faculty over several years about the physics department, any one or a combination of which might motivate the dean to act.

Assuming that the institution takes an action (for example, the dean meets to discuss the situation with the department chair), something might subsequently happen in the physics department (for example, it might apply for and receive a major research grant). But the relationship between the action and the response (*c?*) would be unclear. The application might have been planned long before the meeting, or its award might have been related to unforeseeable events, such as the need by the granting agency to ensure geographical diversity in the disbursement of funds. Finally, the receipt of the grant might be incorrectly seen (*d?*) by the president as confirming his belief that presidents can influence institutional quality by personal intervention in academic activities.

It is possible that in this case the president's intervention *was* in fact responsible for improving academic quality. But it is also possible that because of potential breaks in the loop at various points, the two events were completely unrelated. Acquiring accurate understandings under conditions of such ambiguity is fraught with difficulty, particularly since people are likely to see what they believe, to attribute outcomes to human agency rather than happenstance, and to infer cause and effect when one event occurs after another. When organizational elements are only loosely coupled, "what happened is not immediately obvious, why it happened is obscure, and whether what happened is good is unclear" (March and Olsen, 1979, p. 59).

Tight and Loose Coupling in Anarchical Systems

The traditional organization chart with its boxes representing offices connected by lines representing channels of authority provides one very powerful metaphor for thinking about tight coupling in organizational structure. But a metaphor more appropriate for loose coupling is that of "streams" (Cohen and March, 1974). A stream can be thought of as a flow of "something" that travels through an organization as the Gulf

Stream flows through the Atlantic Ocean. The casual observer would not see it, but it is there. Now consider four relatively independent streams flowing through Flagship University, each only loosely coupled to the others. These four streams consist respectively of problems, solutions, participants, and choice opportunities. Looking carefully at these metaphorical streams can help us understand their composition and the ways in which they may interact with each other.

Problems. Problems are the unresolved concerns of people inside the institution. Problems change constantly, but a snapshot of the problem stream flowing through CLAS at Flagship on a typical day might find, among other things, Professor Smith's failure to be reappointed in the history department because of enrollment shifts and budget constraints, the dean's feeling of job dissatisfaction and burnout, the physics department secretary's difficulty in getting proper room assignments, the comptroller's inability to reconcile this month's enrollment reports, and freshman Green's shortage of funds to pay tuition due this week. These are all problems the individuals concerned wish to resolve, and they must find processes and forums for doing so.

Solutions. Solutions are someone's products. Often, of course, a solution may be developed in order to resolve a problem. But some solutions precede problems and flow in a stream through the organization looking for problems to which they might be the answer. An appealing solution for many faculty in CLAS is "higher standards," and regardless of the nature of the problem, some will suggest greater scholarly rigor as the remedy. A snapshot of the solution stream on a given day at CLAS might include a number of such all-purpose products and answers, such as more computers, a core curriculum, changing from elected to appointed department chairs, more faculty participation in governance, programs for adults, or faculty development. Sometimes the organization itself makes changes that make certain solutions more prominent. For example, the initiation at Flagship of a management information system has led to the appointment of persons likely to identify "more data" as a solution to all kinds of institutional problems.

Participants. Participants are people involved in a decision. In most organizations, certain people are told that they *must* participate in certain decisions and that they *cannot* participate in others. But Flagship is different, and academics there are free to participate in many decisions if they are willing to expend the time and energy, and need not participate in almost any if they wish not to. The number of things to which academics could give attention is therefore quite large; however, their time is limited. Choosing to get involved with one decision is also a choice not to get involved with another. This choice may be based on the importance of the decision or related instead to the time available when the decision is being made. People come and go in decision processes as their interests and time commitments change.

These three streams flow through CLAS. One is problems looking for places to be aired and resolved. The second is solutions looking for issues to which they might be the answer. The third includes decision makers looking for work. (This does not mean that decision makers are idle. Rather, it suggests that the number of matters to which potential participants could devote their attention is so large that they must make choices about the ones with which they will work and the ones they will ignore. And they must often do so without knowing in advance which will later turn out to have been the most important.) Into this somewhat confusing situation we now introduce a fourth stream, independent and only loosely coupled to the other three. This fourth stream consists of choice opportunities—occasions on which the organization is expected to make a decision. Elements in this stream include such things as the approval of the annual budget, actions on promotions and tenure, the appointment of administrators, the approval of new academic programs, or the adoption of the state-mandated master plan. How can Flagship make these choices if it cannot specify its goals, it does not know the best way to achieve them, and it cannot tell in advance who will participate in the decision process?

Garbage-Can Decision Making. Conventional wisdom suggests that, faced with a choice opportunity on budget, for example, Flagship should go through an elaborate process of data collection and analysis, compare the costs and benefits of various sets of expenditures with projected outcomes, and decide which combinations are most consistent with stated institutional goals.

The concept of the organized anarchy suggests instead that choices at Flagship are made through a process that has been called "garbage-can decision making" (Cohen, March, and Olsen, 1976). The stream of choice opportunities can be thought of metaphorically as offering large receptacles, or garbage cans, through which flow the other streams of problems, solutions, and participants. In the garbage can, specific problems, participants, and solutions coalesce with a particular choice point and they become attached (that is, more tightly coupled) to each other. One way of visualizing the relationship is to think of the streams of problems, solutions, and participants as three fluid and wriggling ropes loosely braided together so that the parts that are in physical contact with each other continually shift. A decision point cuts into that rope to reveal a cross section displaying a pattern containing elements of the problem, solution, and participant streams. The unwary observer may mistake the cross section as reflecting the totality of the rope and believe that there is an inherent logic to the decision being made and the observed pattern of connections. An alternative view suggests that the pattern would have been different had the cross section been taken at a different part of the rope, or at the same part but at a different time. The observed patterns of attachment would then not necessarily be logical, but would depend on such matters as the time the decision was made, the availability of other garbage cans, and the particular problems, solutions, and participants in the streams at the time. This indeterminacy introduces ambiguity and uncertainty into the decision arena. Decision making becomes increasingly difficult when irrelevant problems and solutions (that is, "garbage") become attached to choice opportunities.

Take as an example a typical choice point at Flagship.

President Foster has to decide whether to include two new faculty positions for the school of business in next year's budget. Left alone, the president could make this decision easily on the basis of a limited data set (for example, student credit hours in business have increased 10 percent, projections of enrollment for the next five years seem stable, retirements for the next two years will provide needed flexibility) and on intuitive knowledge (based on more grumbling from the business faculty lately about work load, or a hunch that a new subspecialization will be important in the field). But as problems, solutions, and participants get tightly coupled to the decision in the garbage can, the decision becomes increasingly difficult to make. "Extraneous" elements may become attached to the decision. For example:

Problems: Professor Smith (the nonreappointed faculty member in the history department) asks, "How can you fail to reappoint me because of budget constraints, and then go out and hire two new faculty?" The English department states that the new positions represent a loss of intellectual commitment to liberal education. The faculty senate informs the president that proper committee procedures for considering new positions have not been followed.

Solutions: Those who have tried in the past to initiate faculty retraining programs use the Professor Smith situation as a case in point and suggest that his status cannot be resolved without attending to this broader issue. The general education committee says that the matter relates to the issue of small classes, which they believe goes to the heart of the educational process, and they ask the president to conduct a study of class size in CLAS before making a decision on Smith. Deans of heavily enrolled professional schools restate their case for "every tub on its own bottom" funding. The informal "middle-management caucus" suggests that this incident would not have happened had their proposed management information system been adopted, and they propose that better data be collected for this and future cases of this type.

Participants: One of Professor Smith's students, who is editor of the *Flagship Student Daily Courier*, writes an unusual editorial supporting the professor and asking for a mass meeting of students. The faculty of the business school, who have never before become involved in budget issues, transmit a resolution to the president asking to meet with him on this and other previously unmentioned funding problems. The affirmative action office sends a memo to the president requesting representation in the process because of its effect on staffing goals.

What started out as a relatively simple choice opportunity appears now to be exceptionally complicated because of the linkages that have developed inside the garbage can. In the garbage can, it is possible for almost any problem, any solution, and any participant to become tightly coupled with any decision, and it is often impossible to predict with any degree of accuracy which will be. Actions similar to those taken in the Smith case in the past, for example, have not activated the same set of problems, solutions, and participants seen in this situation, and an identical case may not do so in the future.

There are three decision styles related to garbage-can decision making: resolution, flight, and oversight. In resolution, problems are actually worked through rationally until they are resolved. Although we commonly assume that this represents normal practice, in an organized anarchy, decisions may be more likely to be made either by flight or by oversight. Both flight and oversight operate by removing the "garbage" (that is, the extraneous material) from the decision. Of course, it must also be remembered that what one person sees as garbage another may see as the core of the decision; garbage is in the eye of the beholder.

Decision making by flight assumes that while problems attached to choices make decisions difficult, coupling between them is loose and the linkage is not permanent. While a problem (for example, the Smith reappointment) can by chance become attached in the garbage can to the allocation decision, in the course of time another decision opportunity (for example, the formation of an Ad Hoc Senate Committee on Reappointment Procedures) may come along that is more "attractive" to the problem. The Smith reappointment problem may therefore leave (take flight from) the resource allocation arena for the senate committee arena (Smith's time and attention are limited, and he must choose how he will use them), and the allocation decision can now be more easily made. This accounts for the common situation in which a choice that appears intractable over an extended period of time suddenly gets made with little or no difficulty.

A decision by oversight is one made quickly so that people and problems busy in other arenas have no time to get involved in the decision. Had President Foster made the allocation decision before people on campus were aware of it, it is possible that Smith might never have tried to use it as a forum for pressing his case, and none of the other actors and problems would have become activated.

Garbage cans in an organization act like buffers or "energy sinks" that absorb problems, solutions, and participants like a sponge and prevent them from sloshing around and disturbing arenas in which people wish to act. Ad hoc long-range institutional planning committees may be the quintessential garbage cans, temporarily providing "homes" for any conceivable institutional problem, solution, or participant. But there may also be permanent structural garbage cans, such as the academic senate, that function at least in part to draw unwanted participants, problems, or solutions away from decision arenas (Birnbaum, forthcoming a).

What becomes tightly or loosely coupled in this symbolic system is related to a mixture of collegial interactions, bureaucratic structures, ongoing coalitions, chance, and cognitive processes by which people make inferences and judgments under conditions of uncertainty. Flagship, like other universities, can have sophisticated management systems that do not really affect what happens on campus (Bolman and Deal, 1984), approve affirmative action plans that do not increase minority recruitment, and rhapsodize on the importance of teaching while promoting faculty solely on the basis of their research productivity. The anarchical qualities of Flagship allow people to have their cake and eat it too by permitting them to substitute belief for action. The faculty senate can engage in vigorous debate and take a vote deploring grade inflation without requiring behavioral changes in their colleagues, thereby both strengthening organizational claims of concern for quality and minimizing organizational disruption.

In general, loose coupling permits Flagship to give attention to rationalized myths without disrupting the teaching and research programs of the university. They give conspicuous attention to doing things expected by important constituencies, such as the state legislature, as a "signal to the outside world that all is well. If management is making decisions, if plans are being made, if new units are created in response to new problems, if sophisticated evaluation and control systems are in place, then an organization must be well managed and worthy of support" (Bolman and Deal, 1984, p. 168).

This kind of loose coupling is particularly advantageous in a complex and turbulent environment. An organization that has many semiautonomous units can be more sensitive and responsive to changes in different parts of its environment than can a centralized organization whose parts are tied together. The focus on individual activity and the general lack of management controls make innovation possible, and the loose organizational couplings enable the institution to respond simultaneously to conflicting demands. Since people are free for the most part from close management control and able to engage in personally satisfying activity, they are less likely to become alienated and more likely to be productive.

The management of Flagship can, of course, be highly problematic, particularly when dealing with external audiences. To a great extent, this problem is resolved by avoiding it and substituting symbolic for instrumental administrative activity. Because of unclear goals, the difficulty of developing valid outcome measures, and the ability of many institutions to avoid assessment, "symbolic outcomes may be sufficient given the limited aims or the limited interest of social actors in the organization. These factors, taken together, suggest that symbolic administrative responses may, in fact, be sufficient in most instances" (Pfeffer, 1981a, p. 34).

Flagship is driven not by comprehensive rationality but by the autonomous actions of many individuals and organizational subgroups responding to their own perceived interests or to the pressures of the market (Kerr, 1982). Each actor can perceive only a small portion of the environment and can pay attention to only a limited set of elements that can be perceived. If the subunits of Flagship were as tightly coupled as they are at People's Community College, these autonomous activities would quickly tear the organization apart. Loose coupling can therefore be seen not as an aberration but as the functional response of an institution faced with multiple and conflicting demands on attention, priorities, and performance. Flagship may have become one of the world's great universities, not in spite of loose coupling but because of it.

Effective Leadership in Anarchical Systems

President Foster's decisions may have little effect on disparate organizational subsystems; changes in the environment may often overpower any changes that are attempted internally; professional participants may take autonomous action; the institution's most important characteristics, such as enrollment or reputation, are difficult to change; and administrators can attend to only a small number of potentially important matters having no way of knowing beforehand (or often even afterward) whether or not these are the most important. The concept of the larger-than-life heroic leader whose wise decisions and forceful administration solve institutional problems and advance the institution's fortunes appears out of place in the organized anarchy. Instead, "managers must rely on images, luck, and sometimes the supernatural to bring some semblance of order" (Bolman and Deal, 1984, p. 3). And while it is common to speak of rational managers, administration in higher education still appears to emphasize intuition, to avoid quantitative data and new management techniques, and to respond to political groups and influences (Dill, 1984, p. 92). Much of President Foster's effectiveness comes from his ability to project a sense of competence, integrity, and dedication to many different audiences. When he appears before a legislative budget committee, for example, his responses are precise, articulate, and straightforward. The legislators cannot really know much about the programs he is advocating, but because Foster *looks* like a university president and appears knowledgeable and on top of things, they assume that Flagship is well run and worthy of support.

The discrepancy between what leaders are presumed to do and how they actually behave led Cohen and March (1974) to say that the presidency is an illusion and that the role is in large measure a symbolic one with only modest influence on campus life. But while it is true that other organizational constituencies exercise influence that can prevent a president from achieving certain objectives, it is also true that at Flagship, and on most campuses, most of the time, the president is the single most influential person. Presidents therefore can often make a difference, even though perhaps not to the extent that they themselves are likely to believe. In part, presidential influence may be related to "style, an ability to cope, well-publicized actions on noncontroversial topics, and dramatic performances that emphasize the traits popularly linked to leadership, such as forcefulness, responsibility, courage, and decency" (Bolman and Deal, 1984, p. 184). However, effective influence in an organized anarchy may also depend on exhibiting specific behaviors that are not the same as the behaviors expected under other models. Like President Robinson at RSU, President Foster at Flagship is a realist. They both believe that their effectiveness depends on acting with a knowledge of how the system *really* works, and not on the basis of how they would *like* it to work. But Foster gives less attention than Robinson to coalition formation and negotiation to get what he wants. Instead, he is more likely to try to shape the values, symbols, and emotions that affect how other people interpret what is happening at Flagship. He spends much of his time explaining and clarifying events to others so that they are more likely to see equivocal events, messages, and relationships as he does. Robinson tries to convince others; Foster tries to change their perceptions.

President Foster attempted to make some dramatic and swift changes when he first took office, but they almost always activated strong opposition and were often unsuccessful. Over the course of his career, he has come to realize that he could use the natural tendencies of Flagship to move it slowly and marginally in directions that he favored, just as he could move his sail-boat closer to shore by using the winds and currents in the right way. The "eight basic tactical rules for use by those who seek to influence the course of decisions in universities or colleges" (Cohen and March, 1974, p. 207) seemed to him to be sensible.

Spend Time. Most people are indifferent to most deci-sions most of the time, and those who are interested in a spe-cific decision can participate only to the extent that they either have or make time to do so. People who are willing to spend time on any decision are likely to have a disproportionate effect on it. They will know more about it than others and will likely be present when the decision is made. Each year, Foster identi-fies a very small number of important issues to which he will pay close attention, and to the extent possible, he will either delegate or ignore other decisions. One of his current interests is urban education. Because his time is in such short supply, spend-ing it on urban education also has the symbolic effect of dem-onstrating to others through his behavior, rather than just his rhetoric, the importance that he attaches to this issue.

Persist. A unique set of participants, problems, and solu-tions can become coupled with a decision in the garbage can to-day and cause a proposal to fail. Next month or next year, the same program may attract different participants, and the out-comes may be more favorable. Foster does not assume that one of his urban education initiatives that is not well received by the administrative council is lost forever, and he will continue to advance the idea in other forums and at other times. For the same reason, he does not assume that approval of a program to-day means that it will be implemented tomorrow or that it is protected from defeat next week. He agrees with Hutchins that "it is one thing to get things done. It is another to make them last" (Kerr, 1963, p. 33). Persisting requires focused attention and follow-up on a limited agenda.

Exchange Status for Substance. Because the ability of in-dividuals or groups to significantly influence an institution is severely circumscribed, there is often more concern for having one's status symbolically recognized than there is for substantive outcomes. Faculty may fight for the right to participate in committees and then not attend meetings; administrators may announce and attempt to get credit for outcomes over which they had little control. Foster believes in urban education and is willing to let others take the credit as long as the programs he desires are implemented. He has created a prestigious and visible Flagship University Commission on Urban Education. Many important politicians and civic leaders have been appointed, and the group has met frequently with the governor and mayor. The commission holds periodic press conferences to announce progress, and new programs are always presented by Foster to the board of trustees as representing yet another triumph of the commission.

Facilitate Opposition Participation. There is a natural tendency to strengthen and support one's allies by appointing them to important committees and to refuse such appointments to opponents. Those who remain outside the decision-making process are not aware of the organizational and external constraints that limit flexibility in complex areas. Foster's commission appointments included several senior faculty who had always spoken against university involvement in the urban arena, as well as outspoken community leaders with unrealistic expectations of university participation. Membership on the commission has sensitized advocates to the reality of constraints and has given opponents an understanding of a politically charged situation that has long-term implications for university enrollments and funding. Participation in the commission by opponents did not completely eliminate either unrealistic aspirations or conservative reservations, but it did temper them, and commission members found it more difficult to later publicly oppose commission recommendations.

Overload the System. The initiation of new programs on a campus is difficult for many reasons. Systems have high inertia and resist change, new proposals tend to collect garbage, veto tactics are a major means through which participants on campus certify their own status, and sometimes just chance events intervene. In one way or another, almost any individual project can founder. But time and attention are limited at Flagship, and if the system is overloaded with more proposals than it can respond to, at least some of them will be approved through the process of flight or oversight. The commission has made a large number of recommendations, and while some have been the subject of endless campus debate, others were implemented quietly and quickly.

Provide Garbage Cans. There is a limited amount of time and attention available at Flagship. Anyone making a new proposal may find that unrelated problems or solutions (at least from the proposer's perspective) get attached to it and make choice difficult. One way of reducing the chances of that happening is to increase the number of other choices on campus that might prove to be more attractive to those problems and solutions than one's own proposal. These choices might be thought of as garbage cans—that is, as places that attract other people's garbage and keep them away from one's own proposal. At Flagship, there are a great many garbage cans, including the Long-Range Planning Committee, the Committee on the Future of the Undergraduate Curriculum, and the Committee on Faculty Privilege. They are highly visible, they confer status on those participating, and they are instrumentally unimportant to the institution. President Foster has referred many extraneous questions raised about commission recommendations to these committees for "more thorough and complete consideration," freeing the commission to implement the recommendations themselves.

Manage Unobtrusively. Some institutional executives, under external pressure or driven by their own understanding of the meaning of "leadership," seek to manage change through sweeping reorganizations, new academic program emphases, or alternative means for assessing faculty competence or student outcomes. To the extent that such programs are inconsistent with existing cultural expectations, structural systems, and personal interests of other organizational participants, they may trigger negative responses, become coupled with a wide range of problems, solutions, and participants in the garbage can, and fail.

An alternative way of managing is to identify small and unobtrusive changes that can have large-scale effects without generating opposition. Such changes can often be accomplished through minor changes in the bureaucratic or information structures of the organization, which then become amplified through its other social systems. For example, deans at Flagship always prepare a yearly report for the president describing new academic and scholarly activities using a standard format. This year, President Foster added one line to the format: "Please list all activities related to the Urban Education Initiative." He has decided, at least for now, not to bring any additional pressure on the deans, believing that he can exert the greatest influence by "attending carefully to personnel and structural matters, and then by walking away from them. Not only does this strategy ensure a President plenty of free time, but it also represents the best chance for maintaining optimal control from the point of view of his or her own preferences" (Padgett, 1980).

Interpret History. History provides the rationale and precedent for much that happens on a campus. Since the meanings of what has happened in the past are subjective, different reporters writing at different times may present the same event in different ways. Minutes of meetings, summaries of events, and other memorializations of the past should to the extent possible be written long enough after the event so that they can support actions considered desirable today. President Foster has identified several situations since 1900 in which Flagship professors have been interested in urban affairs, and he has used them in his recent speeches to refer to the "historic association of Flagship with the problems of our cities." The phrase has also found its way into the university bulletin. As a result, there is somewhat less opposition to his urban initiatives than would be the case if they were seen as deviating from traditional campus interests.

President Foster is an accomplished man. He hopes that when he leaves Flagship it will be a somewhat better institution than when he arrived, but he also realizes that he is likely to be replaced by someone equally as accomplished as he and that the fortunes of the institution are not primarily dependent on what he does as president. To be sure, some good programs have been developed during his presidency, and he has been identified publicly as having been responsible for them. But he has played for too long on the sloping soccer fields of academe to believe that what has happened during his watch was a result of his actions and intentions. He is more likely to see the reality of academic policy making as reflected in a description offered at another institution:

> Each week at the educational policy committee someone would insist that the future of the university rested on our dropping a given requirement or adding a proposed program. And each week we traded anecdotes and guesses about the effects of the proposals. The most compelling arguments were based on the experience of a relative of a friend or a friend of a relative at another school where the proposal or something like it had been adopted. Through the magic of parliamentary procedure we were able to resolve the same issue at several consecutive meetings with any number of different conclusions. Everybody had an equal chance to win, and everybody did win one week or another. But when a proposal went to the faculty for final approval we all stood behind it. The faculty then repeated the same discussions that we had and voted in their own way, basing their votes on their own feelings and their own anecdotes. And the policy resolutions that came out of the faculty meetings became educational policy [Levine and Weingart, 1973, p. ix].

Anarchical institutional processes flourish when resources are abundant and in excess of the level needed to function. They may be expected to diminish in importance when resources decline and difficult choices must be made. However, as long as rationality remains bounded, effectiveness criteria are in dispute, and nonlinear systems continue to be persistently unpredictable, Flagship is likely to function as the organized anarchy model suggests.

Part Three

Integrating the Models

Four different models of organization and governance—the bureaucracy, the collegium, the political system, and the organized anarchy—have been used to describe different ways of thinking about how institutions of higher education are organized and administered. All four system models are invented social constructs that "make sense" of organizational processes. They reflect our need to impose order and meaning on equivocal events and thereby help us believe that we truly understand the internal operations of colleges and universities. Each of the models is "right," but each is incomplete.

One of these models from time to time may appear to more accurately portray the nature of reality for a specific institution than the other three. But there are no colleges or universities that consistently reflect the "pure form" of any of the models. There are bureaucratic and political elements at Heritage and Flagship just as there are collegial and anarchical elements at People's and RSU. Some elements of each of the models reflect institutional functioning in some ways, at some times, in some parts of all colleges and universities. Because these are nonlinear, dynamic social systems, life on any campus will be predictable at some times but unpredictable at others.

Colleges and universities are inventions that arise from the interaction of social norms, hierarchical structures, contending preferences, and cognitive limits and biases. Different institutions are identified by the relative importance of these processes and by the characteristic patterns in which their elements are loosely or tightly coupled. These patterns define, and function within, the institution's culture. The culture does not prescribe specific behaviors and relationships, but it does establish the likelihood that participants will behave in certain ways rather than in others. Culture thus develops the boundaries of the probable.

Institutions can share similar core cultural elements and organizational subsystems and still not function in the same way. Although organizational patterns appear to systematically differ among institutional types, no two institutions are identical, just as no two people are identical. Nevertheless, certain processes that are characteristic of open systems generally may be found in all institutions. Chapter Eight will take advantage of these common processes by returning to our generic institution, Huxley College, to propose a way of integrating the models by considering colleges and universities as cybernetic systems.

Administration is frustrating. Closure is elusive, systems come undone, solutions create new problems, no group is ever satisfied without another being dissatisfied, and criticisms about process can overwhelm substance. One way of attempting to increase administrative effectiveness is to resolve these dilemmas by seeking more rational ways to make decisions, more structured methods to solve problems, or greater authority to overcome the inertial forces of other participants: if administration does not work, change the institution until it does. This may be effective in some organizational settings, but it is often not helpful in colleges and universities. An alternative approach is to appreciate the cybernetic nature of academic institutions: if administration does not work, then perhaps we should alter our perceptions about what administrators are supposed to do and be more modest in our expectations about what they can accomplish. The implications for administrators of this latter proposal are the focus of Chapter Nine.

Chapter 8

The Cybernetic Institution: Providing Direction Through Self-Regulation

A campus visitor might spend a week at Huxley College observing a buzz of conflicting activities, argumentation over priorities, and shifting alliances. It is difficult to see connections among various offices, policies, and behaviors. Some participants appear only loosely coupled to what is happening on campus but tightly coupled to outside systems, such as those related to their scholarly associations or their research funding agencies. Some see the environment as threatening while others consider it supportive, people disagree about whether the college is being effective, and many are pursuing their own goals without apparent concern for what others are doing. The observer might be tempted to believe that chaos is everywhere and that the only "given" is that participants see what they wish and do what they please. But if the observer were able to view the campus through the conceptual lenses provided by different organizational frames or models, a number of patterns might become apparent.

Some things at Huxley might appear to happen because people follow formal rules and regulations and accept as authoritative the directives of those above them in the campus hierarchy. To be sure, this usually would be more evident in the

purchasing department than in the sociology department, but
even the sociologists adhere to a specified calendar, follow regulations governing grading, and accept (grudgingly) the class
schedule developed by the chairperson. As a result, much of
what happens at Huxley is a consequence of standard operating
procedures, programs, and repertoires.

At the same time, groups of people meet regularly with
others in their offices or departments, or as members of committees, cabinets, senates, and other bodies. They have common
backgrounds and interests, treat each other as equals, and try to
solve problems with solutions acceptable to all. Through their
interaction, members of these groups come to influence each
other's behavior and attitudes, and group norms and values develop that also direct significant aspects of organizational behavior.

These bureaucratic and collegial processes at Huxley regularize organization behavior and reduce the discretion of groups
and individual participants. But there is still room for formal or
informal groups to disagree about institutional programs or priorities, and some patterns of interaction at the college develop
as groups engage in political activities to affect the allocation of
resources to support *their* interests. An observer would not fail
to notice the contact between group representatives engaged in
forming coalitions and effecting compromises with other groups.

Politics can help explain the behavior of people who
make conscious choices, but some of what people do at Huxley
depends on biases of which they are not fully aware. In some
situations, preferences develop to rationalize actions already
taken, rather than to direct behavior. Because individuals and
groups can respond only to a portion of the claims on their attention, they filter out or give prominence to different parts of
messages they receive, and they perceive their environments in
different ways. Beliefs and decisions that are seen as logical and
self-evident by one group may be considered mindless or de-
vious by another. Different versions of reality may lead groups
to become committed to certain courses of action and to lose
the ability to recognize or understand alternatives. Some of
what happens on campus can be explained only by realizing
that people respond to a reality that they themselves create.

Looking at Huxley, a sophisticated observer would be able to see many patterns and signals where a less experienced one might see only noise and confusion. But the patterns would appear to be operating at cross-purposes and to be so complex that they could be only partially understood and controlled. How can such a confused organization survive, much less be effective? And yet it is clear that Huxley not only has survived but has prospered. Students arrive every year, learn, and graduate. Scholars conduct research, publish results of scholarship, and perform community service. Supplies and equipment are purchased, bills are paid, ceremonies are held. And despite the apparent disarray, there are incredible regularity and stability in many aspects of organizational life.

How is this large and complex social system coordinated? One common response is to suggest that it is President Wagstaff who has integrated the work of the various institutional components. But it is virtually impossible to follow the trail of presidential influence through the myriad of actions, interpretations, departments, and decisions that characterize the everyday life of Huxley. Wagstaff is involved in many important activities, to be sure, but he is more often responding to them than initiating them. While it is obvious that Huxley College has some direction, it appears to have evolved in the absence of a director. Yet something has brought a reasonable degree of stability and order to a system that has so many variables that it cannot be understood or predicted using rational paradigms or by the most powerful computers.

In this chapter, I suggest that this is accomplished through cybernetic controls—that is, through self-correcting mechanisms that monitor organizational functions and provide attention cues, or negative feedback, to participants when things are not going well. Systems of negative feedback detect and correct errors so that when something happens at Huxley that moves the college in an undesirable direction, something else automatically happens to bring it back on course (Morgan, 1986). Thus, coordination is provided not by one omniscient and rational agent but by the spontaneous corrective action of the college's parts.

Characteristics of Cybernetic Systems

The four organizational models described thus far give a great deal of attention to the president and to the role of leadership. It is comforting to believe in the efficacy of leaders, but at the same time it is usually difficult to assess the effects of their actions. The importance of strong and decisive presidents is often proclaimed but seldom demonstrated.

Huxley College is analyzed in this chapter through an integration of some elements of the models presented previously. But rather than focus on the president, emphasis is given to how different campus systems interact to keep Huxley functioning effectively.

> The function of the administration is solely to see that the funds are adequate for its purposes and not overspent, that the air is right, that the grounds are tidy—and then to stay out of its way. . . . A good university doesn't need to be headed as much as to be given its head, and it is the administrator's task—not at all an easy one—to see that this happens. The temptations to intervene from the top, to reach in and try and change the way the place works, to arrive at one's desk each morning with one's mind filled with exhilarating ideas for revitalizing the whole institution, are temptations of the devil and need resisting with all the strength of the administrator's character [Thomas, 1983, pp. 169, 172].

Huxley College is a system whose functions are controlled by vertical feedback loops created and reinforced by the institution's structure and horizontal feedback loops embedded in the institution's social system. Political and symbolic processes lead to loose coupling between some loops and tight coupling between others, and the patterns that are created function within and define the constraints of the organizational culture. These patterns of loops and couplings uniquely describe Huxley College, although they resemble in many ways the patterns of comparable institutions.

Huxley College can be considered as a fragmented and hierarchical system; understanding how the college works depends on looking at its subsystems and how they come to form still larger systems. Huxley is fragmented because it responds to multiple and conflicting goals by allocating them to loosely coupled organizational subunits that respond and change their behavior in response to feedback. Huxley is hierarchical because senior administrators monitor and coordinate the activities of subunits beneath them to achieve the "organizational goals." Looking at Huxley College as a cybernetic system (Ashby, 1956, 1960; Lindblom, 1959; Cyert and March, 1963; March and Simon, 1958; Simon, 1961; Allison, 1971; Steinbruner, 1974) helps to explain how Huxley can be successful even though it does not engage in elaborate processes of rational calculation or decision making.

In a cybernetic system, organization subsystems respond to a limited number of *inputs* to monitor their operation and make corrections and adjustments as necessary; organizational responses are *not* based on measuring or improving their output. That means that, for example, nothing is likely to happen at Huxley if its graduates learn less (a measure of output), but that the college is likely to respond when alumni complain (an input) that they have not been well prepared for their careers. Emphasizing the importance of inputs rather than outputs makes it possible to understand how Huxley functions without the need for imputing institutional goals or purposes. It does this by creating feedback loops that tell it when things are going wrong.

Thermostats and Feedback Loops. A thermostat is an example of a self-correcting, cybernetic control system with a feedback loop. It turns the furnace on when the environment's temperature falls below a preset limit (say, 70°) and turns it off when the temperature returns to the desired level. This keeps the temperature within an acceptable range. In the same way, Huxley has a number of goals, or constraints, whose achieve-

ment must fall within an area of acceptability. If any of them
fall outside that range, the energies of individuals or groups at
the college are activated in an attempt to return Huxley to the
desired level.

Activities at Huxley College are regulated by two kinds
of control systems that operate within constraints established
by the organizational culture. These control systems function as
"organizational thermostats." The first system consists of explicit controls manifested in organizational rules, regulations,
and structures. These are structural controls. For example,
when a department at Huxley attempts to make expenditures
beyond its budget (and therefore to move outside the area of
acceptability), the purchase order is immediately returned
marked "account overdrawn," and the budget is returned to its
balanced and desired state.

The second kind of system includes implicit controls developed through the interaction of individuals in groups that
lead them toward shared attitudes and concern for group cohesion. These are social controls. They can be seen, for example,
as Department Chair Chippendale says to Professor Branch,
"students seem to be upset that some people in the department
haven't been available for advisement lately" (noting the receipt of input that an important value has moved outside the
range of acceptability), and Branch responds with a look of
concern that confirms the importance of advisement and that
strengthens their agreement about it. Political and symbolic processes influence which controls are given precedence when there
is conflict between them and how structural and social controls
are connected under different circumstances. The organizational
culture of Huxley within which these controls function provides
the context within which meaning is inferred and data are
sensed, filtered, and interpreted. Because of this, faculty in
comparable positions at People's Community College or at
Flagship University would likely respond both to the "account
overdrawn" notice and to the comment about advising in quite
different ways, although the dynamics of their processes would
be comparable.

Structural controls and social controls are organizational

feedback loops that are sensitive to selected factors in the environment. They do two things. First, they make minor adjustments in ongoing organizational processes as necessary to keep them functioning within acceptable limits (for example, by sending a notice when a department exceeds its budget, or by eliciting behaviors confirming norms). But if these minor adjustments are not successful in keeping the factor being monitored within acceptable limits, they initiate action to alter the organizational processes themselves (for example, by changing the purchasing system, or by bringing the issue of advisement to the faculty senate for debate). These negative feedback loops provide information that something is wrong. They allow Huxley to sense when some important variable is outside its acceptable limits (that is, outside the organization's constraint set) and attempt to correct it. It is this kind of adaptive behavior that creates a reasonably stable institution (Ashby, 1960).

Goals and Subunits. If the environment were simple, undifferentiated institutions could adequately respond to it. As environments become complex, institutions must become equally complex if they are to sense changes and make appropriate adaptations. But as complexity increases, the ability of one person to make decisions is increasingly restricted by the limits to rationality.

Huxley College exists in a complex world, and to cope effectively it must simplify this complexity. One way of doing this is to increase the number of decision makers so that "each decision maker can then focus on some limited dimension, and the effect which his responses produce in other dimensions will become the concern for other decision makers. Complex problems under such a scheme become fragmented into a large number of very specific problems, each addressed by a different decision maker" (Steinbruner, 1974, p. 69).

Huxley responds to complexity by fragmenting into smaller, stable subsystems arranged in a hierarchical fashion. The constraints established by President Wagstaff establish the boundaries within which his subordinates function, and they in turn establish additional constraints that further restrict people at still lower levels. Huxley College has a number of goals (constraints) that are worded in general terms, but they provide little operational guidance, and they are often conflicting. The achievement of these goals constitutes the essential problems of the college, and it responds to these problems by establishing specialized subunits that focus attention on one or another of the organizational "goals" as a subproblem (Simon, 1964).

Limiting Uncertainty. The cybernetic institution has many "goals." One of these at Huxley College has been identified as "moving toward academic excellence." Although people agree on the goal, no one understands the full range of behaviors that would be required to implement it, they cannot measure it in all its complexity, and thus they cannot know when they have achieved it. Uncertainty is discomforting, and decision makers in cybernetic institutions simplify (and consequently distort) their perceptions of the environment and the operations of the college in order to make tolerable the cognitive requirements to understand them. Huxley College deals with the issue of ultimate organizational objectives by avoiding them. Instead, it simplifies its goals to limit uncertainty.

The goal of "academic excellence" could be implemented in many ways. After examining only a few of the potential alternatives, Huxley has chosen several means to achieve excellence, one of which is the honors program. The honors program in turn has identified high SAT scores as one of a small number of indicators of program success. The problem faced by the college in selecting from among an indefinite number of possible programs those that would have the highest probability of maximizing an unclear number of undefinable goals has been significantly simplified; the college has now identified one variable in one program as a measure of one goal. When the college administration is called on to report on its progress in moving toward academic excellence, it is likely to cite as an indicator the SAT scores in the honors program. The decision makers in the cybernetic institution are now able to focus their attention on a small number of incoming variables without having to spend time comprehensively analyzing probable outcomes (Steinbruner, 1974).

Responding to Feedback. The honors program is a subunit created to respond to the organizational goal of "quality." It functions within a series of structural, social, and cultural constraints established at higher levels of the organization. It develops its own programs and procedures as it attempts within these constraints to find satisfactory solutions to its subproblem.

There are an infinite number of matters that might concern the honors program, but because of bounded rationality, the program is able to attend to only a relatively small number. Two of the factors that it emphasizes are the quality of the program and the morale of the program faculty. Feedback loops have evolved to sense and correct undesirable changes in both of them.

The SAT scores of entering students are considered by the trustees, President Wagstaff, and program faculty at Huxley to be one of the most important measures of the quality and therefore the success of the honors program. Of course, the relationship between SAT scores and program quality is not a matter of "fact," but the oganizational culture has made high SAT scores part of an institutionalized myth that is part of Huxley's "reality." Because SAT scores are considered to be so important, Huxley has developed several systems to detect and monitor them. The college's long-range plan has a section on the honors program in which a desired SAT score for admission is specified and identified as a criterion of success. The calculation of SAT scores and reporting of them to the program are standard operating procedure. The data are collected routinely by the institutional research office and sent each semester both to the program and to the academic dean.

When small fluctuations in SAT scores are observed in these reports, the program makes minor adjustments in an attempt to correct them. When the average verbal SAT score declined ten points two years ago, for example, program director Linda Laud sent a note to the faculty suggesting that they give somewhat greater attention to these specific scores in admissions offers in the future. SAT scores returned to their usual level this year, and the basic admissions processes have continued as in the past. But if scores were to drop and minor adjustments no longer sufficed to correct them, Laud would attempt to make significant changes in admissions procedures in an attempt to return the scores to their previous acceptable state. For example, such a serious decline in the past led to the development of a new high school relations program offering college courses to advanced juniors and seniors; within two years, SAT scores returned to their "proper" level.

Faculty morale in the honors program is also part of a feedback loop. In this case, it is a social control rather than a structural one, and morale is not linked to regularized reports or standard procedures. However, director Laud, a former teacher in the program who will return to its faculty after serving her three-year term, is exceptionally sensitive to faculty morale. The program is small, and the faculty and director interact regularly. Laud has always considered faculty griping to be a negative indicator of morale. She responds to gripes with good-natured banter that usually satisfies her colleagues, and program life does not change much as griping fluctuates within a limited range. But when the level of complaints rises to an unacceptable level, Laud begins to alter program processes (for example, instituting a faculty development program) in an effort to bring it back on course.

Changing Behavior. We have seen how the structural and social feedback controls in the honors program permit participants to assess the status of important input variables such as SAT scores or faculty gripes. Minor deviations have no consequences. But when the variables fall outside an acceptable range, the result is a change of "state"—that is, a change in program behavior. When SAT scores decline too far, program participants begin searching for ways to increase them. When griping becomes unacceptable, Laud begins to think about new approaches to increase faculty satisfaction.

In both cases, there are an exceptionally large number of ways in which program behaviors might be changed to lead to the desired outcomes. If Huxley were a rational organization, it would be expected that director Laud would respond to a perceived problem by assessing all the alternatives, calculating the costs and benefits of each, and selecting the alternative providing the best solution to the problem. But as part of a cybernetic organization, Laud responds differently. Instead of searching for all the alternatives and calculating their effects (an impossible task), she begins examining a much more limited set of behaviors that have been found in the past to be effective. Relying on past answers is one of the ways in which organizations can be thought of as consisting of solutions looking for problems. When SAT scores of honors program applicants drop, for example, immediate attention is given to a small number of possible solutions, most of them focused on marketing techniques that have previously been used for recruitment in other programs.

The cybernetic college is unlikely to rationally calculate in advance the probable outcomes of the new activities it selects. For example, Laud does not attempt to quantify the extent to which the proposed change is likely to increase SAT scores. Rather, she implements a proposed solution and then monitors the SAT scores. If the desired changes do not occur, another proposed solution is tried, and then another. The search ends when the SAT indicators return to acceptable levels. The cybernetic college "satisfices."

It is important to note that it is not necessary in this model for director Laud to understand the internal interactions that lead to the desired outcomes. *Why* the new behaviors have the observed consequences is not important, and even random activities may suffice. One way Huxley has typically generated such random activity when it has had a major problem for which there were no obvious answers has been to form a "blue-ribbon task force." These task forces always make a number of recommendations, few of which are ever implemented. Nevertheless, problems for which task forces have been formed have often gone away. No one knows exactly why this has happened, and so the cause-and-effect relationship can be thought of as occurring in a "black box." But since forming a task force in the past has had the desired result, the probability of its use in the future has significantly increased.

Collecting Data. Cybernetic systems can respond only to stimuli to which they are sensitive. The thermostat, for example, is sensitive to changes in temperature and is indifferent to other changes in the environment. Even though organizational cybernetic systems are much more flexible than mechanical or electronic ones, they too are limited. This has implications both for the kinds of changes in the environment to which they will respond and for the assessment of outcomes of changed behavior. At Huxley, program director Laud sees only data that come through well-developed feedback channels. Data for which no channels exist do not come to her attention and therefore cannot be part of her decision process (Steinbruner, 1974).

Both the SAT scores and faculty gripes are part of highly focused feedback channels in the honors program. There is a mechanism in the college for monitoring these outcomes, for comparing them to some desired state, and for taking action to restore the organization to the desired state if minimum criteria are not being met. This cycle is repeated until the variable has returned to the acceptable range. But other potentially important data, which have no focused feedback channels, are not observed at all. The area of moral development is one of these. Although program faculty have frequently discussed their interest in moral development as a desirable outcome of the honors program (among many other desirable outcomes), there is no established process by which data related to moral development are sensed. Decisions about the program will be affected by changes in SAT scores but not by changes that may occur in the moral development of students. Moreover, when the program changes its behavior in order to affect SAT scores, the potential effects of these changes on moral development will not be considered.

Such decisions may usually work out well because many organizational processes are only loosely coupled. There may in fact be no connection between SAT scores and moral development at Huxley College such that raising one will have unanticipated and negative consequences for the other. But while college programs may be loosely coupled most of the time, they are not so all of the time. Decisions to increase SAT scores in the honors program at Huxley may in fact have an impact on other things—for example, the enrollment of minority students. If appropriate focused feedback loops responding to the ethnic distribution of students in the program are not present, such consequences, even if they occur, will not be noticed.

need 4 apprp looks

The honors program, and all other subsystems in a cybernetic institution such as Huxley, are therefore sensitive to only a limited number of stimuli from a relatively small number of sources, do not observe all potentially important data, and have no way of assessing the outcomes of their behavior except in those specific areas in which focused feedback loops exist.

weakness

The Subunit-Organization Hierarchy: Goals and Controls. Commitment to specific subgoals means that the director of the honors program will act to maximize the program's limited objectives with little concern for the effect of these behaviors on the other subunits of Huxley College. This parochial concern for limited goals is not necessarily disadvantageous to the college, since loose coupling means that many changes in that program are unlikely to affect others. In addition, Huxley is complex enough so that some other part of the college is likely to be charged with the responsibility of sensing such undesirable developments and their sources when they exist, and of bringing them to the attention of the upper levels of the organization.

The feedback mechanisms that exist in each subunit also exist at each higher level of the organization. They come into play when a subunit is operating at a level that does not satisfy the lower bounds of the organization's constraint set and is therefore not effective, when the subunit is operating too effectively so that through its aggregation of resources or its level of operations it is overflowing onto the territory of some other subunit, or when the environment has changed and the subunit has not remained sensitive to the information that should prompt altered behavior.

diff forms of correction

Higher levels of administration at Huxley are subject to the same problems of uncertainty, attention, and sensitivity as are lower levels. To reduce the uncertainty of the effects of decisions on such vague goals such as "liberal education," President Wagstaff and other senior administrators do what the subunits do—they select a small number of variables whose values are accepted as reflecting the degree of achievement of the goal itself. If the next higher level in the hierarchy has mechanisms that make it sensitive to the types of failures that have been mentioned, they will serve as attention cues. Rather than initiate their own agendas, senior administrators at Huxley are likely to monitor the achievement of "goals" by assessing the extent to which the honors program and the other subunits responsible for these goals are functioning within the organization constraint set. College executives do not have to pay attention to everything all the time. Once systems are in place that satisfy the criteria of the constraint set, they do not ordinarily require the attention of senior administrators. Administrators deal with exceptions.

Senior administrators at Huxley respond to subunit problems sequentially, and not in an integrated fashion. That is, they attempt to solve problems presented by subunits without trying to understand the effect of the solution on the performance of other subunits or on the achievement of organizational "goals." They fragment the college structure into small units, assign parts of problems to these units, and make decisions in a way that preserves the fragmentation (Steinbruner, 1974).

Allocating the achievement of specific goals to loosely coupled subunits is what permits Huxley to respond to its many ill-defined and often conflicting purposes, and at the same time provides the simplification required for administrative action. "Organizations resolve conflict among goals, in part, by attending to different goals at different times. . . . The business firm is likely to resolve conflicting pressures to 'smooth production' and 'satisfy customers' by first doing one thing and then doing the other. The resulting time buffer between goals permits the organization to solve one problem at a time, attending to one goal at a time" (Cyert and March, 1963, p. 118).

This is how Huxley College manages to respond to goals that may be inherently in conflict, such as "access" and "excellence" (Birnbaum, 1987a). Relatively little attention is given to either goal as a matter of continuous planning, but each may be brought to awareness as a consequence of some specific series of events. When access is threatened or falls below a level deemed by the institution or the social system to be acceptable, changes will be instituted to address it. Little attention is given during that process to the goal of "excellence" or to the impact of programs of access on the achievement of excellence. When the goal of access is largely accomplished (that is, when discrepancies between desired and actual access levels have become acceptable), attention may be given to problems in academic achievement, at which time the goal of access is largely forgotten. The establishment of specialized units to deal with either of these goals increases the probability that the organization itself will deal with them, if for no other reason than that the unit will create products that will serve as attention cues for others. But the sequential attention to goals means that it is unlikely that they will be considered simultaneously, and so obvious contradictions between them can be ignored.

Loops of Interaction in Cybernetic Systems

Huxley College functions relatively smoothly. The organizational culture establishes the boundaries that guide interpretations of reality, the preferences of groups and individuals within these boundaries establish constraints on each other, and subunits establish standard procedures and stable social norms that regularize their activities and permit them to live predictably and at peace with other subunits. Procedures and norms that appear to be related to acceptable measurements of a small number of criteria are maintained. When a variable being measured falls below acceptable standards, the subunit tries new behaviors and monitors the variables. The new behaviors are likely to be adopted if the variables move in the proper direction and abandoned if they do not. The subunit "learns" through trial and error in a process akin to natural selection. The effective operation of the subunit depends on the stability of these procedures and norms, and they are therefore exceptionally difficult to change.

Coordination between the subunits is provided primarily by the constraints established at higher organizational levels, by the cultural context in which the subunits interact, and by the training and experience of the various participants. When these internal control and coordination systems prove inadequate, intervention from the hierarchy is required. This intervention deals with the specific subunit problem without having to attend to the integration of the subunit and broader organizational objectives. If solving one subunit problem creates other problems elsewhere, they will be dealt with in turn.

The cybernetic process is depicted as a causal loop in Figure 18. The process begins when some change in the external or internal environment leads to an organizational response that alters the value of some variable. If that variable is being monitored by some formal or informal group (a sensing unit), and that change of value moves it beyond acceptable limits, the group will attempt to influence the administration (or some other controlling unit) to change the organization response until the variable moves back into the acceptable range. In general,

Figure 18. Cybernetic Loop in Huxley College.

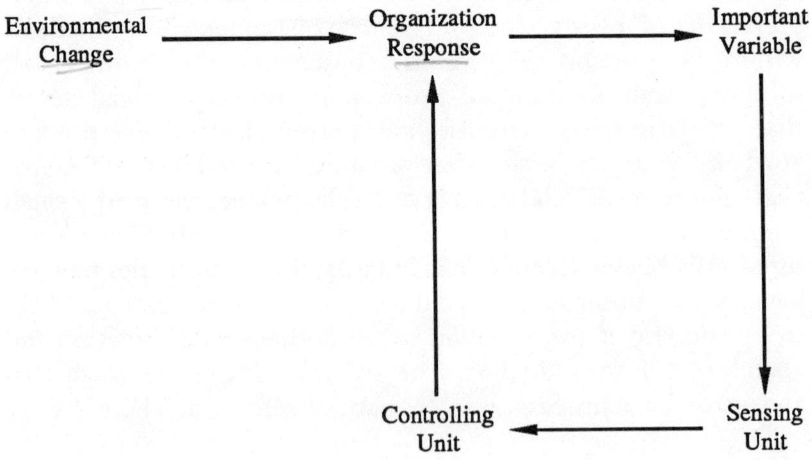

"if the value of essential variables changes to threaten the organization, then we expect to see some sort of internally generated veto of the organization's routine responses to the environment, and a series of trial restructuring of the organization's behavior until the essential variables restabilize" (Mock, 1987, p. 16).

One example of the cybernetic loop at Huxley is the college's response to a salary equity problem. As society became more sensitive to discrimination against women (environmental change) Huxley did little except to form a largely symbolic affirmative action committee (organizational response). The issue of discrimination at Huxley became focused on the salaries of faculty men and women (important variable), and these data were analyzed and discussed each year by the faculty senate (sensing unit). The senate regularly communicated its displeasure to President Wagstaff (controlling unit). As a result of the senate's complaints, Wagstaff continually made changes in salary policy. The effects on the discrepancy, however, were not large enough to satisfy the senate, which continued its criticisms. Not until Wagstaff's proposal for a special salary adjustment policy was approved by the trustees was the discrepancy reduced to the point where the senate no longer considered it a problem. When that happened, the system was returned to a stable state and Wagstaff stopped making changes in salary policy.

The problem of organizational coordination does not end when the variable returns to an acceptable state, however. Actions taken to restore one subsystem to equilibrium often have unforeseen consequences that may negatively affect other subsystems. The processes of adjustment themselves create other imbalances (Blau, 1964), and actions that solve one problem create others. The nonlinear nature of the subsystems and the fact that the output of each subsystem is part of the input for the others make unforeseen consequences inevitable. Unpredictability is predictable, and institutional monitoring and correction are a continuing process.

Tight and Loose Coupling in Cybernetic Systems

Institutional goals have been described as a series of widely shared value premises that set constraints defining effective institutional functioning. Sometimes one constraint (for example, an emphasis on liberal education) is given special prominence and is arbitrarily thought of as "the institutional goal," but other values (such as "minimize employee accidents") may be equally important and exert just as powerful an influence on how people behave.

The goals defined by the constraints of an institution are multiple and often conflicting. The maximum achievement of one can come only at the cost of a lesser achievement of others. When decisions are made affecting priorities or resource allocations, rationality suggests that we should convert all values into a single combined measure, and then select the alternative that has the highest total value. But because of the difficulties of comparing units of "academic freedom" with units of "accountability," for example, this turns out to be impossible to do.

Instead, complex organizations deal with the problem of multiple and conflicting goals in another way—by assigning responsibility for these goals to different subunits. Huxley College, for example, has a number of different goals, among which are "excellence" and "access." It has responded to the goal of excellence by creating a subunit called the honors program and to the goal of providing access to poor and underprepared students by creating another subunit, called the academic opportunity program. Both of these subsystems are themselves relatively stable, but they are only loosely coupled to each other. Indeed, the entire college can be thought of as composed of building blocks of subsystems, most of which can be added or removed from the college without affecting the other subsystems (Simon, 1969a). The linkages *within* most subsystems at Huxley are stronger than the linkages *between* most subsystems, and in the short run what happens in one such subsystem has little to do with what happens in another. The most obvious example in higher education is the multiversity, in which "many parts can be added or subtracted with little effect on the whole" (Kerr, 1963, p. 20). But the principle applies to a greater or lesser extent in other institutional types as well.

Let us turn our attention to how the academic opportunity program and the honors program function as stable but loosely coupled building blocks. Both units have reasonable autonomy, but that does *not* mean that they can do anything they please. In fact, there are a number of potent control mechanisms affecting each unit that increase the probability that certain activities will occur and that other activities will not. Huxley, like every other organization, has a culture that establishes expectations and limits of behavior. Staff in both units understand their organization's culture because of their involvement in the culture of the national educational system, the culture of the profession, and the culture of the institution. In addition, they share the constraint sets, or institutional goals, of Huxley.

But within those limits, the roles of individuals and the extent to which they are coupled to structural or social controls affect the values that each program wishes to optimize. These values are quite different in the two units. And as participants within each unit recruit colleagues like themselves, spend more time with each other, and see less of those in the other unit, they come to share attitudes and behaviors within their unit and to be different from people in the other unit.

Each unit is bound by Huxley's rules and regulations made at higher organizational levels, but these are usually general enough to permit varying interpretations at lower levels. Operating within the cultural framework provided by the institution, the two units have developed different bureaucratic and collegial control mechanisms that limit the discretion of unit members, that regularize and stabilize their operations, and that support the optimization of one of the college's values (Cyert and March, 1963). At the same time, both units have simplified their worlds by developing cognitive biases and filters that permit them to deal with only a small number of variables that they consider to be important. They can usually ignore the possible effects of their program on the program of the other unit, but when their interests are seen as being in conflict, their representatives can meet to negotiate in an effort to change the other's perceptions or values.

That the bureaucratic and collegial systems of both units are not the same is of little consequence, because the two units operate essentially independently of each other. People in the honors program and in the academic opportunity program rarely have to work together, and their students, faculties, and programs are different. What happens in one in the short term has little if any effect on the other, just as the work of the English department has little effect on the mathematics department. Focusing attention only on the limited interests of subunits enormously simplifies rationality and makes organizational life manageable.

Effective Leadership in Cybernetic Systems

Coordination at Huxley does not for the most part require a director, at least not the kind of goal-focused, decision-making, rational director that is commonly associated with the concept of leadership. Cybernetic institutions tend to run themselves, and upper-level participants tend to respond to disruptions of ongoing activities or to improve selected activities through subtle interventions, rather than to engage in dramatic attempts to radically change institutional functioning. This does not mean that leaders are unnecessary to the system, or that they have no effect on it, but rather it means that their effectiveness depends on functioning according to specific cybernetic principles. They can influence which organizational constraints get optimized, but ordinarily they will have little control over how units function within those constraints. Their task is to keep the institution's "lawlessness within reasonable bounds" (Kerr, 1963, p. 35).

Management by Exception. Cybernetic leaders pay attention to what is wrong. They are concerned with identifying and eliminating weakness and problems, and much of their time is taken up with responding to disturbances in the structure (Mintzberg, 1979). The administrative aphorism that the squeaky wheel gets the grease is not all wrong at Huxley. The squeak is an attention cue. It is the leader's responsibility to assess the cause of the squeak and to decide whether it is important enough to attend to. The analytical leader might respond to a deficiency by designing a corrective program, but the cybernetic leader knows that appropriate corrective responses are likely already available in ongoing institutional systems. The problem therefore is to activate or deactivate the appropriate loops. Albert H. Bowker, former chancellor at the City University of New York, once described his job as walking around with two cans from which he poured liquid on fires; one can contained water and the other oil. Cybernetic leaders do not have to start fires; they can usually affect institutional functioning by choosing which can to use on the fires that already exist.

Designing Systems. Cybernetic systems can function effectively only if environmental disturbances are sensed and negative feedback is then generated by organizational subunits that monitor these data. The cybernetic leader ensures that appropriate monitoring devices are in place and that information is generated that will be reviewed by these monitors. Leaders can affect the organization as they "increase the number of participants in the monitoring process, making each participant responsible for a limited number of concerns. Doing so increases the number of concerns they must monitor" (Chaffee, 1987, p. 12), and therefore increases the organization's sensitivity to important changes.

Having identified or established monitors, leaders must then develop the communications systems to ensure their receipt of important signals. If President Wagstaff were concerned about minority enrollments, for example, it would be important for him to design campus reporting systems that clearly identified enrollment data and a communications system that ensured that those campus groups sharing the concern (the system monitors) would be aware of them. These groups would then be activated when the numbers fell below acceptable levels, just as a thermostat activates the furnace when the temperature drops.

Directive Cybernetic Leadership. Much leadership in cybernetic systems consists of carrying out routine tasks when things are going well and making minor adjustments and subtle changes of emphasis when problems are noticed. But there are at least two situations in which leaders in cybernetic systems must become much more directive and intrusive. One occurs when the institution is exposed to an external shock—such as the sudden loss of resources—creating a crisis. Such an event can activate amplifying loops for which the system has no response. It may overwhelm the stabilizing tendencies of the system and even threaten institutional survival. This situation requires a direct leadership effort to make major changes. This task is risky and may fail (after all, no one really knows a good way to significantly reduce an operating budget in midyear), but active intervention of the leader is often widely supported because of the obvious threat.

The other situation occurs when the leader believes that the system is operating at an unacceptable level of performance and there are no institutional processes that can be activated to change it. In this case, the leader can shock the system by attempting to make major alterations in its ongoing processes. The outcomes of such attempts cannot be predicted; the result can be institutional renewal or institutional chaos and leadership replacement. This is the most risky of leadership behaviors in a cybernetic system, because it usually is opposed by campus participants who see it as a threat to themselves, rather than as a response to a problem.

The rules in both cases are what one would expect of dynamic, nonlinear systems: Shocks disturb the system and through the presence of amplifying loops may have large-scale effects—but the effects themselves cannot be predicted in advance.

Administrative Intervention. Good managers are often seen as people who successfully intervene in problematic situations, and equivocal situations are likely to call forth the interventionist responses that good managers are supposed to evidence. But we know that because of the complexity of these systems, attempts to change them can often lead to counterintuitive outcomes. As a result, not only do academic managers "often get in the way of activities that have their own self-regulation, form, and self-correction tendencies" (Weick, 1979, p.

8), but by disturbing ongoing control systems, their interventions may exacerbate rather than moderate the problem. The greater the extent of the intervention, and the more complex the problem, the more it can be expected that the solution will create additional problems (Hedberg, Nystrom, and Starbuck, 1976). The opportunities for false learning in such situations are enormous. Administrators may identify the situation they have themselves worsened as evidence justifying their continued intervention, and erroneously come to believe that things would have become worse still had it not been for their involvement.

Administrators are clearly under pressure to act when something appears to be going wrong. A wise response in such situations is sometimes to do nothing. In the real world of external audiences, of course, doing nothing may be impossible. But administrators must be careful not to overcorrect (Walker, 1979). In general, disruptive conflict can be minimized by limiting the kinds of responses offered to minor problems. William Rainey Harper's injunction that premature action may be the source of more mistakes than procrastination reflects an understanding of the virtue of ignoring some error. The cybernetic administrator follows the physician's ancient creed: *primum non nocere* ("first, do no harm").

The Role of Analysis. Huxley College does not try to implement complete solutions that take all variables into consideration. Instead, it reacts to local short-term problems with local short-term solutions. When new problems emerge as a consequence, they are dealt with sequentially.

The cybernetic perspective does not argue that analytical approaches have no merit but rather that since time, effort, information, and political capital (Steinbruner, 1974) are costly and in short supply, they cannot be applied to every problem. However, it may be worth the investment to develop analytical approaches to a small number of critical institutional issues. The benefits may not be in terms so much of alternatives studied, outcomes examined, and cost-benefit calculations made explicit (although these may be of value) as of both providing cues that symbolize to the organization the importance of a problem and developing forums for analysis that bring people together and therefore alter their behaviors and eventually their attitudes.

Principles for the Cybernetic Leader. Good cybernetic leaders are modest. Recognizing that they preside over black boxes whose internal operations are not fully understood, they adopt three laws of medicine (Konner, 1987, p. 21): "If it's working, keep doing it. If it's not working, stop doing it. If you don't know what to do, don't do anything."

The human body, like the organization, is a nonlinear system whose many unknowns create opportunities for counterintuitive and fluctuating outcomes. The purpose of the "laws" in medicine is to prevent what physicians refer to as iatrogenic illness—that is, illness caused by an inadvertent or erroneous treatment. In higher education, they are meant to prevent what might be termed Caesargenic problems—that is, institutional problems created by the unnecessary interventions of leaders.

Chapter 9 _{see p 176}

Effective Administration and Leadership in the Cybernetic Institution

Practitioners or analysts who typically view an institution —anarchial through the lens of a bureaucratic, collegial, political, or symbolic system are likely to see different organizational environments, select different elements as important or unimportant, and come to different conclusions about cause and effect. The administrative actions recommended by one model are sometimes contrary to those suggested by another. Introducing the concept of the cybernetic institution provides a means to integrate these four models. In this last chapter, I offer some suggestions about effective administration in a cybernetic institution.

To be sure, trying to manage organizations as cybernetic systems is difficult in the real world. The subtle influences of the sensitive cybernetic administrator are often in conflict with the rational myths of what active management and creative leadership are supposed to do. External political or bureaucratic forces may point to obvious institutional shortcomings and demand correction, without understanding either the existing benefits for which they were a trade-off or the significant costs to be paid elsewhere in the institution for improving them. Probably the major argument favoring cybernetic systems is

201

that even though their operational mechanisms are not always obvious or understood, they "work." Cybernetic systems are particularly effective when something is not functioning properly but the reasons are unknown.

Cybernetic systems are notoriously difficult to change; the same forces that make them unlikely to fail also make them difficult to improve. And the complex interaction of elements formed into interacting amplifying and stabilizing loops makes learning exceptionally difficult. A situation may improve or deteriorate with or without administrative intervention, and in many cases the consequences may be independent of the actions taken.

In this book, I have argued that because of the unusual characteristics of academic institutions, attempts to improve the "management" of colleges and universities may reduce rather than increase effectiveness. This should not be interpreted as a suggestion that administrative structures and systems are irrelevant, that sloppy management is as acceptable as thoughtful management, or that nothing makes a difference. But if "good" management is an important aspect of institutional functioning, "better" management as traditionally defined may bring no additional value. In effective organizations of all kinds, "management has to be tolerant of leaky systems; it has to accept mistakes, support bootlegging, roll with unexpected changes" (Peters and Waterman, 1982, p. 145). If the general untidiness of many colleges and universities is taken as a sign of pathology rather than as a normal and expectable response of nonlinear systems that have distinctive technologies and environments, there may be irresistible pressure to adopt new management techniques. Presidents, trustees, and others should beware of thinking of better management as a panacea. Quick fixes and Gordian knot solutions have limited applications in all kinds of organizations and are particularly unlikely to be functional in colleges and universities.

Because administrators experience equivocal environments, are affected by cognitive limitations that require them to make judgments under conditions of uncertainty, and cannot directly measure either their own effectiveness or the success of their institutions, there are relatively few nonroutine decisions or strategies whose outcomes they can predict with complete certainty. Institutions differ on factors such as institutional size, culture, or program, and institutions themselves constantly change, so that following the recipe that led one to triumph at a previous institution—or even in the past at one's present institution—may lead to disaster today.

The contingency perspective warns administrators to be cautious of blanket prescriptions and simple solutions. In a study that asked college presidents to identify their most serious mistakes (Neumann, 1988), many presidents said that they had made a mistake in acting on an important matter too cautiously or too late. But an equal number mentioned that moving on a serious problem too quickly or too early had caused them grief.

Most books about higher education administration call for active and aggressive leadership. Under some circumstances— for example, when an institution is in a crisis that threatens its survival—the need for immediate and dramatic action may outweigh any potential long-term costs. Without denying that this may sometimes be important, this book has presented a perspective meant to provide a balance to those who today criticize higher education and the faculty and administrators who manage the enterprise. It is based on the presumption that, by and large, our colleges and universities are effective, their administrations and faculties are well trained and hardworking, and exploiting the cybernetic tendencies of these institutions to improve them can often be more effective than management muscle, student testing, or fiscal controls. The recommendations that follow are directed to college presidents, but they are equally applicable to administrators at other institutional levels.

Leading Cybernetically

Through their behaviors over time, leaders influence the constraints within which those at lower levels function. Presidents and other administrators may not be able to make dramatic changes in their institutions most of the time, but by recognizing the organizational characteristics of their institution, they may still be able to provide leadership. There are specific expectations of the leaders of bureaucratic, collegial, political, and symbolic systems. But these systems all overlap and influence each other, and administrators play their parts in a complex interaction of other roles and functions. Their responsibility is to keep the institution in proper balance, and not to "run" it.

Presidents should realize the importance of both transactional and transformational leadership. A recent emphasis on the role of leadership in tapping the motivations of followers and leading them to new and better values in the pursuit of leader-intended change has glorified the concept of transformational leadership (Burns, 1978). But establishing such rarely achieved outcomes as the defining characteristic of leadership is in many ways not only misleading but also somewhat demeaning to the actions of the skilled and able administrator who is able to keep an institution functioning effectively in turbulent times. Few administrators are charismatic, but all administrators can be competent.

In a cybernetic institution, most presidents most of the time should be engaged in the expected transactions with the environment and with internal subsystems in an effort to detect problems and to make the adjustments necessary to keep the institution in harmony with its environment. It is difficult to do this well, and administrators who do so should be honored for the accomplishment. Assessing the effects of leadership under these circumstances is difficult, because to an external observer often "nothing" appears to happen. Those who question presidential leadership too often overlook what *does not* happen—that is, the crises that do not occur or the problems that do not lead to disruption because effective presidential action forestalls them (Hollander, 1987). Organizations are constantly changing, and "they require chronic rebuilding. Processes continually need to be reaccomplished. Most administrators know this; most students of organizations need to be reminded of it" (Weick, 1979, p. 44). The constant rebuilding of organizational systems is one way that good administrators provide leadership.

At the same time, presidents should remain alert to the infrequent opportunities to provide transformational leadership. While most administrators operate within the constraints of on-going institutional systems most of the time, there are circum-stances under which they may be able to significantly change those systems. This may be possible in institutions:

- that are in a state of acknowledged crisis, during which zones of indifference expand, participants become willing to em-brace processes and activities that promise to remove threats to the institution's existence, and there is an *expectation* that "the leader" will set the new direction. In such situa-tions, failure of the president to act aggressively may threat-en the president's tenure of office.
- that are small and in which administrators, and particularly presidents because of their higher status, can exert dispro-portionate influence through personal interaction. This influ-ence will be most effective when faculty are locals rather than cosmopolitans, and when traditions of professional au-tonomy and shared authority are weak.
- that are so conspicuously out of date that administrators can use contrasts with comparable institutions as a reasonable basis for change.
- that have trustees who are willing to support autocratic lead-ership and remain indifferent over an extended period of time to opposition from faculty and others.

In the first three cases, through the exercise of expert and refer-ent power, an administrator may enjoy constituent support while inducing major organizational changes. In the fourth case, presidents can use coercive, reward, and legitimate power to make major changes that will not enjoy immediate constituent support, but as personnel are replaced over time, these changes may become part of the institution's culture, and the memory of the means used to achieve them may fade.

Examples of successful transformational leadership in sit-uations other than these are few and far between. If leadership is assessed on the basis of significant alterations of institutional functioning, most administrators must be found wanting. But to call this a leadership crisis is to ask for outcomes ordinarily unattainable in organizations of this kind. Good presidents understand and protect the organization, continue its present level of functioning, and make modest marginal improvements; bad presidents make mistakes without detecting error, do not attend to the proper problems, and allow the institution to fall apart. Effective presidents are part of a cybernetic process; ineffective presidents are bad thermostats.

Presidents should cultivate the emergence of leadership within the various subunits of the institution. Presidents have a tendency to think of leadership as requiring them to decide on the institution's goals and to direct people toward their achievement (Birnbaum, 1987b). But certain characteristics of academic organizations make it difficult for presidents to directly motivate, direct, and control other institutional members. For example, faculty have a need for independence, they have a professional orientation including special knowledge and training, and some may be indifferent to organizational rewards. The task in which they are engaged is often intrinsically satisfying and provides its own feedback concerning accomplishment, and support may be provided by closely knit and cohesive work groups. Factors such as these significantly limit the effects that organizational leaders can have (Kerr and Jermier, 1978).

Organizational leadership is important, but it is a mistake to believe that all leadership must come from "leaders." Cybernetic presidents recognize that their downward influence is limited and that much of the guidance and support in an effective college or university is provided by the qualities of the participants, the nature of the task, and the characteristics of the organization. Goals may arise from the group itself if the presidential role is seen as reducing organizational constraints to enable others to exert leadership, rather than increasing constraints by becoming more directive.

A classic definition of leadership refers to the ability to infuse daily behavior with meaning, to create an "institutional embodiment of purpose" (Selznick, 1957, p. 149). In a cybernetic college or university, the responsibility to "interpret the role and character of the enterprise, to perceive and develop models for thought and behavior, and to find modes of communication that will inculcate general rather than merely partial perspectives" (p. 150) is in large measure fulfilled through the socialization of the participants, professional traditions, and institutional histories.

Presidents should remember that events are equivocal and that many opportunities to interpret organizational meaning afford them unusual influence without inducing the alienation that may arise from giving orders. Cybernetic administrators understand that there are many things at which people can look and that attention is limited. They therefore try to get people to pay attention to matters of interest to the administrator. An administrator can do this by increasing monitor sensitivity, choosing the data to be collected and deciding how they will be displayed and distributed, creating the right information channels, and attending to forums for interaction. Administrators can also influence what is seen and how it is acted on by their decisions concerning organizational structure.

Other simple ways of focusing attention are often either overlooked or minimized. Take, for example, the calling of a meeting, an activity that is among the most important of all administrative actions. Calling a meeting is itself a signal that something is of more than routine importance and therefore commands attention. A meeting is a forum for interaction, and administrators often have great flexibility in deciding who should attend, what material will be distributed beforehand, how long the meeting will last, where it will be held, what the specific agenda of the meeting will be, and in what order the agenda will be discussed. In many campus situations, administrative prerogatives concerning meetings are considered legitimate, even if administrative decisions are not. By attending thoughtfully to acceptable activities such as calling meetings, administrators can exercise considerable influence over people's perceptions and interpretations without creating alienation.

Leaders in cybernetic organizations may have little influence over instrumental activities, but they can be crucial elements in an institution's symbolic existence. The institution is in part a stage, and "problems arise when actors play their parts badly, when symbols lose their meaning, when ceremonies and rituals lose their potency" (Bolman and Deal, 1984, p. 6). As symbolic leaders, presidents who consistently articulate the core values of the institution and relate them to all aspects of instituional life reinvigorate the myths that lead people to create a common reality. A college president who reinforces and dramatizes the importance of access, for example, by symbolic acts such as telling stories of underprepared students who "made it" may have a greater influence on faculty behavior than one who pressures faculty to start a new program.

To emphasize the importance of leadership as myth and symbol is not to denigrate the role of leaders, but rather to identify a particularly critical function that they play. March's (1984) characterization of presidents as light bulbs in a dark room has interesting implications for a cybernetic system. The metaphor recognizes that presidents are essential for the effective operation of a campus. It takes accomplishment of a high order to shed the light that prevents people from stumbling around in the dark. But it also suggests that under normal conditions in a normative professional organization, the presidential role is not to direct order but to provide the illumination needed to permit ongoing organizational processes to continue.

Complicating the Controller

The adaptability and survivability of cybernetic organizations depend on having sensing mechanisms that contain as much variety as the environment they must monitor. Organizations in complex environments therefore require complex sensing mechanisms. One way to do this is to create large numbers of loosely coupled monitors, each responsible for being sensitive to a different portion of the environment. A second and complementary response to complexity is to complicate the administrators who serve as organizational controllers.

Administration is both a science and an art. As a science, it is directed by understandings of structure, schedules, systems, and power. Administrators collect and analyze information, assess relationships, infer causality, and generate and test hypotheses (Nisbett and Ross, 1980). The administrator as scientist must discover how others enact their environment, develop probabilistic theories about cause and effect, and be constantly on guard against false learning. As an art, administration is informed by sensibilities, connoisseurship, and intuition. The administrator as artist tries to create new realities and to influence others as they enact their environment. Trying to lead without science is usually ineffective; trying to lead without art is usually sterile. The best administrators are probably both scientists and artists who are able to integrate the two ways of thinking and of processing data.

Presidents should complicate themselves by learning to look at their institutions using multiple rather than single frames. In a complicated world, it is possible to interpret any situation from a number of perspectives, or frames, *any or all of which* may provide useful administrative insights. Administrators who use only one frame have a narrow framework for understanding a problem, and behaving in the style suggested by one model can be dysfunctional when others perceive a different model (Cohen and March, 1974). Complicated administrators are able to use multiple frames. They can draw on numerous explanations and frameworks to find actions to suit particular situations (Bolman and Deal, 1984). Administrators may find value in many different models during the course of a day; it is important that they have behavioral repertoires appropriate to each and the judgment to know when to use them.

Simple understandings lead to general rules to be applied in all situations; complicated understandings suggest that situations differ and that reliance on experiences of the past may prove dysfunctional. One of the best ways for leaders to develop complicated understandings is to be aware of the various conceptual models of organization and of leadership so that they can generate both multiple descriptions of situations and multiple approaches to solutions. That is why the only thing more useful than a good theory is a lot of good theories. Only complicated understandings can see the many and conflicting realities of complicated situations. There is evidence that such com-

plexity leads to more effective organizational behavior as well as
to more accurate perception (Bartunek, Gordon, and Weathersby, 1983) and that presidents become more complex as they become more experienced (Bensimon, 1987; Neumann, 1987).
Using multiple frames means that a president can disassemble a
process, such as budgeting, for example, and use "political jock-
eying for position, bureaucratic channels for review, and a collegial summary session" (Chaffee, 1983) while simultaneously
engaging in symbolic acts that cause people to modify their perceptions of reality.

There are other ways that presidents can gain more complex understandings. They can practice role reversal, a process
in which people try to see a situation through the eyes of others. A president might better understand possible faculty reaction to a proposed administrative initiative by playing the role
of a faculty senator and responding to the presentation of a
colleague playing the president's role. A president could also engage in frame analysis, and consider how people who use each
of the four frames might interpret an event or proposal. Presidents can also become more complex by engaging in circular
thinking. Presidents would often like to change the behaviors of
others, but that is usually difficult to do. Presidents should consider that the behavior of some people on campus is often a
consequence of the president's own behavior. When presidents
encounter what they consider to be undesirable behavior, they
should ask themselves, "What am I doing that may be influencing what is happening?" In so doing, presidents may come to
understand how they can influence others by changing their
own behavior.

One consequence of being complicated is that presidents
can be generalists rather than specialists. A common debate in
athletic competition is whether a team should draft players to
fill certain roles or instead should select the best all-round
athletes. During ordinary times, institutions should select as
presidents the best cybernetic athletes—complex individuals
who are sensitive to the values of the institution and who are
able to cope in at least satisfactory ways with various and pres-
ently unknown contingencies. During times of presumed crisis,

there may be a felt need to select candidates who appear to offer a specialized talent as an academic innovator, a fund raiser, a hard-nosed budget cutter, or a peacemaker. This may have short-term advantages, but specialists may persist in their specialized behavior long after the need for it has disappeared. This is likely to lead to imbalance and therefore to be dysfunctional in the long run. The medical metaphor provides an appropriate warning: Don't call in a surgeon unless you are willing to undergo an operation.

Even balanced cybernetic presidents will pay more attention to some things than to others. They can focus on these concerns without organizational dysfunction by selecting as administrative colleagues people who share their basic goals but have somewhat different skills and interests.

Presidents should be sensitive to the possibility of unplanned and undesirable outcomes of their behavior. To complicate oneself is not only to see new alternatives but also to become more sensitive to the possibility of unanticipated consequences of one's actions "as each program bumps into others and sets off consequences down the line" (Wildavsky, 1979, p. 4). Recognizing this effect should make administrators more modest in their expectations and more cautious about implementing major initiatives. The question that administrators should ask themselves is not "what program or policy will respond most effectively and immediately to the problem I now face" but rather "what it is within my power to do now that will solve a current problem without creating more serious problems later."

Facts and problems are not givens but may be seen by different people in different ways. Problems are not objectively real but are designed. The most effective administrators are able to define and design problems in a manner that enables them to be addressed by ongoing organizational structures and processes.

Presidents should increase reliance on intuition as they gain experience and are able to understand their organization through multiframe perspectives. When activities involve human beings and human judgments in nonlinear systems, successful behavior cannot be reduced to formal rules. For the cognitively complex administrator, judgments may be formed at least as much by intuition as by rationality and planning. Intuition appears to be related to the ability to see patterns in complex and equivocal situations, much as a chess player is able to find good moves after reviewing the placement of pieces on a chessboard. The chess player (and the experienced administrator) is not able to describe the steps through which that judgment was reached, although after further thought (that is, through retrospective sense making), both will be able to develop arguments that support it. The expert chess player will make a judgment in several seconds but then may take a great deal of time "verifying that a move appearing plausible does not have some kind of hidden weakness" (Simon, 1987, p. 59). This same kind of post hoc consideration may account for the collection of data by administrators that later go underanalyzed; the complex administrator is collecting the data not to make decisions but rather to cross-check and confirm the validity of decisions about which some preliminary judgments have already been made. The complex administrator, functioning in a cybernetic mode, reviews data to be assured that programs are functioning within acceptable levels and to monitor problems that might need attention.

Very little is known about the use of intuition by college presidents. One study of thirty-two presidents from a wide variety of institutions indicated that relatively few gave much attention to data and standard reports, while half of them assessed their own performance by using intuition—a gestalt, instinctive feeling that things are working out satisfactorily (Birnbaum, 1988). Complex administrators, with a large repertoire of potential understandings and behaviors, should have a greater chance than simple administrators to make accurate intuitive judgments and inferences. Intuition and experience should also provide complex administrators with a contingency perspective, warning them that what worked in another setting may not be effective under changed circumstances and allowing them to differentiate the potentially critical from the trivial when confronting new conditions.

Presidents should recognize that acting is thinking. Administrators in higher education are exceptionally busy people. They spend their time on a variety of brief and fragmented activities (Dill, 1984) and move from crisis to crisis. It would be expected that in a complex cybernetic system, administrators would constantly be attending to a multitude of agendas without knowing in advance which of them will prove to be important.

This may lead to a perception that administrators waste their time on trivia. The constant suggestions that greater leadership could be provided if administrators were given enough support to give them time to "think" assume that thought and action are separate, and that one leads to the other. But thinking is as much a product of action as it is a cause; it is by examining the outcomes of one's behavior that the thinking that interprets reality occurs. Indeed, it has been suggested (Weick, 1983b) that action *is* the process by which executives think—that "thinking is inseparably woven into and occurs simultaneously with action. When managers tour, read, talk, supervise, and meet, these actions contain managerial thought, they do the thinking for managers, they are substitutes for thinking, and they reduce the necessity for separate reflective episodes" (p. 222).

Effective administrators act thinkingly (that is, by paying attention, by discovering meanings, and by self-correction) rather than unthinkingly (that is, by rote, by impulse, or mindlessly). We can begin to see why attempting to trace the major decisions of administrators and their institutional consequences often turns out to be an exercise in futility. Particularly in complex, cybernetic institutions with loosely coupled subsystems, effective executives do not for the most part spend their time "making decisions" that have major effects on the institution. Instead, they influence through the smaller things they do— their choices as to which letter they will answer and how, the wording of their state of the college address, or naming the members of a campuswide committee. It is the incremental effects of many actions that together make certain outcomes less likely and other outcomes more likely. As Weick has put it, "the decision making *is* the memo writing, *is* the answering, *is* the editing of drafts. These actions are not the precursors to decision making, they *are* the decision making. And when they are done more carelessly, casually, or absent-mindedly, the decisions they produce are more foolish" (1983b, p. 237).

In some cases, actions can be dramatic and lead to new

perceptions and values, possibilities captured in aphorisms such as "Ready, fire, aim" and "Leap before you look." But acting in a thinking way probably occurs most often in the course of daily routine. Despite our rhetoric about the need for transformational leadership, sophisticated planning systems, or educational reform, effective administrators are probably less likely to be people who engage in heroic activities and more likely to be people who do ordinary things extraordinarily well. As March (1984) has suggested, the way administrators act is often more sensible than the way they talk.

Learning Accurately

Organizations can respond to error by trying to prevent it before it occurs through rational processes, or by trying to detect and correct it afterward through cybernetic processes. We usually spend too much time on prevention and not enough on detection. Recent disasters involving our own advanced technology (which is relatively simple when compared to nonlinear social systems) suggest that complete prevention of error is impossible. Systems for detecting error not only have lower costs and are more effective, but they also enable us to innovate and take risks, confident that unanticipated problems will be immediately sensed and corrected rather than allowed to expand and pose a systemwide threat.

The detection of error requires accuracy in learning, but leaders are subject to cognitive biases that are difficult to avoid. Administrators often must rely on rules of thumb, given the ambiguities of organizations and the human limits of rationality. But heuristics can lead to false learning and improper judgments, including incorrect assessments of the effects of one's own behavior. Administrators must often initiate activity even when samples are known to be biased, data are incomplete, and inferences and judgments are problematic given an equivocal environment. The collection, coding, and interpretation of data can never be done in the ambiguous world of organization and social interaction as carefully as they can be in the controlled environment of a laboratory. And the fact that intuitive understandings are so often correct means that undertaking programs to increase empirical knowledge and reduce error could not usually be justified because of the high fiscal and organizational costs they would require. Nevertheless, there are several simple things that can be done to reduce error somewhat.

Presidents should understand the sources of common cognitive errors and develop habits of thought that question the sources of data and their interpretation. It is important to become aware of and sensitive to the sources of error in judgment such as those discussed in this book. Realizing that we see what we expect to see, leaders should give particularly close scrutiny to information presented by advocates of particular positions, and particularly to information that appears to confirm the administrator's own predilections. Because of the biases caused by our preconceptions and knowledge structures, the difficulties in estimating the strength of relationships, and the basic ambiguities of organizational life, administrators can easily find explanations that satisfy them and then be lulled into a false confidence of their correctness because of the ease of explaining them.

Administrators can respond to this tendency by becoming more active disbelievers. They can ask questions about how data were collected (how adequate was the sample, how was it selected?) and interpreted (how would those on the other side interpret those data; could the results have occurred by chance?). After an initial judgment is reached, leaders can ask additional questions. Given an action on my part, why do I believe that it caused a certain outcome? What are some alternative explanations for the outcome? How plausible are the alternative explanations? What evidence might be available that would refute the original judgment or tend to support the alternatives?

College and university presidents should also try to understand more clearly their real effects on organizational life. Presidents are predisposed to see themselves as causing campus events with favorable outcomes and as not responsible for events with negative outcomes (Birnbaum, 1987c). Confusing skill and luck can have serious consequences for an administrator, who may become inflexible and increase support of an objectively failing policy in order to justify past expenditures (Fox and Staw,

1979). Learning depends on feedback, and learning accuracy
can be expected to decrease if feedback is either constrained or
inaccurate. This may occur because of distortions created by
the status differences inherent in bureaucracies or the appointment to important offices of candidates loyal to the administrator (Gardner, 1986). One outcome is to create administrative
teams whose members have similar backgrounds, interests, and
perceptions. They shield the president from criticism, so that
the office "may become a hall of mirrors. Those around the
president adjust to the presidential style. Furthermore, the several layers of administrative personnel between the president
and the faculty and students provide filters which remove the
unworkable or unreasonable elements of his decisions. The fact
that many decisions are subtly changed often does not reach
his attention. So everything that the president does seems to
work" (Walker, 1979, p. 116).

Cognitive errors in perception, interpretation, and inference can never be totally eliminated in an equivocal world. In
general, however, it would seem advantageous to take advantage of low-cost opportunities to improve administrative learning and practice by minimizing cognitive biases to administrative judgment.

Presidents should encourage dissensus within their staffs.
Subordinates who can help correct leader error are beyond
price, but they may be afraid to be bearers of bad news, or they
may come over time to share the biases of their leaders. Since
cybernetic organizations depend on accurate feedback, leaders
must find ways of supporting norms that encourage deviation
and disagreement in discussion and analysis. It can be helpful to
make judgments in groups rather than individually, since even
one person with persuasive arguments can significantly improve
the quality of a group's decision (Nisbett and Ross, 1980). Erroneous administrative learning can also be reduced somewhat
by focusing explicit attention on the search for evidence that
disconfirms rather than confirms the accuracy of projections or
the reasonableness of assumed cause-and-effect relationships. In
part, this means seeking feedback from groups not ordinarily
consulted, because they are more likely than those close to the

administrator to have a different belief structure and therefore to have different perceptions. This means actively encouraging dissent among one's colleagues and rewarding those with the courage to publicly announce that the emperor's new clothes are not what they should be.

Administering Cybernetically

Presidents influence organizations through statements that stress certain values and make them more prominent, by creating or reinforcing structures that ensure that certain people will interact more frequently, and by designing information systems that collect and disseminate certain data (and ignore other data) and thereby provide attention cues. The processes set up to sense problems and to collect and transmit data affect what is seen. Systems emphasizing structural or social mechanisms will select different cues from the same environment and will prescribe different behaviors. Issues will be seen differently by units that pay attention to different subgoals. Administrators exercise control over organizations by determining the systems of data collection and analysis, the systems of communication, and the allocation of subproblems to subunits. Deciding the area in which a problem should be confronted goes a long way toward deciding how that problem will be resolved. And establishing a subunit charged with the responsibility for a specific subgoal increases significantly the probability that solutions will be generated that will become attention cues for others in the organization. If student learning is not measured by anyone in an institution, for example, changes in learning go unnoticed and cannot affect decisions.

Presidents should make certain that monitors exist somewhere in the organization that are sensitive to variables of particular significance to the president. The cybernetic institution responds to deviations from acceptable levels of operations only if there are mechanisms that monitor the operation and that are sensitive to the variable under question. Many organizational monitors arise naturally from the structural, social, and political dynamics of the institution, and leaders must be aware of these

constraints. For example, most institutions have highly developed systems of committees or unions that sense the adequacy
of faculty salary and fringe benefit levels, and administrators
ordinarily need not worry that such matters will not be monitored and brought to their attention.

But there are other variables that may not be monitored
unless administrators ensure that appropriate sensing devices are
designed. When administrators create an office of freshman
studies, an affirmative action review board, or an ombudsman,
for example, they are increasing the probability that problems
in these areas will be sensed.

The goals of any organization are in large measure determined by the competing interests of the participants, which ensure that parts of the organization can serve as the watchdog
for other parts (Lindblom, 1959). Every executive is a monitor,
and over the long term, the influence of a cybernetic president
will probably be felt more strongly through the selection of personnel than through any other administrative activity. Administrators who rely on a single frame will select people who think
as they do; complex administrators will look for colleagues who
emphasize different values as long as they fall within the organization's constraints. Colleagues who dissent force a more thorough consideration of issues and change the mix of indicators to
which the cybernetic administrator is responsive.

Presidents should be certain that data are collected that
serve as indicators of the issues with which the president is concerned. Setting up monitors is necessary but not sufficient for
detecting problems. Although monitors are sensitive to changes
in operations, their level of sensitivity is related to the availability of data. An administrator concerned about a specific problem should give a great deal of attention to discovering ways the
problem is manifested, and how those data could be collected
and disseminated.

What an institution measures, and how it is presented,
can have a major effect on how the environment is sensed. Obvious arenas for exerting influence through data are systems for
collecting and reporting budgets, enrollments, student achievements, or faculty activities. An institution that highlights ethnic

distributions in its enrollment reports will be more likely to activate certain campus monitors if black enrollment declines than will a campus that describes only the distribution by the number of men and women. A campus that defines faculty work load by distributing reports of student credit hours by academic department is likely to pay attention to different things than a campus that distributes a regular newsletter lauding faculty scholarly activities. Every data system has hidden and unquestioned assumptions built into its design. Data do not speak for themselves, and what is collected and reported—and in what format—can make a critical difference in the way an institution does its routine business (Morgan, 1986).

Presidents should give major attention to the processes through which information is disseminated on campus. On many campuses, important information is collected but not adequately disseminated. Information for the most part does not automatically distribute itself throughout the organization. An administrator facing a crisis may often attribute the apathy of others to selfishness or a lack of institutional commitment, without realizing that those others may not be aware of the situation that has provoked the administrator's concern. Ineffective administrators meet infrequently with faculty leaders, seldom communicate important messages to the faculty by memo or through presentations, and inhibit data comprehension by either distributing few data or else distributing enormous amounts of uninterpreted data. Effective presidents make certain that regularized systems of reporting important data to campus constituents are in place. They meet regularly with faculty leaders, write memos to the faculty outlining emerging issues and requesting comments and suggestions, appear before faculty senates and respond to questions, meet regularly in informal settings with representatives of different internal groups, and in other ways ensure that they have an opportunity both to disseminate important information to others and to hear what others have to say.

If monitors are to effectively fulfill their sensing and feedback functions, they must have access to open channels of communication. Lack of information can prevent monitors from receiving negative feedback, and incomplete communications links can prevent them from reporting error to other organizational levels. A concern for information and for creation of open communications channels between all organizational components may be a factor differentiating successful and unsuccessful administrators. While successful administrators emphasize the importance of communications, "ineffective administrators do just the opposite. As stress and uncertainty build, two-way communication falters and they cloister themselves in an inner sanctum with a few trusted advisors, while the rest of the institution awaits their next crisis-driven action" (Whetten, 1984, p. 43).

Good communication is facilitated by a general sense of openness in institutional governance and climate. To be sure, not everything can or should be exposed to public scrutiny, and there are times when secrecy is necessary to protect individual rights or organizational interests. But openness in an academic community should always be the presumption, and secrecy the exception (Bok, 1983). It is almost certain that disruption is far more likely to be caused by information purposefully or inadvertently kept secret than by sensitive issues inappropriately disclosed. The cybernetic administrator can help to influence this by "open plans, open policy statements, open findings, open reasons, open precedents, and fair informal and formal procedures" (Mortimer and Caruso, 1984, p. 46).

Presidents should provide campus forums for interaction. Wildavsky (1979) has described the formula for effective policy making as consisting of one-third data and two-thirds interaction. Neither alone provides the basis for effective policy making in a cybernetic system; it is the application of data to interaction that permits information to inform preferences and possibilities and that leads to decisions grounded in reality.

The cybernetic administrator therefore not only ensures that systems are in place for collecting, analyzing, and disseminating data but also is concerned that forums exist in which the various constituencies interested in these data can interact. Some forums may be built into the structure as cabinets, councils, committees, or assemblies; others may be temporarily developed in the form of task forces, ad hoc committees, retreats, or colloquia to meet specific needs. In all cases, every opportunity should be taken to ensure the interaction of people who represent different constituencies and interests. Senate presidents who sit as members of administrative councils, deans who attend senate meetings, and students, faculty, and administrators who work on joint committees interact in ways that make campus perceptions more consistent. The cybernetic administrator also thinks about opportunities for informal interaction in social activities that have the potential to increase liking, interaction, and commonality of attitudes and in rites and ceremonies that symbolize adherence to common values and ideals.

The importance of interaction goes to the heart of the usefulness of many administrative activities. Take, for example, strategic planning, a process through which presidents are to "give direction to the college and devise the strategies, make the hard decisions, and allocate the resources that will support movement in that direction" (Keller, 1983, p. 124). No one really knows how to do strategic planning (or everyone has a different idea about it, which is the same thing), but it is often thought of as a management technique for increasing rationality. Institutions hungry for solutions may embrace strategic planning even though there are few data suggesting that it works. People predisposed to believe in strategic planning are likely to incorrectly interpret equivocal data as supporting it (Birnbaum, 1987c), its usefulness is now being questioned by the business firms that originally espoused it, the strategic alternatives open to most institutions are severely limited (Aldrich, 1979), and strategic approaches may have even less applicability to colleges and universities than to other kinds of organizations (Chaffee, 1987).

Institutions select their students and their faculty through self-reinforcing processes that are difficult to change in the short run. These constraints, among others, make the implementation of strategic efforts to develop new goals or purposes difficult indeed. When such changes are effected, their short-term fiscal advantages may be accompanied by long-term competitive disadvantages (Anderson, 1977). Of course, institutions must be aware of their environments, must manage resources prudently, and cannot be indifferent to changing markets without placing themselves in potential jeopardy. These activities are manifestations of institutional intelligence, and most institutions have managed to do these things through processes consistent with institutional purposes and cultures. Some institutions may now give the name of "strategic planning" to these sensible activities, and sensible activity of this kind is important. But the basic purpose of strategic planning in a cybernetic institution is not to develop strategic plans but rather to provide the forums in which interaction may be applied to data. The emphasis is not on producing a plan but on the process of planning itself. The major function of planning should be to serve as a forum in which data inform interaction.

Presidents should know their followers. Leaders are constrained by the limits imposed by their followers. Bureaucrats must operate within followers' zones of indifference if their orders are to be obeyed. Collegial leaders achieve their status by conforming to an unusual degree to the norms of the group. Political leaders function within the constraints imposed by the conflicting interests of various constituencies, and symbolic leaders must conform to group perceptions of appropriate behavior. Administrators who exceed the limits imposed by their constituents will suffer a reduction in their status and lose their claim to leadership. This means that the dramatic, authoritative, and decisive leaderlike behavior we often hear called for may often be counterproductive, particularly in a college setting in which the faculty as well as administrative subordinates *expect* participation. To be leaders, administrators must do what is expected of them. Leaders must do what followers want, even when the followers do not know that they want it!

Leaders often achieve their status through their ability to meaningfully articulate the unspoken concerns and hopes of others. To know what followers want, it is important to encourage open communication and then to *listen.* Acting is easy; listening is hard, particularly for leaders who believe that the leadership role calls for them to *tell* other people what to do. But listening and influencing are reciprocal—the more adminis-

trators listen to others, the more others listen to them. We influence others by allowing ourselves to *be* influenced.

One of the constraints established by followers is their
expectation of appropriate process. In most colleges and universities, the prevailing mood for most substantive matters is apathy—
most people are not concerned about most issues most of the
time. But one thing they are almost certain to be concerned
about is process, because their right to participate and get involved is linked to their organizational status. The right way to
do things is usually the way people *expect* it will be done. In
higher education, process *is* substance, and administrators who
forget that are likely to generate opposition to even the best
ideas.

Presidents should be good bureaucrats. Much of the activity of any college or university is defined in the bureaucratic
routines of its everyday life. The credibility of administrators
and their consequent ability to influence others are to some extent predicated on administering an institution that is seen by
its participants to "work." Late mail, incoherent memos, uncol-
lected trash, incomprehensible personnel forms, or backlogged
supplies give the impression that management either does not
know or does not care. As March (1984, p. 16) has pointed out,
"the importance of simple competence in the routines of organizational life is often overlooked when we sing the grand arias
of management, but effective bureaucracies are rarely dramatic."
Administrative influence is difficult when respect for administrators is lacking, but even recalcitrant faculty will often give the
benefit of the doubt to (and therefore open themselves to influence by) administrators believed to be caring and competent.

Presidents should learn to value inconsistency. Colleges
and universities—and all organizations—are filled with inconsis-
tencies. Cameron (1986a) has referred to these incompatible
elements as "paradoxes" and has argued that their existence is a
hallmark of the most effective organizations. Some of these
paradoxes are that organizations need both loose and tight coupling, that they require both stability and fresh leadership, that
there must be both specialists and generalists, that both ampli-

fying and stabilizing loops must exist, that organizations must break out of old patterns while finding strength in their histories, and that more information must be secured for decision making but the institution must be protected from being overloaded.

The contrary forces that administrators confront are not aberrations to be identified and corrected but essential elements in the self-correcting nature of organizations. One dilemma of administration is to manage these tensions so that no single process, activity, or definition of effectiveness is dominant. Resolving a paradox by minimizing or eliminating one of the simultaneous opposites weakens rather than strengthens an institution, and "extremity in any criterion of effectiveness creates linearity and dysfunction" (Cameron, 1986a, p. 549).

Persistence and Flexibility. It has been suggested that one of the main characteristics of a successful president is persistence—the willingness to pursue a program over an extended period of time until it is implemented (Gilley, Fulmer, and Reithlingshoefer, 1986). Persistence can sometimes yield positive outcomes, but it is also possible for administrators to persist in supporting a program even when past experiences indicate that the program has failed (Staw and Ross, 1980). The pressures to continue a failing program may inhibit the willingness of administrators to experiment with new approaches and behaviors. The administrator must accept the dilemma of appearing to be consistent to maintain the confidence of internal constituents while attempting to respond flexibly to meet the exigencies of external constraints.

Undermanaging and Overmanaging. It is important in some situations for administrators to intervene, make decisions, initiate programs, and take other actions that are generally considered the hallmarks of a good leader. On the other hand, "it's easy to overmanage an organization and . . . an excess rather than a deficiency of intervention . . . lies at the heart of many organizational problems. . . . Any artificial intervention to handle a disruption could destroy the controlled relationships within the system. And if these relationships were destroyed, a host of new disruptions could occur" (Weick, 1979, p. 244). The cybernetic administrator must understand the validity of both conflicting ideas.

Remembering and Forgetting. Presidents rely on their past experiences in order to be able to generalize as they make interpretations about their contemporary world. This permits them to be seen as stable and predictable by those with whom they work and requires them to think and act as if what happens today is similar to what happened yesterday. But at the same time, they must be sensitive to the possibility that their interpretations are incorrect and that these new situations are different from those encountered before.

Administrators cannot approach each event or activity as if for the first time, and effective administrative action requires that presidents respond to situations as they have responded to similar situations in the past. At the same time, presidents must also consider the possibility that important elements of the current situation may be different from those encountered in previous experiences and be sensitive to data suggesting those differences. Less complex administrators credit their past experiences and therefore are less likely to see significant differences. More complex administrators simultaneously credit and discredit their past experiences—acting as experience dictates while remaining open and alert to the possibility that this time they may be in error.

Balancing Administration

In a cybernetic institution, the administrator is not an appendage sitting atop the organization but an integral part of a complex network within it. The matching of a president and an institution can in some ways be thought of as a marriage. There is a courtship during which each tries to exhibit best behaviors and most favorable traits to the other, consummation requires the acquiescence of both parties, there is a honeymoon period in which both parties are pleased and relieved that the strain of courtship has been concluded and nights at the singles bars are

at last over, and each party is almost certainly in for some sur-
prises when the honeymoon ends. As in a marriage, parties enter
into administrative contracts with expectations of a long relationship, while recognizing that divorce on the grounds of ir-
reconcilable differences is always an option. I would carry this
metaphor one step further and suggest that just as it is unwise
for someone to enter marriage with the expectation of changing
the undesirable traits of the partner, it is a mistake for presidents to enter office with the belief that they will be able to significantly change the institution.

The objective of the bureaucratic administrator is rationality. The collegial administrator searches for consensus, the
political administrator for peace, and the symbolic administrator for sense. But the major aim of the cybernetic administrator
is balance. Institutions will find that their technology is supported by mixtures of bureaucratic, collegial, political, and symbolic elements, each responding to certain institutional needs
and posing a constraint on the others. For most institutions,
none of the four systems can dominate the others without causing severe dysfunction. The unique role of the president as
cybernetic controller (and of other administrators in their own
subunits) is to maintain the balance of these organizational systems, giving increased attention to one if it diminishes below acceptable levels and eliciting constraints against another if it
threatens to become all-encompassing.

The role of the balanced administrator is not to achieve
the greatest degree of control and influence for administrative
processes but rather to ensure that at least the minimal levels of
structure, information flow, and decision-making capability are
sustained. Similarly, the administrator must be concerned with
the maintenance of common values and commitments at some
level and with the protection of minority interest groups (and
sometimes with the coalescing of new groups).

The chapters in this book attempt to explain why institutional processes and cultures, like individual habits and depen-
dencies, are notoriously resistant to change. We are all familiar
with situations in which presidents have taken over moribund
institutions and through assertive and bold actions changed

their characters and revitalized their spirit. Because such examples are vivid, they tend to be available and therefore easily brought to mind; because they are consistent with our schemata and our reliance on the representative heuristic (strong presidents appear reasonably related to strong institutions), they seem plausible. They tend to become part of the folklore of higher education. It is from such experiences that concepts of heroic leadership are disseminated and reinforced.

Great credit is due to presidents and faculties when such a rebirth takes place. Less remembered are situations in which dramatic presidential acts generate negative consequences leading to a short and unhappy tenure. There are no data indicating which scenario is most common, but it is my judgment that successful resuscitation is more the exception than the rule. Taking office in order to "turn the institution around" may be more often a prescription for joint misery than for success.

Recognizing the limits on administrative influence, a candidate should consider the presidency of an institution that can be loved for what it is, rather than for what it might be forced into being. Faults can be recognized, of course, and both president and institution can grow and improve as they work together. Although changes can be made, they should be attempted only after a period in which trust has been developed.

A dramaturgical metaphor may help us to appreciate the role of administrators in general, and the president in particular, in a cybernetic institution. Less complex presidents are Hollywood producers of the old school, heroic entrepreneurs able to exercise effective direction through fiscal controls, high energy, and intrusive personal involvement in every artistic and administrative aspect of the production. They write the script, hire the actors, supervise the filming, and expect to sign off on every decision. There may be unhappiness on the set, but the producer discounts the importance of this and justifies the power relationship as reasonable because of having greater vision, more experience, and ultimate responsibility for the outcome.

More complex presidents take over as stage director of a continuing play many of whose acts and scenes have already been performed. There is a script, but it is transcribed *after* rather than before the characters speak. The director has personal goals and ambitions, as well as an idea of what the audience wants and will respond to. But there are many "givens" that restrict to a great extent what can be done. The roles have already been created and the players selected, the scenery and sets have been built and are in use, and the physical dimensions of the stage itself and its proscenium arch delimit the area in which what to this point has been experienced as a melodrama (or perhaps a comedy of manners or a tragedy, a mystery or a passion play) takes place. How can the director have influence?

If the director dislikes the Neil Simon comedy now being performed and tries to quickly mold it into Shakespeare, the actors become angry, the audience is confused, and everyone can walk away with a different (and correct) explanation of the failure. It is better to select a director who appreciates what has gone before and who is satisfied to make minor modifications to focus the play's intentions and make it marginally more compelling and satisfying for actors and audience alike. In this play, there are many activities occurring on stage—too many for any one to grasp. Because the director has some control over the lighting and the sound equipment, some actors and behaviors can be highlighted while others can be left in the shadows. One can focus on Hamlet, or on Rosencranz and Gildenstern, and see different meanings. In the same way, a president can selectively emphasize certain elements in contrast to others and thereby move an organization toward greater consensus and commitment to a course of action. Over time, the incremental changes can have a major effect, but the actors and audience alike have been a part of the change and have not been dragged along unwillingly. In future years, they can reminisce about how *they* transformed themselves from a community theater to a national company.

We have all known faculty or administrators discontented or confused by their inability to make sense of the organizational, governance, and management processes of their institutions. They want to know what new system they can develop that will resolve their dilemmas; they ask, What system is best? Just as there is no one best play, so there is no one best system of institutional governance or management. Governance is just a process that permits people to work together. If people see some sense in what they are doing, if they are excited, if they believe they are making a difference, their governance system is serving its purpose (Carnegie Foundation for the Advancement of Teaching, 1982). Forms of governance make less difference to institutional functioning than we are likely to believe (Kerr, 1982). Probably the most truthful answer that most accurately represents the dynamics of self-correcting cybernetic systems is to paraphrase Pope's famous couplet: "For forms of college organization let scholars contest; Whate'er is best accepted by the constituents is best."

11/1/97 10:15 P.M.

References

Aldrich, H. E. *Organizations and Environments.* Englewood Cliffs, N.J.: Prentice-Hall, 1979.

Allison, G. T. *Essence of Decision: Explaining the Cuban Missile Crisis.* Boston: Little, Brown, 1971.

American Association of University Professors. *Policy Documents and Reports, 1984 Edition.* Washington, D.C.: American Association of University Professors, 1984.

Anderson, L. G. "The Organizational Character of American Colleges and Universities." In T. F. Lunsford (ed.), *The Study of Academic Administration.* Boulder, Colo.: Western Interstate Commission for Higher Education, 1963.

Anderson, R. E. *Strategic Policy Changes at Private Colleges.* New York: Teachers College Press, 1977.

Ashby, W. R. *An Introduction to Cybernetics.* London: Chapman and Hall, 1956.

Ashby, W. R. *Design for a Brain: The Origin of Adaptive Behavior.* (2nd ed.) New York: Wiley, 1960.

Astin, A. W. *Four Critical Years: Effects of College on Beliefs, Attitudes, and Knowledge.* San Francisco: Jossey-Bass, 1977.

Bacharach, S. B., and Lawler, E. J. *Power and Politics in Orga-*

nizations: The Social Psychology of Conflicts, Coalitions, and Bargaining. San Francisco: Jossey-Bass, 1980.

Baldridge, J. V. *Power and Conflict in the University.* New York: Wiley, 1971.

Baldridge, J. V., Curtis, D. V., Ecker, G., and Riley, G. L. *Policy Making and Effective Leadership: A National Study of Academic Management.* San Francisco: Jossey-Bass, 1978.

Bartunek, J. M., Gordon, J. R., and Weathersby, R. P. "Developing 'Complicated' Understanding in Administrators." *Academy of Management Review,* 1983, *8,* 273–284.

Bass, B. M. *Stogdill's Handbook of Leadership.* New York: Free Press, 1981.

Bennis, W., and Nanus, B. *Leaders: The Strategies for Taking Charge.* New York: Harper & Row, 1985.

Bensimon, E. M. "Selected Aspects of Governance: An ERIC Review." *Community College Review,* 1984, *12,* 54–61.

Bensimon, E. M. "The Meaning of 'Good Presidential Leadership': A Frame Analysis." Paper presented at the annual meeting of the Association for the Study of Higher Education, Baltimore, Md., Nov. 1987.

Besse, R. M. "A Comparison of the University with the Corporation." In J. A. Perkins (ed.), *The University as an Organization.* New York: McGraw-Hill, 1973.

Birnbaum, R. *Maintaining Diversity in Higher Education.* San Francisco: Jossey-Bass, 1983.

Birnbaum, R. "Administrative Commitments and Minority Enrollments: College President's Goals for Quality and Access." Paper presented at the Invitational Conference on Minority Achievement of the Baccalaureate Degree, Los Angeles, 1987a.

Birnbaum, R. "The Implicit Leadership Theories of College and University Presidents." Paper presented at the annual meeting of the Association for the Study of Higher Education, Baltimore, Md., 1987b.

Birnbaum, R. "When College Presidents Are Wrong: The Effects of Knowledge Structures and Judgmental Heuristics on Administrative Inferences." Paper presented at annual meeting of the American Educational Research Association, Washington, D.C., 1987c.

Birnbaum, R. " 'How'm I Doin'?': How College Presidents Assess their Effectiveness." Paper presented at annual meeting of the American Educational Research Association, 1988.

Birnbaum, R. "The Latent Organizational Functions of the Academic Senate: Why Senates Don't Work but Won't Go Away." *Journal of Higher Education*, forthcoming a.

Birnbaum, R. "Presidential Searches and the Discovery of Organizational Goals." *Journal of Higher Education*, forthcoming b.

Birnbaum, R. "Presidential Succession and Institutional Functioning in Higher Education." *Journal of Higher Education*, forthcoming c.

Blau, P. M. *Bureaucracy in Modern Society.* New York: Random House, 1956.

Blau, P. M. *Exchange and Power in Social Life.* New York: Wiley, 1964.

Blau, P. M. *The Organization of Academic Work.* New York: Wiley, 1973.

Bok, S. *Secrets: On the Ethics of Concealment and Revelation.* New York: Random House, 1983.

Bolman, L. G., and Deal, T. E. *Modern Approaches to Understanding and Managing Organizations.* San Francisco: Jossey-Bass, 1984.

Bowen, H. R. *Investment in Learning: The Individual and Social Value of American Higher Education.* San Francisco: Jossey-Bass, 1977.

Bowen, H. R., and Schuster, J. H. *American Professors: A National Resource Imperiled.* New York: Oxford University Press, 1986.

Bowen, K. L. "Faculty Voting Patterns and Decision Making: Faculty Governance at the University of Wisconsin-Oshkosh." Unpublished doctoral dissertation, University of Wisconsin, Madison, 1987.

Burns, J. M. *Leadership.* New York: Harper & Row, 1978.

Burns, T., and Stalker, G. M. *The Management of Innovation.* London: Tavistock, 1961.

Cameron, K. S. "Measuring Organizational Effectiveness in Institutions of Higher Education." *Administrative Science Quarterly*, 1978, 23, 604–632.

Cameron, K. S. "The Effectiveness of Ineffectiveness." In B. M.

Staw and L. L. Cummings (eds.), *Research in Organizational Behavior.* Vol. 6. Greenwich, Conn.: JAI Press, 1984.

Cameron, K. S. "Institutional Effectiveness in Higher Education: An Introduction." *Review of Higher Education,* 1985, *9,* 1–4.

Cameron, K. S. "Effectiveness as Paradox: Consensus and Conflict in Perceptions of Organizational Effectiveness." *Management Science,* 1986a, *32,* 539–553.

Cameron, K. S. "A Study of Organizational Effectiveness and Its Predictors." *Management Science,* 1986b, *32,* 87–112.

Cameron, K. S., and Whetten, D. A. *Organizational Effectiveness.* New York: Academic Press, 1983.

Caplow, T. *Two Against One: Coalitions in Triads.* Englewood Cliffs. N.J.: Prentice-Hall, 1968.

Carnegie Commission on Higher Education. *Governance of Higher Education: Six Priority Problems.* New York: McGraw-Hill, 1973.

Carnegie Foundation for the Advancement of Teaching. *The Control of the Campus: A Report on the Governance of Higher Education.* Washington, D.C.: Carnegie Foundation for the Advancement of Teaching, 1982.

Chaffee, E. E. "The Role of Rationality in University Budgeting." *Research in Higher Education,* 1983, *19,* 387–406.

Chaffee, E. E. "System Strategy and Effectiveness." Paper prepared for the State Higher Education Executive Officers Task Force on Role and Mission, Bismark, N.Dak., May 1987.

Clark, B. R. "Faculty Organization and Authority." In T. F. Lundsford (ed.), *The Study of Academic Administration.* Boulder, Colo.: Western Interstate Commission for Higher Education, 1963.

Clark, B. R. "The Organizational Saga in Higher Education." *Administrative Science Quarterly,* 1972, *17,* 178–184.

Clark, B. R. *The Higher Education System: Academic Organization in Cross-National Perspective.* Berkeley: University of California Press, 1983.

Cohen, M. D., and March, J. G. *Leadership and Ambiguity: The American College President.* New York: McGraw-Hill, 1974.

Cohen, M. D., March, J. G., and Olsen, J. P. "Garbage Can Model of Organizational Choice." *Administrative Science Quarterly*, 1972, *17*, 1–25.

Cohen, M. D., March, J. G., and Olsen, J. P. "People, Problems, Solutions, and the Ambiguity of Relevance." In J. G. March and J. P. Olsen (eds.), *Ambiguity and Choice in Organizations*. Bergen, Nor.: Universitetsforlaget, 1976.

Cohen, S. "Ant Wars, 3-Headed Dogs, and Curriculum Changes." *Chronicle of Higher Education*, June 11, 1986, p. 88.

"College Governing Boards." *Chronicle of Higher Education*, Feb. 12, 1986, p. 27.

Commission on Strengthening Presidential Leadership. *Presidents Make a Difference*. Washington, D.C.: Association of Governing Boards of Universities and Colleges, 1984.

Cornford, F. M. *Microcosmographia Academica: Being a Guide for the Young Academic Politician*. New York: Halcyon-Commonwealth Foundation, 1964. (Originally published 1908.)

Corson, J. J. *Governance of Colleges and Universities*. New York: McGraw-Hill, 1960.

Corson, J. J. "Management of the College or University: It's Different." Topical Paper no. 16, Center for the Study of Higher Education, University of Arizona, June 1979.

Coser, L. *The Functions of Social Conflict*. New York: Free Press, 1956.

Cyert, R. M., and March, J. G. *A Behavioral Theory of the Firm*. Englewood Cliffs, N.J.: Prentice-Hall, 1963.

Deal, T. E., and Kennedy, A. K. *Corporate Cultures: The Rites and Rituals of Organizational Life*. Reading, Mass.: Addison-Wesley, 1982.

Demerath, N. J., Stephens, R. W., and Taylor, R. R. *Power, Presidents, and Professors*. New York: Basic Books, 1967.

Dill, D. D. "The Nature of Administrative Behavior in Higher Education." *Educational Administration Quarterly*, 1984, *20*, 69–99.

Diran, K. M. "Management Information Systems: The Human Factor." *Journal of Higher Education*, 1978, *49*, 273–282.

Edelman, M. *The Symbolic Uses of Power*. Urbana: University of Illinois Press, 1967.

Etzioni, A. *A Comparative Analysis of Complex Organizations.* New York: Free Press, 1961.

Etzioni, A. *Modern Organizations.* Englewood Cliffs, N.J.: Prentice-Hall, 1964.

Feldman, M. S., and March, J. G. "Information in Organizations as Signal and Symbol." *Administrative Science Quarterly,* 1981, *26,* 171–186.

Fisher, J. L. "Presidents Will Lead—If We Let Them." *AGB Reports,* July/Aug. 1984, pp. 11–14.

Fox, V. F., and Staw, B. M. "The Trapped Administrator: Effects of Job Insecurity and Policy Resistance upon Commitment to a Course of Action." *Administrative Science Quarterly,* 1979, *24,* 449–471.

French, J.R.P., Jr., and Raven, B. "The Bases of Social Power." In D. Cartwright (ed.), *Studies in Social Power.* Ann Arbor: Institute for Social Research, University of Michigan, 1959.

Galbraith, J. *Designing Complex Organizations.* Reading, Mass.: Addison-Wesley, 1973.

Gardner, J. W. *The Nature of Leadership: Introductory Considerations.* Washington, D.C.: Independent Sector, 1986.

Gilley, J. W., Fulmer, K. A., and Reithlingshoefer, S. J. *Searching for Academic Excellence: Twenty Colleges and Universities on the Move and Their Leaders.* New York: Macmillan, 1986.

Gleick, J. *Chaos: Making a New Science.* New York: Viking Penguin, 1987.

Glenny, L. A., and Dalglish, T. K. "Higher Education and the Law." In J. A. Perkins (ed.), *The University as an Organization.* New York: McGraw-Hill, 1973.

Goodman, P. *The Community of Scholars.* New York: Random House, 1962.

Gouldner, A. W. "Cosmopolitans and Locals: Toward an Analysis of Latent Social Roles." *Administrative Science Quarterly,* 1957, *2,* 281–307.

Gross, E., and Grambsch, P. V. *Changes in University Organization, 1964–1971.* New York: McGraw-Hill, 1974.

Hackman, J. R. "Group Influences on Individuals." In M. D.

Dunnette (ed.), *Handbook of Industrial and Organizational Psychology.* Chicago: Rand McNally, 1976.

Hartnett, R. T. *College and University Trustees: Their Backgrounds, Roles, and Educational Attitudes.* Princeton, N.J.: Educational Testing Service, 1969.

Hedberg, B.L.T., Nystrom, P. C., and Starbuck, W. H. "Camping on Seesaws: Prescriptions for a Self-Designing Organization." *Administrative Science Quarterly,* 1976, *21,* 41–65.

Hills, F. S., and Mahoney, T. A. "University Budgets and Organizational Decision Making." *Administrative Science Quarterly,* 1978, *23,* 454–465.

Hodgkinson, H. L. *College Governance: The Amazing Thing Is That It Works at All.* Report 11. Washington, D.C.: ERIC Clearinghouse on Higher Education, 1971.

Hollander, E. P. "Leadership and Power." In G. Lindzey and E. Aronson (eds.), *The Handbook of Social Psychology.* (3rd ed.) New York: Random House, 1985.

Hollander, E. P. *College and University Leadership from a Social Psychological Perspective: A Transactional View.* Report OP87:11. College Park, Md.: National Center for Postsecondary Governance and Finance, 1987.

Homans, G. C. *The Human Group.* San Diego, Calif.: Harcourt Brace Jovanovich, 1950.

Homans, G. C. *Social Behavior: Its Elementary Forms.* San Diego, Calif.: Harcourt Brace Jovanovich, 1961.

Kahneman, D., Slovic, P., and Tversky, A. (eds.). *Judgment Under Uncertainty: Heuristics and Biases.* Cambridge, Eng.: Cambridge University Press, 1982.

Kahneman, D., and Tversky, A. "Intuitive Prediction: Biases and Corrective Procedures." In D. Kahneman, P. Slovic, and A. Tversky (eds.), *Judgment Under Uncertainty: Heuristics and Biases.* Cambridge, Eng.: Cambridge University Press, 1982.

Kast, F. E., and Rosenzweig, J. R. *Contingency Views of Organization and Management.* Chicago: Science Research Associates, 1973.

Katz, D., and Kahn, R. L. *The Social Psychology of Organizations.* (2nd ed.) New York: Wiley, 1978.

Keller, G. *Academic Strategy: The Management Revolution in American Higher Education.* Baltimore, Md.: Johns Hopkins University Press, 1983.

Kerr, C. *The Uses of the University.* Cambridge, Mass.: Harvard University Press, 1963.

Kerr, C. "Postscript 1982." *Change,* Oct. 1982, pp. 23–31.

Kerr, C., and Gade, M. L. *The Many Lives of Academic Presidents: Time, Place, and Character.* Washington, D.C.: Association of Governing Boards of Universities and Colleges, 1986.

Kerr, S., and Jermier, J. M. "Substitutes for Leadership: Their Meaning and Measurement." *Organizational Behavior and Human Performance,* 1978, *22,* 375–403.

Konner, M. *Becoming a Doctor: A Journal of Initiation in Medical School.* New York: Viking Penguin, 1987.

Ladd, E. C., Jr., and Lipset, S. M. *The Divided Academy: Professors and Politics.* New York: Norton, 1975.

Lawrence, P. R., and Lorsch, J. W. *Organization and Environment.* Cambridge, Mass.: Harvard University Press, 1967.

Levine, A., and Weingart, J. *Reform of Undergraduate Education.* San Francisco: Jossey-Bass, 1973.

Lindblom, C. E. "The Science of 'Muddling Through.' " *Public Administration Review,* 1959, *19,* 78–88.

Lindblom, C. E. *The Policy-Making Process.* Englewood Cliffs, N.J.: Prentice-Hall, 1980.

Lunsford, T. F. "Authority and Ideology in the Administered University." In C. E. Kruytbosch and S. L. Messinger (eds.), *The State of the University: Authority and Change.* Beverly Hills, Calif.: Sage, 1970.

Lutz, F. W. "Tightening Up Loose Coupling in Organizations of Higher Education." *Administrative Science Quarterly,* 1982, *27,* 653–669.

March, J. G. "Emerging Developments in the Study of Organizations." *Review of Higher Education,* 1982, *6,* 1–18.

March, J. G. "How We Talk and How We Act: Administrative Theory and Administrative Life." In T. J. Sergiovanni and J. E. Corbally (eds.), *Leadership and Organizational Culture.* Urbana: University of Illinois Press, 1984.

March, J. G., and Olsen, J. P. "Organizational Learning and the

Ambiguity of the Past." In J. G. March and J. P. Olsen (eds.), *Ambiguity and Choice in Organizations.* (2nd ed.) Bergen, Nor.: Universitetsforlaget, 1979.

March, J. G., and Simon, H. A. *Organizations.* New York: Wiley, 1958.

Martin, J., Feldman, M. S., Hatch, M. J., and Sitkin, S. S. "The Uniqueness Paradox in Organizational Stories." *Administrative Science Quarterly,* 1983, *28,* 438–453.

Masland, A. T. "Organizational Culture in the Study of Higher Education." *Review of Higher Education,* 1985, *8,* 157–168.

Masuch, M. "Vicious Circles in Organizations." *Administrative Science Quarterly,* 1985, *30,* 14–33.

Meindl, J. R., Ehrlich, S. B., and Dukerich, J. M. "The Romance of Leadership." *Administrative Science Quarterly,* 1985, *30,* 78–102.

Meyer, J. W., and Rowan, B. "Institutionalized Organizations: Formal Structure as Myth and Ceremony." In J. W. Meyer and W. R. Scott (eds.), *Organizational Environments: Ritual and Rationality.* Beverly Hills, Calif.: Sage, 1983.

Millett, J. D. *The Academic Community: An Essay on Organization.* New York: McGraw-Hill, 1962.

Mintzberg, H. *The Structuring of Organizations.* Englewood Cliffs, N.J.: Prentice-Hall, 1979.

Mock, C. "Hard Cases and Soft Concepts of Change and Leadership in Universities." Paper presented at annual meeting of the Association for the Study of Higher Education, San Diego, Calif., Feb. 1987.

Mooney, R. "Problem of Leadership in the University." *Harvard Educational Review,* 1963, *33,* 42–57.

Morgan, G. *Images of Organizations.* Beverly Hills, Calif.: Sage, 1986.

Morse, J. J. "Organizational Characteristics and Individual Motivation." In J. W. Lorsch and P. R. Lawrence (eds.), *Studies in Organization Design.* Homewood, Ill.: Irwin, 1970.

Mortimer, K. P., and Caruso, A. C. "Governance and Reallocation in the 1990s." In D. G. Brown (ed.), *Leadership Roles of Chief Academic Officers.* New Directions for Higher Education, no. 47. San Francisco: Jossey-Bass, 1984.

Mortimer, K. P., and McConnell, T. R. *Sharing Authority Effec-*

tively: Participation, Interaction, and Discretion. San Francisco: Jossey-Bass, 1978.

Neumann, A. "Strategic Leadership: The Changing Orientations of College Presidents." Paper presented at the annual meeting of the Association for the Study of Higher Education, Baltimore, Md., Nov. 1987.

Neumann, A. "Making Mistakes: Error and Learning in the College Presidency." Paper presented at the annual meeting of the American Educational Research Association, 1988.

Newman, W. H. "Strategy and Management Structure." *Journal of Business Policy,* 1971, *2,* 56–66.

Nisbett, R., and Ross, L. *Human Inference: Strategies and Shortcomings of Social Judgment.* Englewood Cliffs, N.J.: Prentice-Hall, 1980.

Olson, M., Jr. "The Logic of Collective Action." In B. Barry and R. Hardin (eds.), *Rational Man and Irrational Society?* Beverly Hills, Calif.: Sage, 1982.

"The 100 Most Effective College Leaders, Named in a Survey of Their Peers." *Chronicle of Higher Education,* Nov. 5, 1986, p. 13.

Padgett, J. F. "Managing Garbage Can Hierarchies." *Administrative Science Quarterly,* 1980, *25,* 583–604.

Perkins, J. A. "Organization and Functions of the University." In J. A. Perkins (ed.), *The University as an Organization.* New York: McGraw-Hill, 1973a.

Perkins, J. A. (ed.). *The University as an Organization.* New York: McGraw-Hill, 1973b.

Perrow, C. *Complex Organizations: A Critical Essay.* (2nd ed.) Glenview, Ill.: Scott, Foresman, 1979.

Peters, T. J., and Waterman, R. H., Jr. *In Search of Excellence: Lessons from America's Best-Run Companies.* New York: Harper & Row, 1982.

Pfeffer, J. "The Ambiguity of Leadership." *Academy of Management Review,* 1977, *2,* 104–119.

Pfeffer, J. "Management as Symbolic Action: The Creation and Maintenance of Organizational Paradigms." *Research in Organizational Behavior,* 1981a, *3,* 1–52.

Pfeffer, J. *Power in Organizations.* Marshfield, Mass.: Pitman, 1981b.

Pfeffer, J., and Salancik, G. R. *The External Control of Organizations: A Resource Dependence Perspective.* New York: Harper & Row, 1978.

Plott, C. R. "Axiomatic Social Choice Theory: An Overview and Interpretation." In B. Barry and R. Hardin (eds.), *Rational Man and Irrational Society?* Beverly Hills, Calif.: Sage, 1982.

Reyes, P., and Twombly, S. B. "Perceptions of Contemporary Governance in Community Colleges: An Empirical Study." *Community College Review,* Winter 1986–87, *14,* 4–12.

Richardson, R. C., and Rhodes, W. R. "Building Commitment to the Institution." In G. B. Vaughan and Associates, *Issues for Community College Leaders in a New Era.* San Francisco: Jossey-Bass, 1983.

Richman, B. M., and Farmer, R. N. *Leadership, Goals, and Power in Higher Education: A Contingency and Open-Systems Approach to Effective Management.* San Francisco: Jossey-Bass, 1974.

Ross, L., and Anderson, C. A. "Shortcomings in the Attribution Process: On the Origins and Maintenance of Erroneous Social Assessments." In D. Kahneman, P. Slovic, and A. Tversky (eds.), *Judgment Under Uncertainty: Heuristics and Biases.* Cambridge, Eng.: Cambridge University Press, 1982.

Rourke, F. E., and Brooks, G. E. "The 'Managerial Revolution' in Higher Education." *Administrative Science Quarterly,* 1964, *9,* 154–181.

Ruml, B., and Morrison, D. H. *Memo to a College Trustee.* New York: McGraw-Hill, 1959.

Ruscio, K. P. "The Distinctive Scholarship of the Selective Liberal Arts College." *Journal of Higher Education,* 1987, *58,* 205–222.

Salancik, G. R., and Pfeffer, J. "The Bases and Use of Power in Organizational Decision Making: The Case of a University." *Administrative Science Quarterly,* 1974, *19,* 453–473.

Sanders, I. T. "The University as a Community." In J. A. Perkins (ed.), *The University as an Organization.* New York: McGraw-Hill, 1973.

Schein, E. H. *Process Consultation: Its Role in Organization Development.* Reading, Mass.: Addison-Wesley, 1969.

Schein, E. H. *Organizational Culture and Leadership: A Dynamic View.* San Francisco: Jossey-Bass, 1985.

Scott, W. R. *Organizations: Rational, Natural, and Open Systems.* Englewood Cliffs, N.J.: Prentice-Hall, 1981.

Scott, W. R. "Introduction." In J. W. Meyer and W. R. Scott (eds.), *Organizational Environments: Ritual and Rationality.* Beverly Hills, Calif.: Sage, 1983.

Selznick, P. *Leadership in Administration: A Sociological Interpretation.* New York: Harper & Row, 1957.

Sergiovanni, T. J., and Corbally, J. E. (eds.). *Leadership and Organizational Culture.* Urbana: University of Illinois Press, 1984.

Simon, H. A. *Administrative Behavior.* (2nd ed.) New York: Macmillan, 1961.

Simon, H. A. "On the Concept of Organizational Goal." *Administrative Science Quarterly,* 1964, *9,* 1–22.

Simon, H. A. "The Architecture of Complexity." In H. A. Simon, *The Sciences of the Artificial.* Cambridge, Mass.: MIT Press, 1969a.

Simon, H. A. *The Sciences of the Artificial.* Cambridge, Mass.: MIT Press, 1969b.

Simon, H. A. "Making Management Decisions: The Role of Intuition and Emotion." *Academy of Management Executive,* Feb. 1987, pp. 57–64.

Smircich, L. "Concepts of Culture and Organizational Analysis." *Administrative Science Quarterly,* 1983, *28,* 339–358.

Smircich, L., and Morgan, G. "Leadership: The Management of Meaning." *Journal of Applied Behavioral Science,* 1982, *18,* 257–273.

Starbuck, W. H. "Organizations and Their Environments." In M. D. Dunnette (ed.), *Handbook of Industrial and Organizational Psychology.* Chicago: Rand McNally, 1976.

Staw, B. M. "Attribution of the Causes of Performance: A New Alternative Explanation of Cross-Sectional Research on Organizations." *Organizational Behavior and Human Performance,* 1975, *13,* 414–432.

Staw, B. M., and Ross, J. "Commitment in an Experimenting Society: A Study of the Attribution of Leadership from Administrative Scenarios." *Journal of Applied Psychology*, 1980, *65*, 249–260.

Steinbruner, J. D. *The Cybernetic Theory of Decision*. Princeton, N.J.: Princeton University Press, 1974.

Stroup, H. *Bureaucracy in Higher Education*. New York: Free Press, 1966.

Terreberry, S. "The Evolution of Organizational Environments." *Administrative Science Quarterly*, 1968, *12*, 590–613.

Thomas, L. *The Youngest Science: Notes of a Medicine-Watcher*. New York: Viking, 1983.

Thompson, J. D. *Organizations in Action*. New York: McGraw-Hill, 1967.

Tucker, R. C. *Politics as Leadership*. Columbia: University of Missouri Press, 1981.

Tversky, A., and Kahneman, D. "Judgment Under Uncertainty: Heuristics and Biases." In D. Kahneman, P. Slovic, and A. Tversky (eds.), *Judgment Under Uncertainty: Heuristics and Biases*. Cambridge, Eng.: Cambridge University Press, 1982.

Veblen, T. *The Higher Learning in America*. New York: Sagamore Press, 1957. (Originally published 1918.)

Walker, D. E. *The Effective Administrator: A Practical Approach to Problem Solving, Decision Making, and Campus Leadership*. San Francisco: Jossey-Bass, 1979.

Walton, R. E., and McKersie, R. B. *A Behavioral Theory of Labor Negotiations*. New York: McGraw-Hill, 1965.

Weber, M. "The Essentials of Bureaucratic Organization: An Ideal-Type Construction." In R. K. Merton and others (eds.), *Reader in Bureaucracy*. New York: Free Press, 1952.

Weber, M. "Bureaucratic Organizations." In A. Etzioni (ed.), *Readings on Modern Organizations*. Englewood Cliffs, N.J.: Prentice-Hall, 1969.

Weick, K. E. "Educational Organizations as Loosely Coupled Systems." *Administrative Science Quarterly*, 1976, *21*, 1–19.

Weick, K. E. *The Social Psychology of Organizing*. (2nd ed.) Reading, Mass.: Addison-Wesley, 1979.

Weick, K. E. "Contradictions in a Community of Scholars: The Cohesion-Accuracy Tradeoff." *Review of Higher Education*, 1983a, *6*, 253–267.

Weick, K. E. "Managerial Thought in the Context of Action."
In S. Srivastva and Associates, *The Executive Mind: New In-
sights on Managerial Thought and Action.* San Francisco:
Jossey-Bass, 1983b.

Whetten, D. A. "Effective Administrators: Good Management
on the College Campus." *Change,* 1984, *16,* 39–43.

Whetten, D. A., and Cameron, K. S. "Administrative Effectiveness in Higher Education." *Review of Higher Education,*
1985, *9,* 35–49.

Wiener, N. *God and Golem, Inc.: A Comment on Certain Points
Where Cybernetics Impinges on Religion.* Cambridge, Mass.:
MIT Press, 1964.

Wildavsky, A. *The Politics of the Budgetary Process.* (2nd ed.)
Boston: Little, Brown, 1974.

Wildavsky, A. *Speaking Truth to Power: The Art and Craft of
Policy Analysis.* Boston: Little, Brown, 1979.

Wilkins, A. L., and Ouchi, W. G. "Efficient Cultures: Exploring
the Relationship Between Culture and Organizational Performance." *Administrative Science Quarterly,* 1983, *28,* 468–
481.

Yukl, G. A. *Leadership in Organizations.* Englewood Cliffs,
N.J.: Prentice-Hall, 1981.

Zimmerman, W. D. "An End to Collegial Governance in Colleges
and Universities?" *AGB Reports,* 1969, *11,* 21–26.

Index

245